IN TIME AND PLACE

FLOYD C. WATKINS

In Time
and
Place

*Some Origins
of American Fiction*

Athens
The University of Georgia Press

55093

Library of Congress Catalog Card Number: 76–12682
International Standard Book Number: 0–8203–0415–8

The University of Georgia Press, Athens 30602

Set on 11 on 13 point Caledonia type
Printed in the United States of America

TO FRANK MANLEY
& WILLIAM B. DILLINGHAM

Contents

Preface

The eight novels examined in this book are admittedly a strange assortment. Any one could be deleted without a major effect on the whole. Numerous others could be added. Each of these books treats a particular culture or a diversity of cultures and reveals the author's ignorance or knowledge in his use of the ways of communities. In a sense this volume is a collection of separate essays on different authors writing about various peoples in various ways.

A critic who prefers one great book (at least in his opinion) to a popular one or even to another great one (as I prefer *As I Lay Dying* to *The Grapes of Wrath*) immediately offends a reader with a different taste. One who ventures to judge the greatness of a literary work should measure in terms of the greatest writings that he knows well. Not to be able to recognize the limitations of *Gone with the Wind*, for example, may reflect an inability to appreciate the magnificence of *Absalom, Absalom!* and other novels of comparable greatness. Admittedly, Faulkner is my primary touchstone. The length of a chapter in this study does not indicate a judgment: *House Made of Dawn*, which I discuss in greatest detail, is not, I think, as great as *As I Lay Dying*. To judge, then, is to please or to provoke. Yet not to judge may be to yield to cowardice and not to discriminate.

In this book I disavow all social, racial, and political motivations. My interest lies in cultural and historical and geographical backgrounds and their effects on fiction.

A book may have many fathers. One of these works was assigned to me as a subject at a symposium; I did not know at the time that the study would become part of a larger work. A friend suggested one book and that selection in turn demanded another. Other chapters derive from intensive research over a period of more than twenty years. At least two are here because I found a subject while I was living for months or decades at a particular place and among a particular people. Admittedly, too, I have chosen some of these works on loosely defined cultural, geographical, and literary grounds. In one way, then, these novels are random choices; in another, they add up to a representative whole. But without doubt other works could be chosen on similar principles. The result might be a very similar work or a book altogether on a different subject with even a contradictory thesis and conclusion.

Despite the methods of selection, the diversity of subjects and of artistic techniques, and the choices made, several systems operate within what seems to be at first glance a grab bag of subjects. Geographical diversity and selection is a major principle. Three novels derive from three entirely different sections of the multifarious South; two are from the Southwest; two from the prairies; and one, *The Grapes of Wrath*, begins in a state (Oklahoma) that has been called many things—South, Midwest, West, and Southwest—and ends in California. It might take half a hundred American novels to represent the races of the country, but these eight are at least a fair sample. The Anglo-American plays some role in every work, just as the race appears in almost every community. The Negro has either a major or a minor role in at least four of these novels. Although fiction is a genre alien to the culture of the Indian, that race has minor roles in two novels, is mentioned in others, and is the center of one of the works. The central European immigrants and their cultures are prominent in the work of Willa Cather and Sinclair Lewis, and the Spanish-Mexican-Latin people and cultures appear in several works. A semirandom selection of American fiction, then, covers a wide variety of cultures and peoples.

Although I have paid no particular attention to social class, I have written nothing about the urban aristocrat. There are two reasons: the urbanites of financial means tend to have a standard or homogeneous culture, perhaps; and frankly I do not know first-hand the ways of the Brahmins of Edith Wharton, Henry James, or John P. Marquand. My own upbringing would probably make it easier for me to adapt my life to the ways of the Pueblo Indian than those of a Jamesian character. And perhaps the ways of a Jew like Herzog are as deeply rooted in the mores of a people as those of anyone on earth. One not born and reared an orthodox Jew might never write perceptively of the intricacies of the ways of the people of *Herzog* or Bernard Malamud's storekeeper in *The Assistant*.

To some extent the time of the action has determined the choice of the novels I have studied. The older cultures are more intricate in many respects than the modern. These eight works cover a span from the early settlement of the Spanish explorers in the Southwest in Willa Cather's *Death Comes for the Archbishop* through the slavery of Nat Turner to Abel's life in modern Los Angeles in Momaday's *House Made of Dawn*. An older culture usually presents a more uniform subject matter and tone; but, after all, citizens of Jemez Pueblo may watch "All in the Family," although I hope they do not understand the characters.

Besides the author's relationship to his cultural materials and the critic's choice of author and novel, there is also the problem of how the particular novel fits into the design of all the author's works as well as the peculiarity of his relationship to the materials in the book. I have attempted as much diversity as possible. Perhaps the author here who personally knew the subject of his novel least is William Styron, despite the fact that he is a born southerner who has lived among Negroes and whites a hundred years after the time of his fiction. On the other hand, if Styron could not know at first hand the life of slave or the condition of slaveownership or the personal biography of Nat Turner, history itself (some claims to the contrary) has not been able to make meaningful and significant major discoveries to add to, subtract from, or contradict the cultural structure of *The Confessions of Nat Turner*. Margaret Mitchell, who knew her people by tradition and by research, may, surprisingly, present them as human beings most superficially of all. Steinbeck's *The Grapes of Wrath* is a travelogue with the Okies mostly as passing acquaintances. Faulkner, Momaday, Willa Cather, and Lewis understood their subject cultures most intimately, but even with these authors there are wide variations in knowledge, attitude, and sympathy. Faulkner was writing about his own community, but not about his own class. Yet despite the social disparity, *As I Lay Dying* is probably the richest and most accurate treatment of the southern poor white ever written, and it is sympathetic even though these people have been most abused by many authors with almost complete impunity. Momaday was intimately one of his native people, although he has not returned to live with them after his attainment of the ultimate degree in academic education. Lewis felt ambivalently toward his people, loved them a little, and despised their ways a great deal. In *Main Street* he wrote most personally and most fully about the country of his nativity. Willa Cather knew her childhood prairie as well as the Southwest. I have chosen two books by her to represent an author's treatment of two entirely different cultures. In American literature she may be the author who has written most capably about her own culture and also thoroughly absorbed another and entirely alien civilization and written about it with an accuracy like that of one born to the people.

I have attempted to construct no one well-wrought theory about the relationship of the author to his culture and his use of it in his fiction. The only infallible rules, perhaps, are that the writer must know a people worth writing about and that his art must be capable of revealing something worthy about them and their ways. Often I state principles which I firmly believe to be critically and humanly true. But most of them have some exceptions. And all of them do not fit neatly together. The subjects are the author, his characters and the prototypal people and cultures they represent, his biographical and literary relationships to them, and the understanding the reader may gain about the author, the book, and the cultures in the book. It is almost foolish, I believe, to attempt so much. I have lived among peoples like some of those here all my life, and I have spent weeks or months with others, but no man can ever know entirely his own culture, not to mention half a dozen others. Indeed, in some areas that seem homogeneous on the surface, it is culturally a radical change and even an adventure to cross a county line or to venture into another community. Always theory and principle of culture and the use of it in literature and criticism (or reading) are a subject here, but never is there a consistent system. And there never can be.

This book derives from a wider variety and a greater number of sources than I have ever before used in any scholarly study. I am first of all indebted to the peoples who lived the cultural lives which provided the materials for the novelists to write about. Critics, scholars, and anthropologists before me have made my work easier. For particular assistance with cultural backgrounds I am especially indebted to G. C. King, Leon Covey, Father Meldon Hickey, Mr. and Mrs. Jimmie Wolf, Paul Toya, Mrs. Ella Poolaw, Mrs. Helen Daw, N. Scott Momaday, Mildred Bennett, Viola S. Borton, Bernice Slote, the editor and the staff of the Sauk Centre *Herald*, and William Styron. The Reference Department of the Woodruff Library of Emory University has provided far more help than is usual in the research for a study of literature. Emory University has generously contributed time for work and money for expenses. Fellow scholars who have been helpful are Albert E. Stone, Louis Rubin, and C. Hugh Holman. Thomas Daniel Young, William B. Dillingham, George Core, and Kenneth Cherry have studied the manuscript and contributed numerous suggestions and even larger plans.

My wife, Anna, and I have lived for weeks, months, or years in every community and culture discussed here except one, and she has been clerk, typist, interpreter, and counselor.

Two chapters have been published previously in somewhat different form: that on *Gone with the Wind* in the *Southern Literary Journal* and that on *The Grapes of Wrath* in *The Humanist in His World: Essays in Honor of Fielding Dillard Russell*.

Finally, I am most indebted to my own heritage in the southern hills for providing me with the background, even the ignorance, to enable me to begin to understand the diverse and varied peoples in American fiction.

1

✜§ ONE ৯✜

The Makings of American Fiction

Movement from place to place is a chief distinction of American culture, and except for the camper who leaves Metropolis for brief sojourns in a tamed and often polluted vestige of the American wilderness the movement has almost always had the same direction—from country to town to city. In literature, this change of place has given numerous American authors at least two subject matters—home and voluntary exile—and sometimes several places of exile and many subject matters. Willa Cather's and Thomas Wolfe's growing up in small towns and their subsequent wanderings to the state university and then to northeastern cities, Metropolis, and Europe are two examples of the pattern. The typical American author leaves his world but nevertheless carries it with him as the subject matter he will write about throughout his career.

Cultural changes from one time to another in America have an effect on fiction as great as movement from one place to another. Never has man transformed his ways of living so extensively and rapidly as he has in the last few decades. Never before has he so completely altered or destroyed his relationships with other individuals, with groups, and with nature. Some of the causes are urbanization, rapid transportation, the mass media, mechanization (especially on the farm), cultural nomadism, and a political demand for complete melting in the population pot. The effects are so extensive that they are almost unimaginable. The changes in man's relationship with the earth and nature obliterate whole categories of images which were once available to a writer. Vanishing also are wide and extensive kinships in large families, small communities, ethnic groupings, memories of the past, close associations between men and many kinds of animals, folkways and folktales and folksongs, dialects and languages, and even religions.

A migrant author does not find in Metropolis a community simi-

3

lar to the one he has known. He may be native to the close group-ings in less populated areas but move to a city and a less cohesive occupational community, a religious group, a racial neighborhood. What traditions exist are likely to be more recent. His literary sub-ject matter is likely to be far less traditional—not folk narratives but written fiction and television, not large family groups but iso-lated family units, not single homes but condominiums, not field and stream but park and ghetto, not craft but assembly line.

The places of many older American novels have already been changed and even destroyed. The small Confederate town Atlanta in *Gone with the Wind* has now become a metropolis with a culture on the whole more African and northern than southern white. Steinbeck's Okies have migrated and those who stayed at home own mechanized farms or cattle ranches. Willa Cather's south-western territories in *Death Comes for the Archbishop* have been much influenced by standard Anglo-American culture. Pueblo In-dians, as Scott Momaday's *House Made of Dawn* shows, are mov-ing away from the reservation. In short, many of the subjects of modern writers are beginning to disappear in just one generation. The simple truth is that most Americans have shown by migration and change that they do not wish to live in a way that will provide a novelist with a traditional culture to write about.

If exile in Metropolis provides standardization, the lives of those who stay at home are also altered by movement and loss of popula-tion. Some parts of the South and the backwoods states like Maine, New Hampshire, and Vermont in New England are "areas of de-clining population growth and outmigration, of widespread land abandonment, and of severe local economic depression."[1] Depopu-lated communities, schools, and churches provide a rural subject matter sparse and spindly compared to the world Robert Frost de-scribed in most of his poems.[2] With forests replacing fields, unin-habited homes falling in, and automobiles passing through on the interstate, the lonely and isolated rural landscape provides what-ever author who remains there with less human material to write about. Not only can you not go home again, you also cannot stay at home even in the same place. Wolfe's Asheville and Faulkner's

Oxford contain subdivisions, and much of their past has been changed or bottled up in museums. In Faulkner's later years Oxford had left only the Confederate monument, the courthouse, and the jail "to distinguish an old southern town from any of ten thousand towns built yesterday from Kansas to California."[3] Now the old jail is gone too.

Without doubt a chief distinction of American literature has been its diversity in cultural subject matters. A map of the United States drawn by a cultural geographer (see figure 1) generally corresponds with what a linguistic or a literary map would be. In five major cultural regions there are a total of twenty-five subregions and regions of "uncertain status." Fiction set in any one of these should differ in race, language, customs, and general culture from fiction written about any other. The variety of American literature springs in part from the variations in these areas. One author differs from another not only individually but in heritage and tradition. Cultural dimensions as well as geographic size give breadth to the national literature. The literature of comparatively homogeneous Ireland could never have so great a range as American fiction. Breadth may or may not be a desirable trait in literatures, but in countries like Russia and America it is inescapable.

Choices of cultural subject matter by American authors are almost unlimited. With so much at his disposal, an author is tempted to turn to a variety of cultures without knowing well any but his own. One may be a cultural wanderer like Washington Irving, who wrote not only about Europe and Asia, past and present, but also about the various people of his native New York and also about the prairies and the Rocky Mountains. Willa Cather wrote several volumes about her native peoples and then became deeply involved in the ways of another region, the Southwest. An author may stay almost entirely within his own cultural area as Hawthorne did. If he moves abroad, as Hawthorne did in *The Marble Faun*, his heritage often continues to dictate his art. A novelist may stay within his region for his subject matters and find extensive variety, as Robert Penn Warren does in Kentucky, Tennessee, and Louisiana. Even in a single state a writer may find divergent if related heritages, as

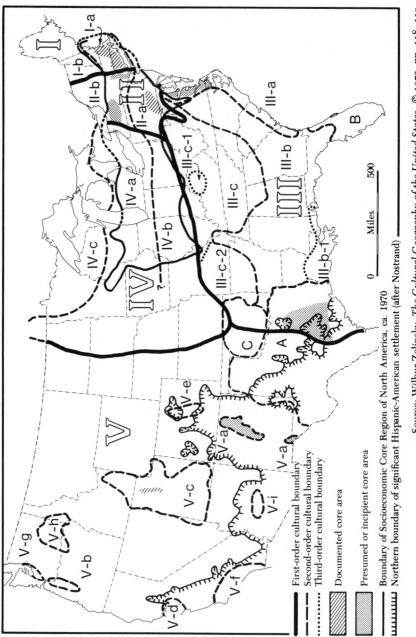

Source: Wilbur Zelinsky, *The Cultural Geography of the United States*, © 1973, pp. 118–119.
Reprinted by permission of Prentice-Hall, Inc., Englewood Cliffs, New Jersey.

First-order cultural boundary
Second-order cultural boundary
Third-order cultural boundary

Documented core area

Presumed or incipient core area

Boundary of Socioeconomic Core Region of North America, ca. 1970
Northern boundary of significant Hispanic-American settlement (after Nostrand)

Miles

0   500

Region	Approximate Dates of Settlement and Formation	Major Sources of Culture (listed in order of importance)
I. New England		
I-a. Nuclear New England	1620–1750	England
I-b. Northern New England	1750–1830	Nuclear New England; England
II. The Midland		
II-a. Pennsylvanian Region	1682–1850	England & Wales; Rhineland; Ulster; 19th Century Europe
II-b. New York Region, or New England Extended	1624–1830	Great Britain; New England; 19th Century Europe; Netherlands
III. The South		
III-a. Early British Colonial South	1607–1750	England; Africa; British West Indies
III-b. Lowland, or Deep South	1700–1850	Great Britain; Africa; Midland; Early British Colonial South; aborigines
III-b-1. French Louisiana	1700–1760	France; Deep South; Africa; French West Indies
III-c. Upland South	1700–1850	Midland; Lowland South; Great Britain
III-c-1. The Bluegrass	1770–1800	Upland South; Lowland South
III-c-2. The Ozarks	1820–1860	Upland South; Lowland South; Lower Middle West
IV. The Middle West		
IV-a. Upper Middle West	1800–1880	New England Extended; New England; 19th Century Europe; British Canada
IV-b. Lower Middle West	1790–1870	Midland; Upland South; New England Extended; 19th Century Europe
IV-c. Cutover Area	1850–1900	Upper Middle West; 19th Century Europe
V. The West		
V-a. Upper Rio Grande Valley	1590–	Mexico; Anglo-America; aborigines
V-b. Willamette Valley	1830–1900	Northeast U.S.
V-c. Mormon Region	1847–1890	Northeast U.S.; 19th Century Europe
V-d. Central California	(1775–1848) 1840–	(Mexico) Eastern U.S.; 19th Century Europe; Mexico; East Asia
V-e. Colorado Piedmont	1860–	Eastern U.S.; Mexico
V-f. Southern California	(1760–1848) 1880–	(Mexico) Eastern U.S.; 19th & 20th Century Europe; Mormon Region; Mexico; East Asia
V-g. Puget Sound	1870–	Eastern U.S.; 19th & 20th Century Europe; East Asia
V-h. Inland Empire	1880–	Eastern U.S.; 19th & 20th Century Europe
V-i. Central Arizona	1900–	Eastern U.S.; Southern California; Mexico
Regions of Uncertain Status or Affiliation		
A. Texas	(1690–1836) 1821–	(Mexico) Lowland South, Upland South; Mexico; 19th Century Central Europe
B. Peninsular Florida	1880–	Northeast U.S.; the South; 20th Century Europe; Antilles
C. Oklahoma	1890–	Upland South; Lowland South; aborigines; Middle West

Eudora Welty does in the frontiersmen of the nineteenth century, the planters of the Delta, the yeomen of the hills, and the neighbors in a small town.

If American literature has a greater cultural variety than Irish literature, its scope is not a great deal wider than that of the British, where the central culture has several satellite cultures (to use T. S. Eliot's term). "The survival of the satellite culture," Eliot believes, "is of very great value to the stronger culture. It would be no gain whatever for English culture, for the Welsh, Scots and Irish to become indistinguishable from Englishmen—what *would* happen, of course, is that we should all become indistinguishable featureless 'Britons,' at a lower level of culture than that of any of the separate regions." A man should live at the place of his birth, Eliot adds, and be "a citizen of a particular part of his country, with local loyalties."[4] Economically and materialistically in America, the central culture is the Midland, New York and Pennsylvania mainly, an extension of New England (see figure 1). Culturally, this is a region of "a markedly urban character" and "polyglot ethnicity." It has imposed "its image upon . . . much of the remainder of the country."[5] Compared with New England, the South, and various areas of the West, it has not retained a regional tradition and identity.

The writer without an inherited tradition may turn to history, perhaps in a bookish way. He may write a historical novel. It is easier for a sophisticated writer to go to the books than it is to search out and learn a traditional community and culture. Country people are usually well mannered and communicative with strangers, but it takes a native to know a native. The degree to which it is possible for a novelist to learn a people well across time and space is the question addressed, but one which must be answered in a different way with every work of fiction. I believe that a novelist or a critic with talent and patience may with great labor cross long distances, as Willa Cather does in *Death Comes for the Archbishop*, or that he may fail to do so, as Steinbeck does in *The Grapes of Wrath*. The severest view is that a historical novel is virtually impossible. "Most historical novels are fraudulent," Donald E. Stanford has said. "It is extremely difficult, no matter how much research is done, to give a completely authentic picture of the past. The exact ways of thinking, speaking, acting, and feeling of a century or more ago are lost forever and no novelist can reproduce the daily life of the past with the same accuracy that he can reproduce the life of his own time. Nevertheless, the attempt is constantly being made."[6]

Great literature, however, can spring from false history—but very rarely does there appear a literary genius, a writer who knows the wellsprings of the human heart, who chooses a human historical subject and infuses it with something to transcend historical inaccuracy. History is not the thing of literary importance in Shakespeare's history plays. The characters of *Julius Caesar* are not Romans but Elizabethans. Shakespeare was accurate in what he wrote about his time and about what his time thought of history. To some extent, the nature of the audience or reader must affect response and even perhaps, strangely, the quality of the literature. That is to say, one who knows very well the tradition or history written about in fiction cannot completely suspend his disbelief and dislike even when the work is humanly accurate but historically or socially false. If Romans could step across the barrier of time and read *Julius Caesar*, necessarily the play would seem false to them historically and even perhaps esthetically.

A native usually does not wish to see his traditional community written about in fiction. One who reads novels written about his people or a historian who reads fiction written about history requires that the work of art correspond exactly to his conception of the subject matter. If one does not know the history, the literature may seem to be historical fact itself. One who sees a beloved source—history, community, or fiction—tampered with automatically objects on grounds other than esthetic, and he usually proceeds to object on esthetic as well as factual grounds. The historical inaccuracy of the number of slaves on the plantations in *Gone with the Wind* is more important to a historian than to a gentle reader. Factual accuracy and human accuracy have a loose relationship but not a precise one. The human spirit in literature, of course, outweighs the factual. Margaret Mitchell wrote about a past she had both inherited and researched, but she represented both northern and southern cultures falsely, and she created stereotyped characters who are untrue in human as well as historical terms.

What in the vehicle of a traditional culture carries meanings which are unavailable to an urban writer? The best answer to such a question lies in fiction itself. The families and places and stories of Yoknapatawpha County represent the inexhaustible variety of life there. But fiction exemplifies usually without explaining, and some explanation is possible. Psychologists, for example, know something physically demonstrable about what Karl Jung calls

> the mystery of the earth. . . . One only needs to see how, in America, the skull and pelvis measurements of all European races begin to indianize themselves in the second generation of immigrants. That is the mystery of the American earth.
>
> The soil of every country holds some such mystery. We have an unconscious reflection of this in the psyche: just as there is a relationship of mind to body, so there is a relationship of body to earth. . . . There are people—quite a number of them—who live outside and above their bodies, who float like bodiless shadows above the earth, their earthy component, which is their body. Others live wholly in their bodies.

Jung provides no information about possible psychic effects of living separated from the earth by steel and concrete as compared with living close to the soil. But he does link the earth and culture (and therefore the artist's subjects): "Certain Australian primitives assert that one cannot conquer foreign soil, because in it there dwell strange ancestor-spirits who reincarnate themselves in the new-born. There is a great psychological truth in this. . . . I would not speak ill of our relation to good Mother Earth. . . . He who is rooted in the soil endures."[7] Even in translation, Jung's vocabulary as well as his meaning resembles Faulkner's language and his themes in the novels about Yoknapatawpha.

The peculiar significance of small towns in American culture is of course the cause of the centrality of small towns in fiction. They "have occupied," Peirce F. Lewis writes, "something of the same place as Paris has to the French, or the green countryside to the English." America's "literary tradition" associated with the small town is "peculiarly American, and absolutely central to our national psyche." A Gallup poll in 1966 revealed that twenty-two million American "city dwellers . . . thought they would prefer small town living."[8] "The life of a village," Graham Greene says, "is intimate and dramatic. There is a sense of community. People talk." And of course their talk is what a good novelist must write about. "In a city," Greene says on the other hand, "there may be a suicide in the next street and you will never hear of it."[9]

Regardless of population density, however, the standardized subdivision and the apartment house provide little of that kind of life. Perhaps urbanism is one cause of the recent intensification of the interest of author and reader in pornography. That is a subject matter without much community, and at least it is available anywhere there is a sexy body. One of the most representative novels of the life of our time may be Updike's *Couples*, and it is a pretty good indication of the limited possibilities of the life and of the fiction about it. It is impossible to imagine the world of *Couples* as the subject of as many books as Yoknapatawpha is. A talent of the dimensions of Shakespeare's or Faulkner's which survives childhood in modern Metropolis may have to look elsewhere for a reservoir of subject matter.

Particulars in life on the earth and in the small town and even in the city have vanished from place and with time. American authors have created magnificent animal characters—Moby Dick, Brer Rabbit, the dog Buck, Hemingway's marlin, Old Ben—but they have lived at sea or in the forest, with the elemental. In a motorized world animals disappear. The approximately twenty million horses and five and a half million mules in 1920 had diminished in 1960 to approximately three million of both combined.[10] The characterization of the mule in Faulkner now has few referents even on the farm. Instead of a horse, a car; instead of a mule, a tractor. The family milk cow, the cow raised for beef, the farm pig, and the other animals which provide food now are raised in huge herds. A child sees milk only in bottles or cartons and beef in trays covered with plastic. The chickens which ran loose in the farm yard are now raised in coops of thousands, and many city dwellers have never seen a living chicken. A reader's way of life may be so changed from his father's that he cannot recognize the very names

11

of objects in his father's world. Some university students, for example, refer to Janet's *hen* in John Crowe Ransom's poem with the masculine pronoun *he*.

This is not a pastoral lamentation, but a discussion of subject matters. Even in Oxford, Mississippi, since the ascendance of the automobile Faulkner could not write "Spotted Horses." Strangely, even the autos have lost their identity. Mr. Buffalo's home-made car and Ratliff's Model T Ford in *The Town* exist only as antiques, and their replacements have become standardized. The earth itself is not exempt from mechanization. Farm employment of ten million in 1950 decreased to a little over four million in 1972. Thus neighbors in fact and potential characters in fiction have been replaced by machines.

Communities are lost as subjects. Fewer novelists know "that sense of shared experience that comes from living within, and as a part of, a group of people who share basic assumptions, a common system of values, including morals and manners, the same historic experience, the same traditions, and all other things that cause men to feel that they are not alone in an alien world or surrounded by an unfeeling society."[11] The extensiveness of loss of community between 1920 and 1970 is apparent in figures of urban-rural population: 1920, about 54 million urban and 51 million rural; 1970, about 149 million urban and 54 million rural.[12]

The problem in America is that cities tend to reach a certain size that prevents tradition and individuality. The more people a man has to write about, the less subject he may have. "The bigger the crowd," Karl Jung believes, "the more negligible the individual becomes. But if the individual, overwhelmed by the sense of his own puniness and impotence, should feel that his life has lost its meaning—which, after all, is not identical with public welfare and higher standards of living—then he is already on the road to State slavery and, without knowing or wanting it, has become its proselyte." On the individual level the results of "statistical truths and large numbers" are "the nullity and futility of the . . . personality."[13] The consequence "in great world cities like New York . . . [is] the most anguished and angry alienation on the part of the intellectuals."[14] The novelist and the editor who chooses his novel must pick a mode and a subject that will be bought and read. One executive in a great American publishing house saw the trends in 1973 as "stress on writing that probes into the buried life of the psyche, on the confessional novel, and on the tendency to give up fiction in favor of history and biography."[15] The community here seems to be removed from the purview of the writer and the interest of the reader. Lost are the forms which provide patterns for the individual. The world promises fiction of existentialism and the absurd and determinism. Metropolis confronts characters with worlds they cannot influence or modify. The consequences are rebellion and violence.

The architecture of the typical American home has provided national characteristics in settings for American fiction. In some traditional American novels houses have been intricately involved in the action and the lives of the characters. Among the most elaborate architectural creations of this sort are the house of the seven gables, the boarding house of Wolfe's Altamont, and Thomas Sutpen's mansion. The most "important peculiarities" of American housing have been "the lavish use of space" in the house and its lot, "the one-family . . . free-standing unit with at least a token patch of space between it and its neighbors" even in urban settings, "a disproportionately small fraction of the population . . . in apartment buildings or other multiunit structures," and the lack of "row housing" except in "urban neighborhoods in the Northeast that were built about two centuries ago." The economic cause of these attributes has been the abundance of inexpensive land, "but the urge toward very large, isolated, individual properties seems to go beyond any rational economic reckoning."[16] These attributes, of course, have been characteristic of homes in fiction as well as in fact. Even Jay Gatsby's lavish residence is distinctively American. One wonders now whether America is changing its character as fast as it is its housing. Since World War II the move to Metropolis has caused, perhaps even dictated, the change from single unit to multiunit, niggardliness with space, more and more subdivisions and row housing, and so on. The American novelist born after midcentury probably will not himself have an intimate and hereditary relationship with any house. The very repetitiveness of multiunit living will be carried into fiction in ways which must affect characters, meanings, techniques.

If the novelist has shown better than anyone the life of traditional societies, he has also begun to describe the loss of that way of life. Forerunners of this kind of fiction were the naturalists (especially Crane, Dreiser, Norris, Farrell) and some of the members of the Lost Generation (Fitzgerald most of all). More recent figures who create fiction about a standardized world are Updike, Cheever, O'Hara, Mailer, Heller. It is too early now to determine the character of much of the fiction being written about standardized America. The sociologist and the cultural geographer can much more quickly describe patterns of life than can the critic, who waits first for the novelist to create what he has observed, then waits longer for the trends to become apparent, and finally deduces what their effect is on a body of fiction. It is easier to define social effects than it is to determine cultural and literary consequences.

The observer can, however, witness the kind of cultures which will be subjects of fiction in the future. It is not easy to predict what pockets of culture will produce the most fiction and the best. Most settings may be Anyplace, where "motels, filling stations, magazine racks, drug stores, high schools, radio program formats, chain restaurants, and the seemingly unlimited array of franchise retail enterprises are all very much peas in a pod, whatever the city or state."[17]

Also standardized are products and athletic events and television. The works of craftsmen have become museum pieces and curios. Those leather wine bottles from which the Basques drink in *The Sun Also Rises* are now souvenirs of a different time as well as of a strange people, and perhaps plastic containers are a new thing under the sun. The interest here is American, but culturally even the world is becoming standardized. "Such things as the bicycle and plastic raingear have penetrated almost every part of the world, including some primitive societies otherwise adamantly set against any sort of change."[18] Whenever it rains, then, in any modern novel in the world, the raingear has already been predetermined and stereotyped for the novelist.

With few exceptions a novel presents itself as the past. If the reader knows well the world re-created in the work, he reads from his own perspective (remembered or vicarious) as well as the novelist's. Most good novelists provide clutter of a world accurate for the knowing reader and yet clear to the reader who does not know the time and place. Esthetic laws governing the relationship between a novel and its referents are numerous, adaptable perhaps from one situation to another, sometimes mysterious, and imprecise. But they are numerous, and they do exist. What follows is an attempt to investigate in several instances the relationship between a writer and his materials and then the relationship between the reader and the author's materials.

Dorothea Lange Collection, The Oakland Museum

Migrant Mother, Nipomo, California. 1936

Tractored Out, Childress County, Texas. 1938

Dorothea Lange Collection, The Oakland Museum

❧ TWO ❧

Flat Wine from *The Grapes of Wrath*

A character in fiction is known in part by his relationship with things; he is defined by the clutter of his world. If the things are vague or false, the character is unlikely to be genuine. In a novel with sparse details, the people usually share the vagueness of the environment. Nature may be a large part of the raw materials of fiction. When an author does not know the natural objects of the world he is writing about, then he also gets the manufactured products and the people wrong. A skyscraper or a horse trough or a churn helps to make characters what they are. A writer who does not know a world well should not write about it. But that is precisely what Californian John Steinbeck did in *The Grapes of Wrath* when he wrote about Okies, a people he did not know.

The effect on fiction of an author's ignorance is difficult to measure. It may also be difficult for a critic who is ignorant of a culture to try to interpret fiction about it. One who knows a country or small-town culture can perhaps understand the mores of another country people better than he can understand his own city kinsmen. A rural southerner might read a novel about a Pueblo Indian with more comprehension, for example, than he would have of the urban world of *Herzog*. Can a critic who does not know the culture of the people discussed by an author tell whether or not the author knows that culture? What can he measure by? Some critics presume to judge the truth of fiction when they do not know its background. Reviewers of *The Grapes of Wrath*, for example, thought it was "true"—"great art" and "great sociology."[1] Can a critic or a reader who is well acquainted with a folk culture of his own measure a writer's accuracy when the writer treats a culture foreign to the critic? How long must a writer study an alien culture before he can write about it? Can he acquire such knowledge merely from books? These questions, of course, can be only pondered, not answered.

"Genuine history," Hippolyte Taine has written, "is brought into existence only when the historian begins to unravel, across the lapse of time, the living man, toiling, impassioned, entrenched in his customs, with his voice and features, his gestures and his dress, distinct and complete as he from whom we have just parted in the street."[2] The novelist and the critic after him may have to cross a barrier of place or culture instead of time as the historian does, but the distance may be just about as great. The novelist is as subject to error as the historian. Hawthorne maintains that a romance must be true to the human heart. Likewise, a social novelist must be true to the cultural as well as to the human. Steinbeck has written what poses as a study in fiction of social reality, but the facts are wrong. Can a credible truth of the heart be embodied in cultural untruth? As *The Grapes of Wrath* is often false and vague, so the characters are false also.

People in a small town or the country are never truly pleased to be the subject of fiction. Mountaineers have objected to James Dickey and Thomas Wolfe, Mississippians to William Faulkner, Indians to Scott Momaday. Many Oklahomans have been infuriated by what they regarded as the insult of *The Grapes of Wrath*. They attacked it on social, factual, and moral grounds, but most of them did not point out many of the specific errors. Lyle H. Boren used the *Congressional Record* to object to the facts: Steinbeck "had tractors plowing land of the Cookson Hills country where there are not 40 acres practical for tractor cultivation. He had baptisms taking place in the irrigation ditches in country near Sallisaw, Oklahoma, where an irrigation ditch has not run in the history of the world." But the congressman did not consider his people exposed with justification. "The truth is," he said, "this book exposes nothing but the total depravity, vulgarity, and degraded mentality of the author."[3] Grampa longs to go to California, where he can have enough "grapes to squish all over his face" while in Sallisaw, Oklahoma, he already lives "in one of the greatest grape growing regions in the nation."[4] Frank J. Taylor has disputed almost all the social details about the lives of the migrant workers in *The Grapes of Wrath*—their food, shelter, medical treatment, wages. His bias seems as strong as Steinbeck's when he defends

California businesses and governments.[5] Carey McWilliams, on the other hand, writes that "the LaFollette Committee came along in 1939 and verified the general picture of conditions in the state as set forth in *The Grapes of Wrath*."[6]

Most of Steinbeck's errors about Oklahoma and country people like the Joads have never been pointed out. Some of the mistakes are entirely factual; that is, they can be proved wrong without involving any critical judgment. Including the three errors above, *The Grapes of Wrath* contains nearly twenty plain linguistic and factual inaccuracies:

In the dust bowl "ant lions started small avalanches."[7] Native Oklahomans do not know what ant lions are. Like southerners instead of Californians, they call them doodlebugs.

The famous old "land turtle" (p. 21) which crosses the highway early in the novel is also not native to Oklahoma. The Joads would have called him a terrapin.

Steinbeck's "land turtle" has an armored tail, a biological impossibility. Armadillos have armored tails, but not "land turtles."

Steinbeck's vocabulary is sometimes wrong. By a far stretch of the imagination, a coyote might squawk (p. 31). But flies do not roar (p. 8).

Tom Joad would not speak of a "leg" of pork, a wrong term for the meat. It should be ham or shoulder.

Ma Joad says salting down meat is woman's work (p. 146), but that task belongs to men on an Oklahoma farm.

Muley eats prairie dogs in eastern Oklahoma, where prairie dogs have never lived.

Tom Joad wears a coat as he walks on the highway in hot weather (p. 9), and Muley wears "an old black suit coat" over his "blue jeans" (p. 61), which he would call overalls or overhalls. The dress is authentic, but not in this season. Two Oklahomans told me that no one would wear such clothing except a preacher or an idiot.

The driver of a truck looks out at cornfields and sees that "little flints shoved through the dusty soil" (p. 12). First, the perspective is wrong. The driver could not see them from a truck moving on the road. Furthermore, small flints are not visible through plowed and dusty earth. I have hunted arrowheads in plowed fields in

Oklahoma. They are not visible until after a rain, and obviously there had been no rain in the dust bowl in *The Grapes of Wrath*.

The truck driver has had a course in mind-training. After he passes someone on the road, he tries to remember "ever'thing about him, . . . how he walked an' maybe how tall an' what weight an' any scars" (p. 16). Scars would not be visible from a passing truck.

When Muley comes toward Tom Joad and Casy, they "can't see 'im for the dust he raises" (p. 61). Oklahomans who remember dust bowl storms say that you could hardly see a man for the dust, but Muley is not in a storm, and a walking man did not raise that much dust.

Wages are wrong. Tractor drivers in the novel were paid $3.00 a day (p. 50). Actually, $1.50 would have been good pay for the time.

The Joads have chopped cotton for "fifty cents a clean acre" (p. 63), but that is not the custom. People chopped by the day rather than by the acre.

After Uncle John is baptized, he "jumped over a feeny bush as big as a piana" (p. 39). Feeny bushes are not known to Oklahomans, and I have not been able to find out what one is. Raymond John Taylor, an Oklahoman and a biologist, tells me that a typical bush at a creek where a baptizing occurred would be a button bush. A novelist writing authentically about a region would use a bush common to the area but unknown to many other places and then make it visual. Steinbeck does not do that.

Oklahoma has no lobo wolves.[8]

Besides the factual errors, there are a number of improbable occurrences in *The Grapes of Wrath*. An ant runs "into the soft skin inside the shell" of the "land turtle," and the terrapin crushes it (p. 21). It would be close in there, but not insecticidal. The Joads' house is pushed down by a tractor (pp. 54, 62, 70). I learned of one such occurrence near Caddo, Oklahoma, in the 1940s, but again the event was not sufficiently representative for Steinbeck to use it in fiction aiming at social truth.

The variety of geography and the diversity of cultures in the United States make a single national literature impossible. In a sense there is no national literary history in America, but there are many different ones. Certain things are nationwide; I believe doves appear all over the country. When a novelist uses only objects that are as universal as the dove, he does not describe a region. Steinbeck did not know Oklahoma well enough to attempt to write a novel about it. The particulars he uses are either from California, or universal, or wrong. The Joads are a kind of people that Steinbeck did not know very well; they have individual identities, but they are not peculiarly Oklahoman. Such things as scissortails and horned toads are not found in *The Grapes of Wrath*. Nor are Indians, and it is impossible to travel far in Oklahoma without seeing some of them. The novel here is incomplete if not erroneous. On one occasion Steinbeck publishes his ignorance of his subject. Casy and Tom Joad see a "dry watering trough, and the proper weeds that should grow under a trough were gone" (p. 55). Now Faulkner would know what kind of weeds were there. The botanical life of Yoknapatawpha County is lush with honeysuckle, heaven trees, dog fennel, jimson weeds, wistaria, verbena, and many other particular plants. "Proper weeds" is plain bad writing. In this case Steinbeck did not even provide a dove, much less a scissortail.

The Grapes of Wrath is sometimes wrong and often vague, but many details also ring true. Much of the nature is right. Water did have "surface dust" after a storm (p. 6). Jackrabbits do have boils (p. 67). A hungry man could eat skunk meat after washing the musk off the fur (p. 66). The anatomy of the hog-killing is right (p. 143). The gophers (p. 3) and wild oats (p. 21) and the big owl with a "white underside" (p. 70) are natives of Oklahoma. Some unusual customs in the novel were practiced by the poor people during the Depression. Farmers lashed barbed wire to fence posts with baling wire because they had no money to buy nails or staples (p. 24). Urine is used as a medicine by Oklahomans. Farmers have urinated on animals to stop bleeding, rubbed urine as a cure on horses' sores, and used urine as a medicine for earache (p. 235). That "picture of an Indian girl in color, labeled Red Wing," is on a can of Calumet Baking Powder, an item once found in every farm kitchen.

So what if the facts are wrong and omitted? Does that make the fiction bad? In a way it does because it becomes allegorical, invented. It is fantasy, and it is false. The people are usually wrong in much the same way the facts are. They live in a flat universality instead of among the clutter of their daily lives. Poverty is not an absence of things in the daily world. The poor have different kinds of things from those who are more fortunate, but they may be surrounded with objects which depict them, as in homes in a junk-yard. But Steinbeck's Okies are too much without objects.

A comparison of Steinbeck's journeying Joads with Faulkner's journeying Bundrens in *As I Lay Dying* shows the emptiness of the world of *The Grapes of Wrath*. The Bundrens are relatively poor, but they are culturally rich. During Addie's illness and her death and her funeral she is surrounded by children, her husband, neighbors, a doctor, and a minister—all functioning in their personal and ministering roles with the tools and the clothes and the objects that belong to their characters. The long and almost ridiculous cortege moves through the cultural world of Yoknapatawpha County. Grampa and Granma Joad die outside society and their familial cultures. They have been uprooted. They have no funerals, no neighbors, no ritual, no chance to love. This is an essential difference between the life of a yeoman society still functioning in its tradition and the life of an uprooted society thrown out into a world where all the forms are dead and past. In part, the cultural vacuum of the Joads is a thematic representation of the life of migrants. But they had no cultural richness in their life before they left, as the Bundrens did. They live in a void not so much because Oklahomans left their ways at home as because Steinbeck did not know them well in the first place. The Bundrens and Eudora Welty's poor people and Robert Penn Warren's yeoman farmers have more folk manners than a middle-class society. And wandering peoples take their traditions with them. Country people such as the Joads must be given credit in fiction for the gentility they do have. Without all their trappings, they are reduced to caricatures and buffoons. They may also be made ridiculous even when the author is trying to portray them favorably. As Sinclair Lewis, another writer about the ways of the little man, said, "Steinbeck did not quite get those Okies. . . . He got so lousy sentimental he read sounds into their mouths they could never have uttered."[9]

When *The Grapes of Wrath* violates the mores of people like the Joads, the result almost every time is a reduction of the humanity of the characters. Grampa's leaving his underwear unbuttoned and his fly open is a violation of conventions in the rural Protestant ethic, and even if he is "lecherous as always" (p. 105) his misbehavior would not have been tolerated by members of his family, especially the females. Pa's language before his wife and daughter seems incredibly exaggerated when he refers to his lecherous son's "nuts just a-eggin' him on" (p. 112). Grampa calls a brother, a daughter, and a grandson "sons-a-bitches," and that cuss-word is almost never taken lightly by people of his class and place. Except in foolish and drunken situations, such name-calling usually has dire consequences (as is potentially true in *Light in August* and *As I Lay Dying*). But Grampa's language provokes not even a shrug. For the sake of sensationalism, perhaps, Steinbeck momentarily forgets the abstract philosophical goodness he attributes to most of the migrants, and he does not even allow them the dignity they do possess. Granma has "survived only because she was as mean as her husband" (p. 105). She opposes him "with a shrill ferocious religiosity that was as lecherous and as savage as anything Grampa could offer." After she rips "one of his buttocks nearly off" with a shotgun blast, he admires her. Grampa and Granma "both sleeps in the barn" (p. 102). The humanity of these characters is so utterly destroyed by Steinbeck's treatment of them that no dignity can survive even when they die. They are ruined by a tone of amused tolerance of near-murder with a shotgun. And their manners at the table leave them with no measure of dignity.

> Granma said proudly, "A wicketer, cussin'er man never lived. He's goin' to hell on a poker, praise Gawd! Wants to drive the truck!" she said spitefully. "Well, he ain't goin' ta."
> Grampa choked, and a mouthful of paste [pork, biscuit, thick gravy] sprayed into his lap, and he coughed weakly.
> Granma smiled up at Tom. "Messy, ain't he?" she observed brightly. (p. 108)

Actually Steinbeck is demeaning his own characters whom he presumably pities and loves. He is condemning them on social grounds even though the book thematically protests economic abuse of them. At times Steinbeck's amused treatment of them is as inhumane or inhuman as the capitalists are to the migrants. Tom Joad's family are as unloving as they are illiterate when he spends four years in jail and his mother writes him only a postcard after two years and then granny sends him a Christmas card a year later. Yet the Joads should be a writing family. Witness the extensive correspondence between uneducated soldiers and their families during the Civil War. In other incidents caricature occurs because Steinbeck, unintentionally perhaps, reveals how his poor people are unfeeling. The truck they travel on is crowded, no doubt. Yet it is implausible to take all the mattresses and barrels of pork and cooking utensils yet to be unable to find a place for the single stationery box of letters and pictures which Ma burns before she leaves (p. 148). Surely she could sew the most precious into the mattresses.

That pig that "got in over to the Jacobs' an' et the baby" (p. 56) becomes a curious social and cultural generalization about poor Oklahomans instead of being merely a statement of the hardships of their life and the animalism of pigs. The author may intend no slur on the nature of the human beings here, but it is conveyed nevertheless. Pigs do not break into houses and eat babies except in situations too extraordinary for the author to select as representative details. The reason is that families guard their houses too well to admit hogs. Basically the episode attacks the humanity of the people by reflecting on their care of their children. Even if there is a factual precedent, the atrocity is so unrepresentative that it is too sensational for fiction which intends to be socially true. Here the novel is more like lurid journalism than fiction intending to depict the character of a people.

The same anecdote in two different contexts may produce entirely different effects. In Old Southwest humor like that written by George Washington Harris or Johnson Jones Hooper, cruel jokes and brutal fights are more slapstick comedy than social generalizations. Steinbeck writes tall tales in *The Grapes of Wrath*, but the overriding social theme cannot be detached from them. The integrity of the characters is affected and even destroyed. Steinbeck exaggerates absurdity in supposedly good people as much as Faulkner does in the evil Snopeses. Worse, he assigns the absurdities to all the people, creating a wide social generalization, and even the good people threaten violence. Albert, for example, visits the city and returns to find that the folks decided that he had "moved away without sayin' nothin' " (pp. 58–59). They stole the stove, beds, window frames, "eight feet of plankin' . . . from the south side of the house." When he returns "Muley Graves was goin' away with the doors an' the well pump." Albert collected his stuff from the neighbors, but not the pillow stolen by Grampa, who said he would "blow his goddamn stinkin' head off if he comes messin' aroun' my pilla" (p. 59).

Steinbeck denies the Joads and their kind the dignity of their religion, and he does it for a social cause. Casy, the approved philosopher and prophet of the novel, believes in a religion of man which permits meaningless sexual promiscuity. Walter Fuller Taylor has argued that "A reader who really 'buys' *The Grapes of Wrath* has bought . . . an elaborately illustrated and reiterated philosophy of casual sexual indulgence."[10] In the Bible belt and among southern yeoman whites their education as well as their religious beliefs derive from the close and intimate knowledge many of them had of the Bible. Steinbeck ridicules this knowledge. Tom Joad does not know whether the Bible is the origin of a country saying: "Don't roust your faith bird-high an' you won't do no crawlin' with the worms." Grampa Joad gets the Bible and *Dr. Miles' Almanac* all "mixed up" (p. 123). Granma has a "ferocious religiosity" (p. 105), yet her ecstatic pentecostal experience, "speaking in tongues," is still going on when she shoots her husband's buttocks nearly off. Religion is thus associated with humorous violence. She ardently desires a blessing at the table, but she has not "listened to or wondered at the words used" for years (p. 109). Despite a Christ figure or two, every Christian in *The Grapes of Wrath* is belittled. Steinbeck's animosity to Christianity shows clearly through once when he writes that they "had been trained like dogs to rise at the 'amen' signal" (p. 110). Why dogs instead of monarchs or holy men? How else should they rise and at what other time? There are no alternatives. Steinbeck is objecting to their Christianity rather than the method or time of rising. He attempts to demean it by comparing them to dogs, and yet he has diminished the presumably good people who are his admired and suffering souls.

Steinbeck's derogatory views of fundamental religionists are presented extensively in the novel. The woman religious fanatic at the government camp in California is nearly as evil and destructive as the agents of the large landowners who wish to use the migrants and to destroy those who object. A preacher virtually makes war on his congregation when he preaches near an irrigation ditch. He "paced like a tiger, whipping the people with his voice, and they groveled and whined on the ground." He shouted, "Take 'em, Christ! and threw each one in the water" (p. 450). All Steinbeck's Christians are attacked; the only religion he respects is one like his own belief in the "one big soul ever'body's a part of" (pp. 570–572).

Fundamentalists and Christians in fiction do not all deserve contempt. The Reverend Shegog's sermon in *The Sound and the Fury* is probably the best example in fiction of admirable uneducated Christianity, and other such sermons appear in *Mosquitoes* and *Moby-Dick*. James Weldon Johnson, Robert Penn Warren, and Scott Momaday have also created good but plain ministers. Steinbeck uses the rule passed against taking up collections in camp to suggest that all ministers in the camp are interested only in money. Casy's religion of man is more in harmony with Steinbeck's social views. To substitute a kind of biological transcendentalism like that in this novel for religion is not true to the Protestant ways of the characters. Orthodoxy and tradition in Oklahoma are a part of the way of life. There are many irreligious souls, but most of them are skeptics or hell-raising unbelievers or the indifferent. Casy must surely be the only uneducated rural minister converted to Emersonianism who ever lived in Bible-belt areas like the South and Oklahoma. Tradition, experience, and culture make preachers in these areas fall to the flesh or to the demon rum, not to freethinking. If a preacher did fall as Casy does among a people like the Joads, their own religion would damn him more than one who fell to the flesh.

It seems strange that a novelist of the stature, talent, and humanity of Steinbeck should get the culture, the facts, and the religion as wrong as he did in *The Grapes of Wrath*. The reason may be simple. The tragedies of the dust bowl and the migrant workers grabbed his interest. He set out to write about them with humanity and for a social purpose, but he was too ignorant of his characters' ways. In this book Steinbeck is what Robert Penn Warren has called a "doctrinaire; that is, he appreciated a work of art to the degree in which it supported his especial theory."[11] Mildly, Steinbeck has allowed social purpose to control him as it has some Russian authors and critics, who, naturally enough, admire this novel especially. He was not a great enough artist to be able to put aside his social beliefs and prejudices. The theme and the practice of the novel show that he could not lift himself to that level. *The Grapes of Wrath* resembles those novels which make all good characters white and all bad ones black or vice versa. But Steinbeck does worse than categorize characters by whether they are good migrants or bad capitalists. He did "conspicuous violence to his laborers" because he tried to blend "left-wing . . . dialectics and the country people together."[12] Communal and biological forms of a unified society do not conform to the fiercely Anglo-American culture which has been established in farming areas like eastern Oklahoma.

3

The Life: The plantation home of Philip Fitzgerald,
great-grandfather of Margaret Mitchell, Clayton County, Georgia

The Fiction: Tara

⋞ THREE ⋟

Gone with the Wind as Vulgar Literature

At the end of a good historical novel, do the fiction and the reader discover the meaning of history as Jack Burden does in Robert Penn Warren's *All the King's Men*? Or, as in William Faulkner's *Absalom, Absalom!*, do the mysteries of history remain undiscovered, the private belief of different meditators? How much history must a historical novel have? How much meditation? How much story? The practices of many modern novelists present meditation above all other things. Story in the sense of straightforward, chronological narrative may matter little or none. The popular and romantic novel like *Gone with the Wind* is written and then revered as a story; the folderol and paraphernalia of history are presented ostentatiously and defended vigorously as plain and true. But meditation? Who wants it? Leave that, they say, to the symbol-mongers, the pedants, and the myth-masters.

The dominant critical tradition in our time demands that the novel contain meditation; even if a writer like Faulkner in *Absalom, Absalom!* does claim that it is impossible to deduce the past, every man—and novelist or reader—must try for himself. According to Lion Feuchtwanger, creative writers who write about historical subjects "desire only to treat contemporary matters."[1] This theory has flaws: it denies the pleasures of antiquarianism and some of the accomplishments of the historian and the human imagination. When Feuchtwanger maintains that the "sole purpose" of a historical novel "is to enable the reader or the viewer to re-experience the author's immediate experience of history" (p. 142), he again excessively limits the human mind. But he does state the aim of the best kind of novelists. William Styron is thinking of a similar principle when he describes *The Confessions of Nat Turner* as "less an 'historical novel' in conventional terms than a meditation

33

on history." The thinking of an author in our time may be of such value artistically and philosophically as to justify even the deliberate invention if not misrepresentation of history.

In a "Foreword" to *Brother to Dragons* Warren maintains that "the relation" of his work "to its historical material is, in one perspective, irrelevant to its value. I am trying to write a poem and not a history, and therefore have no compunction about tampering with facts." Warren continues by arguing that a poem cannot violate "what the writer takes to be the spirit of his history" or "the nature of the human heart." Here Warren is careful to distinguish his work from run-of-the-mill historical novels. Perhaps literature would be more blessed if the historical novelist would be willing to take some of Warren's risks in the hope of reaching some of his achievements.

The facts which are the proper subject of a meditator on history must be sufficiently complex to represent the human heart and the mortal condition in our time or any other. No one can defend chattel slavery now. Then how can a reader sympathize with a good poet like Henry Timrod, who defended slavery while sympathizing with the new Confederacy in the 1860s? Is it possible to shut out from the mind the ironies of Timrod's praise of a lost cause and to appreciate the poetry as poetry? Was the southern white soldier so completely wrong that it is impossible to sympathize with him? If fiction is to be written about the Civil War in 1936 or 1970, the men on both sides must be human enough to be potentially tragic figures. Not many historical novels may attain such greatness. But the potentialities do abide in the genre, and a model in some respects is Styron's *The Confessions of Nat Turner*.

Good historical novels in some way are meditative. They are not written merely to make history come alive.[2] Mere dramatization or fictionalizing of history may be a service to history—if it is accurate enough—but it is a disservice to literature. It is unnecessary because one may know much factual history without the embroidery of art. There must be, however, a limit to meditation. Obsessive interest in archetypes and mythology ruins the brew, and the contemporary and the humanity in the work are obscured. When a novel is false to historical fact and also false to the human heart in

34

the contemporary age, then it must be simply a poor novel. Despite an immediate popularity which excelled that of all other books, that is the category of Gone with the Wind—a bad novel. It creates a myth which seems to ease the hunger of all extravagantly southern and little romantic souls, but it propagandizes history, fails to grasp the depths and complexities of human evil and the significances of those who prevail. Gone with the Wind is what William Dean Howells called vulgar literature: "what is despicable, what is lamentable is to have hit the popular fancy and not have done anything to change it, but everything to fix it; to flatter it with false dreams of splendor in the past, when life was mainly as simple and sad-colored as it is now."[3]

Never has a book been more praised than Gone with the Wind for what it omits. A friend of mine in the business office of Emory University became heated in anger recently when I told him that Gone with the Wind is a bad book partly because of what it leaves out. It is a good book, he maintains, because it tells a good story and does not expose itself to the nit-picking analyses of scholars and pedants. As a child, Margaret Mitchell evaluated a book about the Rover Boys: "The story is all that matters. Any good plot can stand retelling and style doesn't matter."[4] And Stephens Mitchell, the brother of the novelist, asserts that she "repeated this early opinion, almost word for word," not long before she died.

The most laudatory article about Gone with the Wind praises it for its little subtlety, the lack "of the complexity of the imagination of William Faulkner or the art of Robert Penn Warren." The "lack of subtlety . . . is in its favor," or said to be, because society was "unself-conscious . . . as opposed to the analytic and introspective."[5] "Story" is better than "study." Other critics praise the novel for the lack of obscenity and the failure to include "the inductive vagueness of the stream-of-consciousness school."[6] One who lauds the absence of subtlety later maintains that Ashley's "self-knowledge" gives him tragic stature; his is the "tragedy of every man who cannot be what he was born to be or would be."[7] And Scarlett, the same writer finally says, deliberately chooses "to return to . . . the life of tradition" and is "redeemed into the life of tradition" (p. 149). And the true conflict of this epic-like novel "will

35

never" be presented "more excitingly or appealingly than it is here" (p. 150).

The real difficulty in criticizing *Gone with the Wind* seems to be coping with half-criticism. All it has to be is a good story. Now, the real question is whether this is possible. Ultimately, no one can prove the impossibility. Unfortunately, it is a matter of faith and taste rather than knowledge. That *Gone with the Wind* does need more analysis may be shown by claims for excitement, for tragedy, and for profound tradition and meaning—all these in what is said to be a simple story. How is one to judge whether these may be in a simple story if "story" and "simplicity" are the main characteristics? Obviously, one cannot. And that is why, perhaps, little direct frontal assault has ever been made on the novel which has outsold any other fiction. The critic faces a difficult task and a hostile audience of nations of readers.

When a critic ventures to say what a novel should have included, he has begun to write his own fiction—like the reviewer who says what a book should be without ever considering what it is. Perhaps the only way to avoid this arrogance is to turn to the writings of good novelists and good scholars and to see—in comparison—what greater literature and greater characters or human beings are. After all, isn't this the only real literary purpose of the discipline of comparative literature? (Isn't all else that is comparative really a study of the fashions and trends of ideas and techniques?) What can history and myth be besides icing for the antiquarian, a sop for those looking for color and extravaganza, and escape to ardent romance for those wishing to forget the arduous moment? Myth for Robert Penn Warren is "a fiction, a construct which expresses a truth and affirms a value." When "history is blind," the individual "man is not."[8] History is where we find out what man is that makes God or even man mindful of him. A historical novel, if it wishes to claim as much greatness as it claims popularity, must present characters whose accomplishments, with the Hebrew prophets, we exalt to the heavens or whose shames, with Melville, we wish to cover with the "costliest robes."

There are many works about history and the Civil War which accomplish things that by comparison indicate *Gone with the Wind* is no better than it should be. The Pulitzer Prize Committee chose *Gone with the Wind* over Faulkner's *Absalom, Absalom!*, published in the same year; and *The Unvanquished* is cut from the same cloth of history as these two novels. Faulkner's two books alone contain much which can never be found in the gaudier romance. There is history in the works of Faulkner and Mitchell, but the depths of humanity appear only in Faulkner. In Scarlett's marriages and aspirations and Rhett Butler's ruthlessness there are parallels to Sutpen.[9] But no one in *Gone with the Wind* is capable of Sutpen's tragic failure.

Gone with the Wind lacks true depth for one reason: it leaves evil out of the garden of Tara. The "clumsy sprawling building," the old oaks, the lawn "reclaimed from weeds," the "avenue of cedars," and the slave quarters have "an air of solidness, of stability and permanence" until the Yankees come. In shallow romantic fiction except for occasional bad manners all evils flow entirely from without. The houses of great literature fall before enemies, and usually they simultaneously crumble or at least struggle from within. Consider the complex forces in the Sutpen mansion as Sutpen builds it almost with his bare hands and as it is burned by its founder's mulatto descendant. And compare the house of the seven gables and even the establishments of the Montagues and the Capulets. It is almost as if *Gone with the Wind* shares the simplicity and the callousness of its heroine, who endured struggles which "passed over her without touching any deep chord within her."[10]

The determined and vengeful Drusilla in *The Unvanquished* is a greater enigma and tragedy than Miss Mitchell's willful and selfish Scarlett, and Bayard Sartoris' struggles in killing Grumby and renouncing the sword are deeper than any of the petty issues of the "sub-pornographic" romance *Gone with the Wind*.[11] With Scarlett we enjoy being titillated by the hope of sexual promiscuities for the sake of material security, and then foolishly we are disappointed that she did not keep her Rhett in the end. Faulkner's Drusilla is unsexed by the loss of a lover in war; John Sartoris is violently destroyed with some justification and Bayard is redeemed by his courage and conviction in renouncing violence. *Gone with the Wind* has no character with their consistency, sacrifice, courage, and suffering. No prominent character except for the weak Ashley and the too-perfect Melanie is constant in depth and integrity. Romantic stereotypes cannot even confront the decisions of great characters created by a great and noble mind.

Movements through the city during the burning of Atlanta magnificently but superficially portray the shiftings about of small men caught in terrible forces, but *Gone with the Wind* never catches all the complexity of the Negroes marching for freedom and "homemade Jordan" in *The Unvanquished*, caught in a tangle of forces they cannot comprehend, rejected by the very soldiers who freed them, understood by some of the owners from whom they flee. The battle of Atlanta in *Gone with the Wind* is good pageantry, but its accomplishment stops precisely there. The victor is victor in romantic fiction, but Faulkner's greater work shows a victor overrun by those he liberated and harassed by those he defeated. In contrast, Margaret Mitchell's novel, in the words of her brother, "struck a blow for her Southland."[12] The freed slave here is just another mean nigger who causes an uprising by the Ku Klux Klan, punishment of southern whites by the Yankees, and the death of another of Scarlett's husbands. In Faulkner, he is a massive physical force or a minor character and a political issue. The great drama of the forces of history appears in Faulkner's work but not in Mitchell's. This is negative criticism, almost pure judgment. But the wise critic can make it from a perspective and with taste which cannot be shared by the large popular audience which admired *Gone with the Wind*. In the final analysis, pure assertion must have some critical place. Fiction has often fought the Civil War, and the soldiers in Warren's *Wilderness* and *All the King's Men* and in Crane's *Red Badge* engage in profounder personal and massive struggles. It is possible to bury one's head among the rapidly shuffling pages and insist that *Gone with the Wind* is good because it is an engaging story, excellently told; but when proof is not forthcoming, the same claim can also be made about "Marse Chan," *The Little Shepherd of Kingdom Come*, and Thomas Dixon's *The Clansman*. Damning a novel with faint praise because of what it does not contain is inadequate criticism, but at least it is a beginning point.

But all the errors of *Gone with the Wind* are not of omission. Much in the novel is bad, false to the facts of rural and southern life particularly, false to history, and, worst of all, false to human nature. Grandiloquent claims have been made for the historical accuracy of *Gone with the Wind*. Margaret Mitchell, we are told, "did write the truth, and because she did her novel is the authentic historical study as well as a fascinating love story."[13] And her biographer wrote in 1965 that "so far as can be determined, there is not even a minute error of fact in the novel."[14] Patently, such a claim may be wrong; Andrew Lytle believes that the novelist may create only "the illusion of past time . . . because finally . . . we must leave the truth to God."[15]

Factual errors in *Gone with the Wind*, however, do exist, though most of them are negligible. The most obvious mistakes lie in the field of pyronomics. One burning southern plantation home has its fire remarkably extinguished: "The wooden wing of Mimosa had burned and only the thick resistant stucco of the main house and the frenzied work of the Fontaine women and their slaves with wet blankets and quilts had saved it." (p. 471). John Carter, a fire investigator for the city of Atlanta, comments that their methods of fire-fighting were "surely impractical" if not impossible. "Three years of stored cotton" go up in flame which lights "up the place lak it wuz day . . . , and it wuz so bright in this hyah room that you could mos' pick a needle offen the flo" (p. 418). But loose cotton burns with a tiny blue flame, and baled cotton only smolders.[16] The statistics of slave-owning in Margaret Mitchell's Clayton County do not conform to actuality. Poor white trash in *Gone with the Wind* never own more than four Negroes (p. 17), but in Clayton County only thirty-six farmers owned more than ten Negroes, and only 134 owned from one to ten. To reach even the lowly status of poor white, a man in this county in fiction would have to own as many slaves as a middling slaveowner in fact. The Tarletons own one hundred Negroes (p. 6), and apparently several other plantations in the novel are about that same size. But the census of 1860 lists no slaveowner with that many slaves in Clayton County, and only one owned between forty and fifty slaves. The luxuriousness of class has been exaggerated for poor white and large plantation owner. False romance is created by increasing the number of slaves. In *Gone with the Wind* during Reconstruction a citizen could not vote "if he was on the tax books for more than two thousand dollars in 'sixty-five" (p. 523). Mitchell exaggerated and dropped a digit. Those denied amnesty in fact were the ones whose taxable wealth surpassed twenty thousand dollars.[17]

The romance is also false because Miss Mitchell reaches too low into the barrel for her chief poor white family, the Slatterys. They own a "meager three acres," where they grow a "few acres of cotton" and a poor vegetable garden. Slattery begs cotton seed for planting or a side of bacon "to tide him over" (pp. 48–49). The economics and the culture are wrong. In 1860 only two farm families in Clayton County farmed as few as three to ten acres, and only seven as few as ten to twenty. Probably no one with the name of farmer tilled as few as the three in fiction. When the poor white begged in the South, he asked only for those things his wealthier neighbor could not use—such as corn cobs which might be soaked and fed to the cows. Usually he begged for nothing, as is shown in Faulkner's more accurate representation of the yeoman farmer in the fiercely independent convict of *Old Man*, and the Bundrens, who refuse to be beholden.

But many errors are more serious than factual errors though less definite. Romances of the Civil War and southern history and the admiration for romances have had a pernicious influence. Southern readers—and foolish romantic readers anywhere—dream of an impossible past, expect more of the present than can be realized, ignore an authentic culture while praising a false culture that never existed, foolishly defend themselves against attacks from the North, use false defenses of illogic and rhetoric, become vulnerable to attacks that could be avoided, fall victim to false and pretentious characters in dreamers and political demagogues, ignore and condemn the yeomanry and the peasantry. False history causes sentimentality about the past and hopelessness about the present. For other reasons false history can fail. Sheldon Van Auken has indicated that the old southern way of life could be defended only after it "is no longer regarded as a menace" and that then "the North listens to its voice with interest and appreciation."[18] In part, of course, it has failed to continue to be a menace to northern and modern culture because it has been falsely romanticized and made aristocratic. A true picture of the values of yeoman Clayton County might form a threat to the monolithic patterns of progress in our culture. *Gone with the Wind* is no menace to anything false. It has what Richard Chase calls a "fatal inner falsity."[19] It is like chamber of commerce advertising, which can sell almost anything but a true picture of the complexity of life in the South (or anywhere else, for that matter).

Formal manners and dress in *Gone with the Wind* give a false picture of the old South, idealize its flaws, and suggest that people who are perfect in the social proprieties are also perfect or nearly so in their human relations. Scarlett's "seventeen-inch waist, the smallest in three counties" (p. 3), may be possible. But it surely is improbable considering her buxom flesh. Even on weekdays she wears stays "laced too tightly to permit much running" (p. 24). Maybe on certain streets in older towns such as Charleston and New Orleans this might be the fashion, but so much style in Jonesboro, Georgia, seems most unlikely. The rather stereotyped Irish head of the O'Hara plantation, Gerald, wears a cravat when he goes on a trip to buy a slave—even on a weekday (p. 29). And before he married, this rough, florid forty-three-year-old bachelor had a valet who served his "meals with dignity and style" (p. 51). These formalities sit better in the *Ladies Home Journal* or with Peggy Marsh in Atlanta in the 1920s than with an Irish farmer in Clayton County before the Civil War. During the summers "the County averaged a barbecue and ball nearly every week" (p. 86), and lusty girls like Scarlett were supposed to "eat lak a bird" at the barbecues until their marriages. The intimate details of going to bed move almost with the formality of a barbecue. The chief Negro slave leads the family upstairs "with the pompous dignity of a first chamberlain of the royal bedchamber lighting a king and queen to their rooms" (p. 71). Presumably the social amenities and formalities reflect a society untroubled by most human frailties before it is destroyed by depraved Yankees. The problem is not that these things never happened. Southern society has its manners, even its going-to-bed rituals, but I suggest that these concentrations of formalities in

Miss Mitchell's novel are propaganda instead of history. Social purpose is in control when Negroes come home from their field work and the whites hear "the shrill careless laughter of Negro voices" (p. 8). There is no mention of sweat, of exhaustion, of the arduousness of field work. *Gone with the Wind* is a world without sweat, except for that caused by the Yankees.

The contrast in manners is completely apparent when women follow northern soldiers into Atlanta. "They were so lately come from nothing and so uncertain of themselves they were doubly anxious to appear refined" (p. 879). Some have been chambermaids; some grew up in a room over the family saloon; and one "had come out of one of her husband's own brothels" (p. 879). But they foolishly strive to be as gracious in their manners as ladies on a southern plantation.

Perhaps *Gone with the Wind* is one of the last books to be openly patriotic and popular in our time. It defies all the lessons of restraint which Miss Mitchell could have learned from the early Hemingway, and it blatantly defends what Stephens Mitchell called "the Southland." It is sentimental and patriotic and melodramatic—and shallow, enough to make shallow readers, even radical modern integrationists, suspend their disbelief. The home guard, the militia, and home-front patriots sing the "Bonnie Blue Flag," and tears come with "a deep hot glow in eyes" (p. 170). Ashley and Miss Mitchell define the Civil War and the cause of the war in a sentimental fashion which is altogether foreign to the twentieth century except among some readers of a vast popular audience: "Perhaps," Ashley says, "that is what is called patriotism, love of home and country. . . . I am fighting for the old days, the old ways I love so much but which, I fear, are now gone forever, no matter how the die may fall" (p. 211). Sentimentally, but truly, they are gone with the wind; and not all the weeping and wailing can bring them back. Obviously, Miss Mitchell satirizes Scarlett's chivalric dreams, but by creating characters like Scarlett and Ashley and making them admirable, Miss Mitchell also is a victim of their sentimentality. Given the plot and characters, there is no way to make "Marse Chan" or *Gone with the Wind* truly realistic. Ashley is "a young girl's dream of the Perfect Knight" (p. 214), and every female heart that ever dreamed of Walter Scott or soap opera falls victim along with Scarlett.

The irony of defeat—an irony that could not be treated by a contemporary like Timrod—is conveyed mainly through the character of Rhett Butler. No patriot, Rhett predicts defeat. He even sees the flaws of the Confederacy, represented by the contract holders who sell "shoddy cloth, sanded sugar, spoiled flour and rotten leather to the Confederacy" (p. 228). But Rhett is not enough to remove the stigma of sentimental patriotism. Truth breaks in to encourage the woebegone reader: "But even with this loss on the top of the others, the South's spirit was not broken. True, grim determination had taken the place of high-hearted hopes, but people could still find a silver lining in the cloud" (p. 278). Such triteness is followed by tear-jerking sorrow over the retreating army. Even the sardonic Rhett finally makes a patriotic speech (and it is only half-comic) before going to join the Confederate army. There is a "malicious tenderness" in his voice as he speaks to Scarlett (p. 389). Rhett is a tough guy who could get along well with the roughest of Hemingway's characters, but when he softens he is a blithering patriotic old sentimentalist, for all his rough ways with women. And his sentimentality is as false as the falsest thing of the sea. He goes to war purely for feeling, not because the South had any kind of true cause. Rhett and Miss Mitchell might have learned a great deal from a poem like Donald Davidson's "Lee in the Mountains."

An oversimplified regionalism in *Gone with the Wind* is the source from which nearly all evils flow. There has been all too much of this in southern fiction. *To Kill a Mockingbird*, for example, a Pulitzer Prize winner as was *Gone with the Wind*, divides humanity into good blacks and good white southern liberals versus bad white southerners. *Gone with the Wind* is on the opposite side. Yet both books take sides so superficially that one wonders if the authors would not have switched sides with the times. Nothing southern is so inglorious as the Reverend Hightower's grandfather, shot while he was stealing chickens from a henhouse. No northern soldier is so kindly as the Yankee officer who refuses to drag the children Bayard and Ringo from the protection of an old woman's skirt. No scalawag is so admirable as Redmond in Faulkner's "An

Odor of Verbena." He refuses to shoot even to protect himself when the young Bayard Sartoris comes to see him apparently seeking vengeance. Instead, despite such foolish and extreme claims by historians as the contentions that slavery was the only issue or that it was not a main issue at all, *Gone with the Wind* is one of the most oversimplified treatments of the Civil War. The chief contention of the book and its author is that Yankees are bad and southerners are good. Yankee soldiers burn and loot; southerners visit folks on the home front and encourage them without taking their foodstuffs. The scalawag of *Gone with the Wind* is unalleviated evil. Mulatto babies increase after northern soldiers come to town; northern mothers refuse to trust their babies "to a black nigger"; and Negroes give northerners who fought for them "the creeps" (pp. 671–672). The only good scalawag was Rhett Butler, who merely acted like one so that he might learn information useful to the defeated South. The manners of Yankees who visit Scarlett are so bad that they use the rugs to spit on "no matter how many spittoons she might put out in plain view" (p. 879).

Yankees are romantic and false because they do not conform to human nature. A novel may legitimately portray a just cause, and most of the good people in fiction can fight on just one side. But when *all* the good soldiers belong on one side and *all* the bad ones on another, then the novel has become propaganda, even if it was written more than seventy years after the physical conflict ceased. But if Yankees are evil and if some southerners are guilty of some foibles, perfection on the southern side does represent the regional perfection of Miss Mitchell's romantic Southland. The most unbelievable character in the book, perhaps the heroine, is Melanie Wilkes. Typically, the chief goodness belongs to a woman; the novel, after all, was written by a woman; and in the plantation tradition the South was a matriarchy, with fumbling but kindly men and competent and altogether loving women. Miss Mitchell explicitly attributes complete goodness to Melanie: "In all her sheltered life she had never seen evil and could scarcely credit its existence, and when gossip whispered things about Rhett and the girl in Charleston, she was shocked and unbelieving" (p. 222). (The narrow puritanism of the novel at times is indicated by things like

the equation here of evil and immorality which is only sexual.)
Melanie's trivial flaw is that she is physically so "small-hipped" that
she has great difficulty bearing a child. Attended only by Scarlett
during the birth of her baby while the Battle of Atlanta is raging,
she says, "Don't bother about talking, dear. I know how worried
you are. I'm so sorry I'm so much trouble" (p. 356). But Melanie,
confronted by Yankee evil embodied in a soldier in Tara, can turn
to steel. She rises from her bed and gets her dead brother's saber to
defend Scarlett. When she speaks after Scarlett shoots him, Scarlett sees "beneath the gentle voice and the dovelike eyes . . . a thin
flashing blade of unbreakable steel [and she] felt too that there
were banners and bugles of courage in Melanie's quiet blood" (p.
441). Melanie starves herself to save food for hungry soldiers. She
can confront necessity more boldly than Scarlett. After her Ashley
has been shot while carrying out a chivalric mission by the Ku Klux
Klan, Rhett Butler brings him home. Since hostile soldiers can
hear the conversation, Melanie calls in a loud clear voice, "Bring
him in, Captain Butler. . . . I supposed you've gotten him intox-
icated again. Bring him in" (p. 802). Melanie has too few flaws to be
human—and none of any significance. But she is more than an
idealization of a perfect woman. Miss Mitchell intended her to be
representative of southern regional goodness to counteract northern regional badness. She is "the gentle, self-effacing but steel-
spined women on whom the South had builded its house in war
and to whose proud and loving arms it had returned in defeat" (p.
1026). If Scarlett is all a repressed Atlanta debutante and matron
might wish to be in her most fleshly moments, Melanie is what
Miss Mitchell knew a woman ought to be. But she is so perfect that
she is not a sound basis for good fiction. She contains no evil. She
sins too little.

Gone with the Wind is far too prudish to be a good novel. Miss
Mitchell flirts with the risque. Four times Scarlett is called one
kind of "piece" or another, and I suggest that Miss Mitchell would
have enjoyed protesting her innocence while appreciating the in-
nuendos. Except for the women visited in offstage trips to Belle
Watling's brothel, there is no true piece in *Gone with the Wind*.
The point of the love scenes between Rhett and Scarlett even dur-

ing their marriage is Scarlett's frigidity. The chief sexual characteristic of the women in the novel is an unhealthy curiosity about
the life of prostitutes. When Dr. Meade's wife asks him about life
upstairs at the whorehouse, the good doctor is "thunderstruck";
and several times women are just this curious. Once Miss Mitchell
writes that "most innocent and well-bred young women . . . had a
devouring curiosity about prostitutes" (p. 248). But prudishness
becomes even more incredible. The devoted Melanie does not
wish to have to be so frank in a letter as to tell her husband that she
is going to have a baby (p. 282). Scarlett delivers the baby. Later,
she kills a soldier who is looting Tara and asks Melanie for her
shimmy to "wad it around his head" in order to avoid leaving a
bloody trail (p. 444). Melanie's face turns crimson, but all of Scarlett's bluntness and directness do not prove that the "nicey-nice"
way is wrong. Girls are auctioned off to dance with men and to
make money for the southern cause, but their reaction is too
ridiculous to appear in any believable novel. When Maybelle Mer-
riwether was bid on, she "collapsed with blushes against Fanny's
shoulder and the two girls hid their faces in each other's necks and
giggled."

Gone with the Wind is narrowly patriotic, prudish, melodramatic, and sentimental. Belle Watling is as good a whore as ever
lived; her patriotic sacrifices, her philanthropy for the Confederate
cause, and her protection of good Ku Klux Klansmen make her as
fine a woman as Bret Harte's Mother Shipton. It is a pity that
Thomas Wolfe never had a chance to turn his parody on Gone with
the Wind. Rhett is as straight out of melodrama as Wolfe's Faro
Bill. Two men are killed during a raid by the Klan. To protect other
Klansmen, Rhett gives instructions to "put them in that lot and put
pistols near them—in their hands. . . . Fire one shot from each.
It's got to appear like a plain case of shooting. You understand?"
"Archie nodded as if he understood perfectly and an unwilling
gleam of respect shone in his cold eye" (p. 808). When Wolfe's
Faro Jim fixes his "vulturesque eye" on the "little dance girl" with
"suave murder in his heart, . . . the cold gray eyes of the Stranger
missed nothing. Imperturbably he drank his Scotch, wheeled from
the mirror with barking Colt just one-sixth of a second before the

gambler could fire. Faro coughed and slid forward slowly upon the floor."

> There was no sound now in the crowded room of the Triple Y. . . .
> "By God, stranger!" . . . [the sheriff] ejaculated. "I never knew the man lived who could beat Faro to the draw. What's yore name?"
> "In the fam'ly Bible back home, pardner," the Stranger drawled, "it's Eugene Gant, but folks out here generally calls me The Dixie Ghost."
> There was a slow gasp of wonder from the crowd.
> Gawd!" some one whispered. "It's the Ghost!"[20]

In Miss Mitchell's scene Rhett Butler apologizes like a gentleman after he has saved Melanie's husband and almost called her Miss Melly. Then

> "I beg your pardon, I mean, Mrs. Wilkes. . . ."
> "Oh, Captain Butler, do not ask my pardon. I should feel honored if you called me 'Melly' without the Miss!"

Similarly, *Look Homeward, Angel* parodied this overformal melodrama before it was written. Bruce Glendenning, cast away with the beautiful Veronica on a desert island, has never told the damsel he loves her. When a band of natives charges, at last he feels free to speak. Then a destroyer steams into view.

> "Saved! We are saved!" cried Glendenning, and leaping to his feet he signalled the approaching boat. Suddenly he paused.
> "Damn!" he muttered bitterly. "Oh, damn!"
> "What is it, Bruce?" she asked.
> "A destroyer has just entered the harbor. We are saved, Miss Mullins. Saved!" And he laughed bitterly. (p. 107)

Gone with the Wind is much more than a simple story. It also consists of melodrama, sentimentality, perfect characters, evil and good in black and white, anti-Negro racism, discursive essays on history and politics usually at the beginning of a chapter in the manner of Theodore Dreiser, writing in the spirit of a chamber of commerce, artificial dialogue, exaggerated Negro dialect almost at times in the speech of Irwin Russell's Negroes. The flaws of *Gone with the Wind* are not merely those of omission. It is a simple story, almost simple-minded at times. Great literature can occasionally be popular, and certainly popular literature can occasionally be great. But with a few notable exceptions, such as the Bible but not *Gone with the Wind*, greatness and popularity are more likely to be contradictory than congenial.

4

William Sidney Drewry, *The Southampton Insurrection*.
Washington: The Neale Company, 1900. Facing p. 50.

Home of Mr. Nathaniel Francis

Dwight Lowell Dumond, *Antislavery: The Crusade for Freedom in Americ*
Ann Arbor: The University of Michigan Press, p. 11

The Capture of Nat Turner

✺§ FOUR ॐ

The Confessions of Nat Turner:
History and Imagination

The Confessions of Nat Turner, by William Styron, begins with
Nat's view of a "barren, sandy cape where the river joins the
sea"—a landscape that provides for the reader an image of the
teeming life of the sea, which Nat had experienced only through
the bars of his prison and in his imagination. He knows that there is
a river estuary below a cliff, but he is physically and mentally
locked within a totality of physical, spiritual, and civil imprison-
ments as well as within chattel slavery. He does not know which
river estuary, the name of the river, or the appearance of any landscape where the land joins the sea. William Styron says that he
intended the landscape to be vague, in congruity with the enforced
blindness of Nat's prison cell.[1] Nat had never been "allowed the
opportunity of a trip to Norfolk and the ocean."[2]

The other gaps in the mind of the protagonist in this section of
the novel are appalling. He can see that the day is clear, but this is
a vision of a sky without a world. Time is so out of joint with him
that he does not know whether it is the beginning of spring or the
end of summer. The world to him, as prisoner and slave, is essentially a vacuum—"benign and neutral, windless, devoid of heat or
cold" (p. 3). His helplessness is envisioned as an approach to the
place in a boat merely adrift: "I do not row" (p. 3). That he is at the
mercy of his world is shown by the boat's "moving obediently" to
the currents of the river. The shores of Nat's world are peculiarly
devoid of life and habitation, "unpeopled, silent." There are "no
deer," no gulls, only "great silence and . . . even greater solitude"
(p. 3).

As Nat drifts in his imagination on the river he sees one building,
and so far as he can tell it does not even have an aperture, "neither
doors nor windows" (p. 4). He does not venture an interpretation

51

but envisions only a "profound mystery which to explore would yield only a profusion of darker and perhaps more troubling mysteries, as in a maze" (p. 4). The reader can understand Nat's impenetrable mystery: physically it is a complete enclosure, so far as we can see without the exit or egress even of air. It is the structure, the box, the tomb, even the pyramid of slavery. Nat does not himself know its meaning. Its enclosure is emphasized by Nat's ignorance of the sea (the world), which he has not seen but only heard about from "a few Negroes of Southampton" (p. 5). But slavery has its extraordinary hungers, intensified so much that Nat's imagination is "inflamed." Slavery, of which all this is symbol or image, provides Nat no release, and he has to content himself with "recurring phantasm" (p. 5).

Styron has been accused of not describing the real places of Nat's life.[3] In reading or writing there are different kinds of associations between the place of fiction and that of the source. When I read about Faulkner's Compsons, for example, I see one of my grandfather's old farm homes, the barn and the pasture. Styron's places seem to be much more inventions of the mind. He built his own homes and established his own terrain. Thus those charges that he looked at the wrong Whitehead home when he made a short visit in Virginia seem irrelevant as long as the home is true to the kinds of homes some families lived in during the time of Turner's rebellion (interview). It is, Styron says, just a combination of all the old country homes in Virginia of this style, but not a thing of grandeur in the manner of Westover.

History leaves gaps about the feelings and the things of slavery—such as, for example, what a slave took with him when he was sold to another owner. Fiction must fill in. When Samuel Turner sold Nat to the Reverend Eppes, "My Bible was the only possession I had to take away from Turner's Mill save for these things: a single change of denim pants, two cotton shirts, an extra pair of what are elegantly known as nigger brogans, some little bone crosses I had carved, a needle and some thread, a pewter cup left to me by my mother, and a ten-dollar gold piece which Marse Samuel had given me" (p. 229). Compared to the traded slaves, Steinbeck's migrant Joads were wealthy. What Nat takes with him defines slavery. These are the images and things of human chattel. History does not provide a list of the objects, and consequently the symbolic meanings of the objects are lost except to the imagination. This is not merely to say that history is limited but that it is circumscribed by the stated conjecture and the absolutely known. Here is fiction's virtue. It does not have to be minutely accurate, but if it contradicts too many facts or the spirit of the times it can be historically flawed.

Of course any item of the life of white or black is subject to a racial, a historical, or a social interpretation. Styron's very selection is subjective. The cultural data of the everyday world, for one thing, show how much the slave is acted upon, how little he may do for himself, how passive he is. Objects which revealed many independent actions of the slave and thus freedom would depict a false culture, erroneous history. Readers may judge (as I do) that Styron's view of the liberty of action allowed the slave is about right, but no kind of critical or social study can furnish a measurement of this accuracy.

The beginning of *The Confessions of Nat Turner*, then, provides a set of images designed entirely to show the state of mind of one who is both civil criminal and chattel slave—at least in the mind of the dominant class. The succeeding pattern reveals the physical abasement of the slave. In prison Nat has a cedar plank for a bed, leg irons to limit movement and prevent escape, no heat to relieve the "wintry touch about the morning" (p. 6), and no warm breakfast on arousal. The glimpses of life Nat may see from his open barred window reveal a world only somewhat less miserable than the cell. He sees a moving candle, a woman emptying the accumulations of the night's chamber pot, and the privy. The first real activity of the morning comes when "a distant drumming noise, a plunging of hoofbeats" (p. 7), signals the arrival of fresh soldiers and the changing of the guard to prevent the escape of this least free of all mortals. Slowly the life of the prison begins to stir.

This is an extensive account of the imagery of Nat's pitiful world at the beginning of the novel. Styron has chosen a wretched circumstance for the beginning. It is a time of all the despair as well as the dullness of life in prison and in chattel slavery—which is worse one might question without answer. Hope is gone; all the action but confession and execution is over; and the intensity and trauma of the final emotional moments have not begun. There is a particular reason for this point of departure. In a sense every single aspect of *The Confessions* is a revelation of slavery, its objects, and, most importantly, the states of mind created by the condition. Nat's mind in the beginning is a metaphor for the most abject slavery, yet every other slaver and indeed the mind of every white man in the book is to be seen somehow in its relationship with slavery. Slaves and even slavery have at least brief moments of triumph. Schematically and in structure the novel starts with the darkest hour of the rebellious and revolutionary slave at the physical and psychological mercy of his oppressors.

Knowing that it is still impossible to cut through all the rumors and records and lies about Nat and even slavery itself, Styron attempts what he has been so defamed for, "a meditation on history." Styron made some efforts to get at previous subjective impressions of the facts of the case: He read Frederick Law Olmsted, Stanley Elkins, the Grimké sisters, Malcolm Cowley and Danille Pratt Mannix's *Black Cargoes*, B. A. Botkin's folklore, excerpts from slave narratives, Fanny Kemble, and others. And he had lived in Virginia. Necessarily, he did not read Henry Irving Tragle's *The Southampton Slave Revolt of 1831: A Compilation of Source Material*—it had not been written. He might have learned some more facts from Tragle, but rumors and errors are so great in that work that one would not expect greater accuracy on the whole from it than from the novel. History is generality, social fact, a violent but impersonal episode as it is written. Slaves and their masters in history, for example, seldom speak in direct quotation. Journalistic accounts collected from the time seem to possess less truth than the rumors of war and battle in *The Red Badge of Courage*.

A good novelist must create a living man. Even the supposedly factual slave narratives are different from life; a diary is an interpretation. Slaves and ex-slaves have written narratives, but they admittedly are colored by the slaves' memories as well as by the propagandistic intent of the slaves' amanuenses and editors. Thus even an account of a slave by the slave himself is a meditation. The life of a slave is revealed as he *remembers* his past and meditates on it at the present moment. This is a flaw of any history, of course, but it is much more so a flaw in the remembered works of folk history and an illiterate people. Slave narratives strove for truth and effect, but *The Confessions*, I believe, is the only significant novel by a white man which attempts to re-create the immediacy and intensity in its presentation of the moment-to-moment events and thoughts of a slave.

In the twentieth century the oppression of slavery has not existed except in isolated primitivistic situations and criminal cir-cumstances. Parallels to slavery may exist in folklore, printed his-tory, and racism. Analogies to slavery exist in any oppression—in the family, military service, prisons, and concentration camps. But in no situation in the twentieth century does a man legally own the body as well as the services of another man. A great chasm must be leaped when one attempts to get back to the ways a slave and his master spoke and thought. The paucity of objects in a slave's world must reveal his oppression; and the objects and ways of the life of the master must reveal the effect on him of being the oppressor, willing or not. These objects are not vast social issues, but they are the furniture of daily life, things like the cradle that the slave "flang" down on John Hartwell Cocke's plantation when he became disgusted at work not for his own gain,[4] the food and the toilet, the hoe and the musical instrument. This was the task William Styron set himself. History has not preserved what Styron wanted except as some well-sanded and polished and painted or varnished curio on the wall of an antique shop. Some things have not survived at all. Coffles have been endured and witnessed, but any modern narrator's mind must imagine them at a great distance. At the mo-ment of its existence Styron's coffle is experienced from the perspective of a pampered black man living in the abjectness and deprivations of a coffle's food, sanitation, and toiletry. Nat Turner thinks a story that no living person has ever seen, recounts it, and recounts the reactions of the other characters.

So long as fiction re-creates rather than violates the spirit of the times and the mysteries of human nature, it may be superior to or truer than history. Fiction must be fuller, more personal, more dramatic. As the historian follows his method and creates the life-blood of a man, he cannot say what he does not know. The novelist must present and enact scenes whether he knows them factually or not. History may have to accept gaps in the Watergate tapes; fiction must create material to fill them. The historian may conjecture what happened; the novelist has to know. There is a small body of facts agreed on by many of Nat's contemporaries and the historians, but they do not get at the lifeblood of the man and his times. Styron's Nat is a meditation, and not enough is known about the real Nat to make him anything else. The Nats of Styron's critics and historians are also meditations, but there is not enough characterization of him to make him a person. Their syllogism runs that all rebellious Negro slaves of some success were heroes; Nat was a slave and a rebel; therefore Nat was heroic and without blemish. In general Styron invents in a way different from that of the presumed historian. He creates details from daily living, sexual episodes for example, which are unknown to the historian. But ideologically what he does is no more far-fetched than the writings of pseudohistorians, no more so than Thomas Wentworth Higginson's essay or the writings of the crusader William Wells Brown. Styron had to extend the range of his imagination beyond the ken of many historical novelists. He had to find what he could about slavery in history, imagine the rest of it in human terms, and draw analogues from autocratic authority in relationships outside slavery. His task was difficult because the life of the slave, like that of the yeoman white, had been recorded only in folklore and in the writings of others about black and yeoman white.

Practices of fiction do not demand that Styron follow true history in relating what happened to Nat in the places where he lived and with the families who owned him. Fiction must conform only to the possibility of life at the time and in the place and according to human nature. Cultural and daily facts of life in a historical novel may derive from sources besides known events in the life of the subject. A credible historical character must conform to the novelist's experience of people. Manners may derive from the recorded facts of personal history, but such detail varies from person to person and from farm to farm. One who knows rural life in one age may with some success transfer folklore and culture to another time. A washpan in one time is like a washpan in another, even if one is of tin and another is of china. To the extent that an attitude is valid in general human terms, it may be transferred to another era.

The totality of the world of *The Confessions*, then, is known in our time only by limited analogues. Styron assumes the incredible obligation of creating a world which is unknown to us but which must seem as real to us as our own kitchen stove. Every image, every object, is related to the world of slavery, and besides having its own reality it must impinge on the mind of the reader and that of the character as being routinely real. On the whole, with some exceptions, authors do not choose from the humanly imagined so much as from the factually known or historically researched. Obviously, Styron has failed for some readers from an ideological perspective; from the human and cultural perspectives, however, I believe that he has succeeded in terms of what men might have been in that remote world.

Not a single character in the book has an entirely correct view of the relationships between the races. Even Nat's condemnations of whites are not always to be trusted. Although he recognizes that there is "a kind of *love*" felt for him by his owner, he maintains that his education "began as surely an experiment as a lesson in pig-breeding or the broadcasting of a new type of manure" (p. 155). Nat's prejudice is understandable, but the statement is unfair to his white owner. In a time when many believed that the "darky is an animal with the brain of a human child" (p. 162), when Negroes did not read, any change could be unfairly called an experiment no matter what the personal feelings of the master. Nat first hears himself called a slave when he is old enough for Samuel Turner to plan to teach him to read. Then "a wicked chill like cold water filled the hollow of my gut as the thought crashed in upon me: *Yes, I am a slave*" (p. 164). Thus the idea of slavery first invades the consciousness of a child. And Nat as well as Styron has condemned the system. But Nat's view is not the whole truth. He lived in such a kindly situation that he remained ignorant of his chattel status for a long time. The phenomenon was not unusual. The historian John W. Blassingame has shown that "many young blacks had no ideas they were slaves."[5] Nat's insurrection is not attributable to the physical horrors of slavery but to his spiritual and psychological rebellion despite the comforts of his own situation. Provided education, training, and opportunity, Nat revolts because his owner did not give him promised freedom and because he lived a life soft enough to enable him to plan and lead a revolt. Styron has thus depicted primarily not the physical horrors of slavery so much as the moral and psychological aspects of it, which are especially demeaning.

No one can defend slavery now. Because slavery is indefensible, slaveowners in Nat Turner's time were wrong. From this point, it is easy to proceed and to maintain that the white was inhumane, monstrous, absolutely evil. The defenders and justifiers of Nat, similarly, demand almost absolute heroism. Any flaw in the character is an attack on a George Washington of the Negro race, an emasculation of the black race by the novelist. But fiction cannot be created about perfect heroes. Extremism denies humanity, and humanness is the first principle of art.

Styron, I believe, is less bigoted than any significant novelist who has extensively treated the race question in recent decades. Black and white are credibly human. One relationship in the novel, for example, attributes great humanity to white and black, to the judge and to his prisoner whom he condemns to death. Nat and the judge are human as well as racist. Judge Cobb, who has suffered greatly, lives in physical pain. He has lost stables, horses, and a Negro groom in a fire; his wife and two daughters have died of typhoid. At first Nat takes joy in Judge Cobb's disasters. He mutters to himself, "Feel sorry for a white man and you wastin' your sorrow" (p. 58). Cobb overhears him and still condemns slavery in a vehement rhetorical tirade. "Oh, Virginia, woe betide thee! Woe, thrice woe, and ever damned in memory be the day when poor black men in chains first trod upon thy sacred strand." When two whites drive the lovable Hark up a tree to punish him by his fear of heights, Cobb pities him (p. 83). Then Nat does precisely what he had said the Negro should not do—he feels "sorry for a white man." When his mission comes to pass "and Jerusalem is destroyed," he says, "this man Cobb will be among those few

58

spared the sword" (p. 75). The humanity of Nat and Cobb encloses the inhumanity of the punishers of Hark. More than that, Nat can feel sorrow for Cobb even as the judge passes out the death sentence. Seeing Cobb's eyes "sunk deep within their sockets," Nat realizes "that he too was close to death, very close, almost as close as I myself, and I felt a curious pang of pity and regret" (p. 105). Nat Turner is a fanatic, but not only that: he is compassionately human too. Again there is a general source rather than a particular one. Styron derived the compassions of the two from a mere hint, he says, in the original confessions (interview).

The purpose of *The Confessions* is not to take us back to history. All the searchings and researchings seem to indicate that the story of Nat Turner can be known only in rumors and small and fragmentary parts. One purpose is to get back to a social and cultural world. So far as I can tell, Styron is culturally correct except in one instance. He erred, I think, in regard to cemetery customs. Lucy Skipwith, the "Black Ma" on the John Hartwell Cocke plantation, was buried in the family cemetery, and "others of their caste received similar respect."[6] Similarly, Nat's mother, "alone among all the Negroes at Turner's Mill, had been laid honorably to rest in the family plot among white folks" (p. 185). But the graves of the other Negroes rest idle for a brief respite, then are returned to agriculture. As one cemetery is plowed up at the Turner place, one Negro man observes, "Dem old dead peoples is sho gwine grow a nice passel of yams!" (p. 132). The incident is one of moment in Nat's understanding of slavery. To me this is Styron's worst misrepresentation of culture of black or white. Slaves in many family cemeteries in north Georgia were buried in the same graveyard with whites—though only the latter might have tombstones. Southern respect for the dead prevented abuse of all cemeteries both black and white. (I have compared my views with those of Bell I. Wiley and others.) At most churches black and white cemeteries were adjacent rather than integrated. There may be, however, a direct source for the plowing up of the cemetery on the Cocke plantation. There was a Cemetery Field on the plantation, but whether it was named that because it had been a cemetery or a field close to a cemetery is now an imponderable. Styron defends himself: "Anything that was possible," he says, he "could use. If that places fiction above history, I am willing to do so if it does no disservice to the spirit of the time. An out and out lie is not acceptable. If plowing up the cemetery is wrong, it was an honest mistake" (interview).

Perhaps the final question about *The Confessions* is whether the system of slavery as Styron presents it allows for the "great variety of personality types in the quarters,"[7] whether there are characters other than some rebellious Jack, a fawning Sambo, or a decorous house butler—and whether there are whites other than blessed white Massahs, Simon Legrees, poor whites, and cruel overseers. Precisely here, I think, Styron has been fairest to black and white of any novelist writing primarily about a race question in the American novel. Even slavery per se does not altogether govern the character of a man, does not determine his goodness and badness by his blackness and whiteness. Styron has said that he was not consciously aware of attributing good or evil to any character on racial grounds (interview). The pattern was human nature, which tends to survive any system with some modifications. Indeed, slavery, Styron says, was a human situation in which people reacted very much as they do now (interview). That is, they are true to their natures in any racial or human situation.

Nat's own failings and accomplishments are seen basically in human terms. Styron has bestowed on him the mixed blessings of humanity and complexity. He is in twentieth-century terms a visionary and even a meditative intellectual. He thinks and meditates more than he acts. Faced with a confrontation, he is as impotent physically and spiritually as Faulkner's Gail Hightower or the man before the gate in Allen Tate's "Ode to the Confederate Dead." To the modern militant black his failure to kill whites (except for the beautiful Margaret) is a cop-out by Nat Turner and a blatant example of white racism by William Styron.

In a work where virtually everything relates to race, the difficulty lies in making everything also human and credible. One critic has charged that Styron is "overly schematic" in showing the variety of relationships which exist between master and slave.[8] Nat himself describes the categories of whites: "I think it may have been seen by now how greatly various were the moral attributes of white men who possessed slaves, how different each owner might be by way of severity or benevolence. They ranged down from the saintly (Samuel Turner) to the all right (Moore) to the barely tolerable (Reverend Eppes) to a few who were unconditionally monstrous" (p. 299).

Nat's statement reveals Styron's determination to be human and artistic rather than racial, not to allow color of skin to determine goodness of character. Race and personage are of course inseparable. Some may believe that they can look at others with absolutely no regard for color. But as some black militants have discovered, culture and race are not clearly distinguishable. In complex interrelationships it is often extremely difficult to tell what is racist and what is not. In the best fiction the racism of a thing may be ultimately undefinable.

One statement, depending on the speaker, the perspective, and the context, may be antiwhite or antiblack or not racist at all. Sometimes Nat himself seems antiblack. Negroes, he says, are "a people not notably sweet-natured around domestic animals." And he knows why: "what else but a poor dumb beast could a Negro mistreat and by mistreating feel superior to?" (p. 293). The possibilities of interpretations here are numerous. A sociological field investigation might discover that the statement about the black man's mistreatment of animals is a factual error. That hostile critic to slavery, Fanny Kemble, the English actress who resided for a time in the South, agreed with Nat. She saw no gentleness in the manner of Negro to animal. "I was constantly struck with the insolent tyranny of their demeanor toward each other. . . . They are diabolically cruel to animals too. . . . These detestable qualities, which I constantly heard attributed to them as innate and inherent in their race, appear to me the direct result of their condition."[9] But who is to say after so long a time that it was "almost a universal characteristic," and who is to define the cause? One can only stumble through the blind corridors of history wondering whether there is any conclusion at all. Indeed, Negro slaves could have been kinder to animals than whites because their bondage induced them to be sympathetic to chattel beasts. See, for example, the love of the old Negro for the dog in "Marse Chan," Thomas Nelson Page's sentimental story. Here Styron's fiction is as complex as race and life. There is no clearly correct attitude. This again is what Styron aimed to write—a kind of meditation in which the historical novelist makes a statement but gives no precise clues as to how it is to be interpreted. Only in this way can fiction allow the human truth to prevail over a bias.

Even praise of the black by the white may be biased racism. T. R. Gray is a gross and callous white racist whether he condemns or praises. Negroes who attempt to carry out an "insurgent action" are cowardly. They are weak men marked by "irresolution, instability" (p. 88). But the blacks who defend their masters, on the contrary, are heroes who can "fight as bravely as any man" (p. 86). Gray's bigotry decides whether he will praise or damn the black.

Styron obtains balance by refusing to measure a character by the system, by setting one event against another, one character against another. A black extremist offsets a white one. A good white man is a counterweight to a good black in the novel. The moral system balances almost like balancing scales. A black sells his racial brother for his own material gain and returns the runaway Hark to his master and slavery. Benjamin Turner, who is more hostile to Negroes than his brother, Samuel, is also a gross and callous alcoholic. Styron's design makes the racist bad in other ways. Those whites unmarked by the system of slavery, those "reared outside the tradition of slavery often made the most callous taskmasters" (p. 343), at least according to Nat. A white mob casts stones at Nat and Ethelred Brantley when Nat baptizes the white man. This mob is a counterweight to Nat's own insurrection. And the white uprising after the insurrection kills more Negroes than the blacks had killed whites. Styron does not portray heroism as much as violence among the revolting Negroes, but even here slavery may be responsible for the Negroes' hatred.

The necessity and the extent of imagination is a baffling aspect of *The Confessions*. There are two slave coffles which Nat sees close by, and both of them had to be cut from the cloth of invention. On one occasion Nat rides back home from Richmond "in joy and exultancy" (p. 195) because he has been given the chance to work his way to freedom in Richmond by the time he is twenty-five. At this moment of penultimate hope of the higher-caste slave he sees a coffle of some forty men "skimpily clad; linked to each other by chains . . . and manacled with double cuffs of iron" (p. 196). They do not talk while one pisses in the ditch and a small boy weeps. After elaborate accounts of their drovers and of the slaves, who derive from the Ryder plantation, they pass on.

But Nat is not one of them. He is a house slave, and with inhuman lack of compassion he tells the poor devils in the coffle that his master is going to set him free in Richmond (p. 200). But even slaves are human. One from the coffle speaks and tells Nat, "Yo' shit stink too, sugah. Yo' ass black jess like mine, honey chile" (p. 201). The story is from the offal of history. Indeed it may be excessive in the descriptions of the slaves, their drovers, their destitutions, and the methods of travel. The intimate details of the coffle could be precisely based on a first-hand documented witness of the coffle, but so far as Styron knows the whole scene came to him in a flash and at a single second and with no particular recollections that he could recall separately (interview). When he was a little "boozed up," as he says, the scene came to him in its entirety as if it were already written. With no research and no correction, he says, it came to him as if he had been a witness.

Fiction must see a slave coffle personally. Despite its small part in the action of *The Confessions*, it is filled with living detail: a weeping child, an anxious father, a leader of slaves, drovers, a plantation owner grieved by another owner's need to sell his slaves, and, most important of all, the consciousness of an arrogant house nigger vain of himself and contemptuous of the shitty shepherds of his time. On the whole Styron's mind seems to have worked (this is a guess on my part) from a very broad and general social situation to render it in such particularity that it is a representation of the utter inhumanness of slavery.

Just after the creation of the mass coffle and its representation of the life of the slave, Styron turns to a different condition and situation in an extended account of Nat's relationship with his friend Willis. Nat leads him to an acceptance of the light of Christianity, fishes with him, joins in a sort of homosexual masturbation with him, prays with him for forgiveness, and finally baptizes him. He plans eventually to help free Willis and immediately to go with him to a Baptist camp meeting. Abe is supposed to carry four boys to be sold to a coffle at night. But Abe gets sicks, and Nat has to carry them. Instead of carrying Willis to the camp meeting, Nat finds himself carrying him off to be sold into slavery clandestinely in the night. Not only does this episode magnify the evils of selling slaves, but it shows the inhumane separation of friend and friend. Yet even this, Styron argues, is carried out in somewhat human terms (interview). The white felt a tremendous reluctance to sell off slaves, and when he was compelled to do so, he sold the slaves—like Willis—who had no family ties. Willis was an orphan and was therefore least vulnerable to a profound grief (p. 219; interview). Once John Cocke sold some of his brother-in-law's slaves at low prices rather than sell them to traders, and the brother-in-law was distressed. Cocke sold his own slaves to the Deep South only after they had committed a crime.

Amost without exception in *The Confessions* Styron has had to build structures with scarce materials. Usually the detailed and personal life of Negroes has had to be imagined more than that of most slave-owning whites, many of whom kept journals, diaries, ledgers, account books, and records of plantings and harvests. When the Negro improved a tool or a toy, he left no record. Owners left extensive diagrams of wooden wheels and lengthy records of the quantities and kinds of food they gave to their slaves. The library, clothing, hiring out of Nat to an architect, the newly invented Carey plow, the cleanliness (or filth) of the Negro quarters, Negro songs and sayings and wisdom, the transporting of slaves to America in inhumanly crowded circumstances (see the account of Nat's fierce Coromantee grandmother)—the world exists in historical fullness in *The Confessions*.

The manners and everyday events and personal relationships of white culture are revealed in elaborate detail and always carefully from the perspective of a slave narrator with the character of Nat Turner. He overhears white secrets, as when he hears Miss Emmeline Turner making love during an assemblage. Styron and Nat present social customs as fully as the earlier writers of Old Southwest humor did. There are revivals of fundamentalist whites, a camp meeting, a church service, allusions to Negro songs ("Sweet Woman Gone," "Old Zip Coon"), a Christmas on a plantation, and all the details involved in the knowledge of complicated occupations like carpentry and blacksmithing. There are unusual musical instruments, a Jew's harp, and a banjo made of fence wire and pine strips. Study, research, culture, history, fact, characters, imagination—all of these and much more must come together to create the life of an older time.

In some fashion all the materials of *The Confessions* are in Nat's original confessions, Coyner, Fanny Kemble, Olmsted, and other sources. But the novel itself is not there at all. Styron could have taken the appearance of John Hartwell Cocke (whose plantation and life he knew extensively), for example, and with a little transmogrification have made it his Samuel Turner, but despite Styron's admission that Turner derives from Cocke, they bear little physical resemblance. Cocke is a sterner man than Turner even though he is more radical as an opponent to slavery. Cocke is tall and weather-worn:

> "tall, commanding"
> "rough-hewn"
> "pleasant blend of sternness and kindliness"
> "dark haired"
> "large featured,"[10]

but Turner is softer, perhaps, more kindly to slaves, but less effectual in his dealings with the system:

> "a curious abiding sweetness"
> "kindly, shrewd, luminous strength in his face"
> "patriarchal and venerable grandeur"
> "cheek whiskers . . . which end in small tufts whiter than a cotton tail's butt"
> "wrinkles around his mouth . . . lines"
> "singular face too long and horselike"
> "ugly as a mushrat"
> "the nose too prominent beaked"
> "Lawd didn't leave Marse Sam a whole lot of jawbone."
>
> (p. 26)

The two men are not the same. Not only has fiction filled out the portrait more fully, but it has made the man more contradictory, complex enough even to be hard to visualize. Cocke may be even harder to see because his features have been taken from an historian's facts rather than an artist's conception of the appearance of a whole man.

Again and again it is in this fashion that the critic and the source-hunter proceed from whatever source to the novel. The generalities of the novel appear in history over and over; the particulars, never. The particulars are invented as are, necessarily, the meditations. In almost tabular fashion one can see the difference between Cocke's life as reported by Coyner and life on the Turner plantation as reported by Styron. Often to a flaw, historians fail to speculate and interpret.

Anything belongs to the province of the novelist, Styron believes, as long as it is in the interest of his fiction. He does not name Coyner or Cocke or the source of quotations from them with footnotes. A footnote even to a plagiarized passage in a novel, if that is what it should be called, is in a sense a betrayal of fiction. It would make fiction history and when the novelist finds exactly what he wishes somewhere else, he may use it as Styron did here and as Momaday did in his fiction without any regret or respect for property rights.

I have long and do still steadfastly believe that Slavery is the great Cause of all the chief evils of our Land—individual as well as national . . . eating upon the vitals of the Commonwealth.[11]	I have long and do still steadfastly believe that slavery is the great cause of all the chief evils of our land. It is a cancer eating at our bowels . . . . (p. 159)

"The novelist," Styron says, "has a right to appropriate anything" (interview). In a way also, it is curious what Styron chose to use. The only direct quotation is an unspecific passage chosen from a general letter about a rather commonplace opinion and cast in a rather commonplace vocabulary. Strange are the vagaries of novelists.

The sources of fiction *not* found in history may be stranger than those that are. Indeed, if one were to read somewhat cursorily the long dissertation of Martin Coyner, Jr., he might not be at all aware that it is a source of *The Confessions*. The historical source and the art derived in part from it are a world apart, as perhaps they should be. In general Styron takes an episode or principle and has his Turner talk about it. The drama and the talk come from the principle, and indeed the historian may have no obligation at all to entertain as the novelist has. As the fiction is more human and particular and heightened than the source, so it may also in many instances be much more heightened than life itself. The artist may choose from all the things he has known in order to create. As he often chooses the most colorful, so also he may leave out the dull. Finding a source may be a disappointing experience for the scholar. And he must turn, not to the source, for the mysteries of the work of art, but to the totality of the author's experience as well as the associative cerebrations of his mind in putting a work together. The deep well of the author's mind from which the creation springs may exist in monumental proportions, but it may also be picked from tiny debris and filaments which have no connection at all except in the final product.

What is not in any source for a work of fiction may show ultimately more about the work and the mind of the author than about factual history. The bare fact of history takes on flesh and blood and drama in art. A couple of instances may prove the extensive difference between the bland world of academic history and that of the flesh, indeed the carrion, of actual history. Styron does not recall reading about a communal slave privy, seeing the picture of one, or ever seeing an actual privy once used by slaves on a southern plantation before the Civil War. No plantation privy has been preserved in the twentieth century in all its fecal abundance. If there is a modern analogue, it would be the lines of commodes or outdoor latrine holes used as depositories in the modern army. The sad but comic account of the scorching of Nat's private parts when someone pours oil in the latrine and sets it afire during a moment of Nat's solitary cogitation after the morning rush (p. 137) has its analogues in stories of at least hundreds of episodes of latrine humor during World War II.

The novelist's cleverness in inventing sociological and antiquarian phenomena out of whole cloth, so to speak, is not a mark of artistry; his ability to use such inventions to illuminate personality, however, is artistry. Negroes had to use the woods or go to some kind of structure. Visual and odoriferous as the latrine may be, it conveys vividly the lack of privacy in the rural South, especially among gangs of Negroes in the morning rush. "Hit's a shame in dis world," Nat's mother complains; "Us folks in de house is *quality*. And we ain't got no outhouse for our own selfs, hit's a cryin' shame!" (p. 136). That is a general condition portrayed in the fiction, but the ultimate aim must be personal: how does our protagonist react to the filth and the stench? With all the sensibility and finickiness of one reared with indoor plumbing, black or white, Nat avoids "the morning rush, training my bowels [obviously with discomfort] to obey a later call when I can enjoy some privacy" if not dry sanitation (p. 136). From a little experience and much imagination Styron has created a situation and a character indeed remote from any facts that he may have ever learned from historical sources.

Other situations in *The Confessions* concern strictly the private life of the slave. No man in the twentieth century—no child like Nat—has witnessed the rape of a mother house-slave cook in a plantation kitchen. Doubtless there have been numerous analogues, but ultimately the entire scene must come solely from the imagination of William Styron. The journalist or the historian of the nineteenth century would be interested in the general effect of master- or overseer-slave sexual relationships, in their extent and in their social and moral and economic effects. Except in very general terms, however, he would not provide a full account of the intercourse of one person with another. Search as he would through history, the source-hunting novelist would find few such incidents or none. In Coyner's dissertation, for example, the episode of overseer-black sexual relationships is but a detail under the assertion that "Cocke's luck with Alabama overseers [that is, on the plantation of which he was absentee owner] was more uneven." Elam Tanner was an outstanding problem. He was "a little hare brained" but smart. Cocke thought his plantation problems were due "to Tanner's contrariness and failure to attend to his business." And "in the end, charges against Tanner of cohabiting with several slave women became substantial enough for the overseer to confess in part." He refused to marry and therefore find sexual solace in one woman, so he "was released."[12]

That is history, history of the entirely respectable kind, perhaps history of the most common sort. But it does not furnish the materials of the situation in its intimate details. Fiction in most of its usual modern forms enacts the episodes on stage. After a stark warning by the black driver Abraham, Nat's mother Lou-Ann refuses to leave her kitchen. She sings a song of her desire for protection:

> Bow low, Mary, bow low, Martha,
> For Jesus come and lock de do',
> An carry de keys away.   (p. 145)

Jesus does not lock the door for Lou-Ann. Styron enacts the scene of her rape by the white overseer McBride. In an antique kitchen which would delight the heart of an antiquarian, a brutal white man rapes a gentle black mother while he holds the splinters of a broken brandy bottle to her throat. The small son of the woman watches the force, the denial, and the sexual experience itself. The humanness of the scene is apparent in Nat's mother's ultimate relinquishment. The scene begins as rape and ends in acquiescence: "her brown long legs go up swiftly to embrace his waist, the two of them now joined and moving in that . . . strange and brutal rhythm" (p. 148). The complexity of the scene is not that it ends merely in the semirape and oppression and miscegenation, but that it ends with the impingement of this new experience on the mind of a sensitive young Negro boy. The rape is not itself so spectacular to him as its ultimate meanings. With his mother involved he sees "that same strange and brutal rhythm I have witnessed . . . through the cracks of half a dozen cabins and which in the madness of complete innocence I had thought was the pastime, or habit, or obsession, or something, of Negroes alone" (p. 148). Despite the enactment of a scene which reveals a knotty entanglement of many of the situations of slavery, the supreme accomplishment of Styron here has been the creation of the effect of the mystery of a small boy who knows not where he came from, what he is, and what he is to be. And there was no specific source for this. It is an enactment of all of history selected from tiny shards of experience derived from biography, history, the daily newspapers, and the witnessing of many trivial acts of violence. The jagged bottle, Styron says, for example, leaped into his mind from he knew not where (interview).

All the analogies do not enable the historian or even the novelist to turn back the clock to the facts of slavery. Whether *The Confessions* is a success or a failure, it is to the everlasting credit of Styron's fortitude that he was willing to attempt to create the mind of a black man living in a system that does not now exist and one that was not accurately or fully recorded when it did exist. Few records provided what Styron had to tell about Nat Turner. Some of the physical realities existed, but the records of observers were unreliable, much more so than usual in history. Not only is *The Confessions* more fiction than most, but also the resolution of the debate about its accuracy is more difficult than in most instances. The final decisions about the authenticity of the novel are personal, racial, historical, subjective. I believe with C. Vann Woodward that the general portrait is "informed by a respect for history."[13] But if the ghost of Nat Turner himself were to return, he might not recognize his own life. Such is the diversity of life that it can be deeply human and true whether or not it is fact.

5

Vern Walters Studio, Red Cloud, Nebraska

Willa Cather's Childhood Home

The Prairie near Red Cloud, Nebraska

⏳ FIVE ⏳

My Ántonia:
"Still, All Day Long, Nebraska"

In seven novels written between 1912 and 1926, Willa Cather created fiction mainly about the people and the land of the Nebraska prairies. Between 1925 and 1940 she published only one novel partly about Nebraska and four with settings not native to her. Her best and most profound creation about life in the country and the towns of the prairies is, I think, *My Ántonia* (1918). The materials in the composition of this book are rich but limited in scope. She writes about the old cultures of the immigrant peoples from eastern America and from Europe; about the land, the country of the prairies; and about the ways of life in a small Nebraska town and later in Lincoln. The dominant element in the lives of the characters of *My Ántonia* proves ultimately to be the land. The prairie takes the settlers as they are, slowly but inevitably destroys their older ways, destroys even some of the people themselves, and compels the survivors to adapt their ways to the land. Those who endure eventually adapt the land to their wishes, but not much more than superficially.

The great shock of moving to the prairies is the first adjustment of the immigrant or traveler. Traveling through Nebraska on a train in 1879, four years before Willa Cather herself moved to the Midwest, Robert Louis Stevenson saw and described the relationship between the land and a frontier woman in a way that strongly foreshadows *My Ántonia*. Newcomers like Stevenson, Cather, and Ántonia confronted "this spacious vacancy, this greatness of the air, this discovery of the whole arch of heaven, this straight, unbroken, prison-line of the horizon." Yet, Stevenson reasons, perhaps "the settler may create a full and various existence." He remembers seeing a frontier woman who has beauty like Ántonia's; her eyes are "kind, dark, and steady." In this "naked and flat" world which

73

seems "almost ghastly" to the visitor, the woman "sold milk with patriarchal grace" and "spoke of an entire contentment with her life."[1] Here in miniature is a figure for the accomplishments of the magnificent and happy heroine of *My Ántonia* and also for the achievements of Willa Cather in creating the novel.

Creative artists certainly give more attention to man's relationship to his natural world than critics do. Anthropogeographers have studied in general terms the effect of the natural habitat on countries and peoples, on beliefs, the arts, literature. No specialist I know of has made a study of a particular work of literature in anthropogeographical terms. Criticism often writes of setting, nature, and images, but not much has been written about the extensive effect of a geographical world upon the culture and the characters in a novel. The reason for this lack is obvious—seeing fiction from the perspective of geography requires caution. The novelist creates a complex character and places him in an intricate natural world and culture. That this created world has numerous and drastic effects on the personae is certain, but a good author usually does not sort them out and provide interpretations for his own fiction. The good reader, the critic, should conclude as much as he possibly can, but often he can go no further than the uncertain but meaningful speculation about geography.

With fiction about the rather unvaried terrain of the Middle West it may be possible to speculate with some assurance. On the other hand, one who has not lived for years with the prairies may never be able to know them. Jim Burden and the "I" of the "Introduction" agree "that no one who had not grown up in a little prairie town could know anything about it."[2] Even Willa Cather (like Stevenson but younger) came a stranger to the world she was to write about. Until just before adolescence, during many of the most impressionable years of childhood, she lived in Virginia, a much more varied world. If one who is not a native cannot know the country, how does a stranger learn to know it in a book? A good writer can tell the stranger, but it is a difficult task, and he cannot tell all in fiction. An author may not himself know fully the relationship between his own geography and his characters. One of the marvels of literature is that it may contain profundities the author

74

never articulated for himself. Writing about his own people and culture, an author may have in mind a facet of his characters' lives and may transport that into his fiction without ever analyzing the causes and effects of the culture and place. The reader or the critic may then see the relationships in true ways the author never consciously visualized for himself.

Confrontation of the prairies must first be physical. The usual traveler from hills to flat lands faces only a few things; in place of variety there is quantity—more horizon, for one thing, than anywhere else in the world except on the sea. The early pioneers confronted even less variety and more quantity. In their time the world was a sea of red grass with a few cottonwoods along the streams and almost no other trees, no evergreens except "a few little cedars" (p. 64), and few berries and natural grapes and fruits. Stevenson called it "a world almost without a feature."[3]

The pioneer on the prairies had to bring with him the materials to make a varied world: seeds, plants, creatures, tools, and so on. A southern family like the Cathers began adding numerous kinds of garden plants, domestic animals, and fruit trees to the midwestern landscape. By 1895 one Cather family on their farm in Nebraska raised corn, oats, rye, fish, turkeys, chickens, ducks, cattle, sheep, cherries, apples, peaches, plums, grapes, gooseberries. Even yet, however, most of the midwestern land lies in large tracts of a few things: corn, wheat, maize, pasture. The greatest variety on the prairies occurs, strangely, in elevation. In some places Willa Cather's prairies are approximately as hilly as the Piedmont South. There is a strange effect, to me at least, of being fenced in by nearby hills but at the same time of sitting at the top of a world stretching to a distant horizon on every side. Although rainfall is usually comparatively scanty, there is much variety and quantity in seasons and the weather: much heat and many dust storms, floods, tornadoes; much cold and snow and wind. Varied seasons in one place, according to a geographer, produce "differentiations" and emphasize existing "ethnic difference."[4] Man's crops and animals and trees now provide more variety than did the original prairies, but laying out the roads in uniform square-mile blocks has created a pattern of repetitive geometrical figures.

If a terrain of landscape is physical, it is also a country of the mind. Seen by many men, it becomes a country of many minds. In *My Ántonia*, the land is one thing to Jim Burden, another to Mr. Shimerda. But perhaps first it is best to look at the country through many eyes and then to see what it is in the novel and what it does to the characters. The prairies look different to the mere sojourner, to the naturalized immigrant, and to the native. Most lifelong Nebraskans love their homeland. The prairies make them feel religious, bring them "much closer to life and death,"[5] draw them back to the cornfields when they leave, give them a feeling of indescribable freedom (this was said to me many times), offer a landscape that is "beautiful, rich, and strong,"[6] provide "inexhaustible" features.[7] Whether a deep lover of the prairies has an adequate basis for comparison or whether he himself may know the effects of his prairie life on his psyche cannot be determined from life or fiction.

The sojourner on the prairie feels exposed; he cannot imagine what the old prairie dogs like about them. If a wind comes, there is nothing in the vast expanse to anchor to. The newcomer fears monotony. One early pioneer said when seeing his first snow on the prairies, "There wasn't much to see, no matter how hard we looked."[8]

The fear and esthetic dissatisfaction of the immigrant Mr. Shimerda in this strange world are utterly different from his old responses to the fields, forests, and civilization of Bohemia. He commits suicide. Shimerda fails while changing habitats; he is a victim of the elemental forces which controlled the primeval migrations of history and which affected man's psychology, race, economics, entertainments, learning, culture—all. The environment of Nebraska in Shimerda's time as surely killed him off as primeval environments in certain situations "killed off the animals which could not walk erect, which did not know how to use their hands for holding tools, and which were not able to take refuge in caves."[9]

A visitor does not know the prairies; a lifelong resident may not know fully the extent of the esthetic and psychological effects of his habitat. No science or philosophy or other field of knowledge can spell out objectively what landscape means to individuals or peoples. Perhaps those who have tried most are geographers or anthropogeographers. The classical American scholar of this field in the twentieth century, certainly in the early twentieth century, was Ellen Churchill Semple, a student of the German Friedrich Ratzel. Her conclusions seem rather speculative, and modern scholars reject in part her work. She published her most outstanding book, *Influences of Geographic Environment*, in 1911, seven years before the publication of *My Ántonia*. Whether or not Willa Cather knew Ellen Semple's work, the ideas were well known at the time. Generally they explain aspects both of prairie life and of *My Ántonia*.

Unrelieved lowlands, Semple says, affect the development of peoples and of individuals. They produce "a monotonous existence, necessarily one-sided, needing a complement in upland or mountain."[10] Low mountains, on the other hand, are "gentler, stimulating, appealing, and not overpowering. . . . [They] have produced many poets and artists."[11] Balance and variety, according to Semple, seem to produce a richer life. At the time of the frontier, when Mr. Shimerda killed himself and Tony became coarsened by field labor, the conclusions of Semple may especially apply. It is a time and place of "much labor and little leisure, of poverty to-day and anxiety for the morrow, of toil-cramped hands and toil-dulled brains."[12] These brief citations perhaps overstate and exaggerate Ellen Semple's ideas and the truth, but they are not far from the target.

Another anthropogeographer, Roderick Peattie, writes that he is "not yet ready to construct a map of regional psychologies, . . . but that regional differences exist all will grant. Certain psychological qualities have locale even though there are no boundaries." Peattie regards the prairies as a beautiful world of "unbelievable orderliness." It is "a land with a psychological consciousness," and he quotes descriptions of the people and the climate in *My Ántonia*.[13] Indeed, a scholar can turn to a geographer for understanding of fiction, but the geographer may also turn to the novelist for understanding of his own field. According to Peattie, "This being in harmony with one's physical habitat is by some curious chance better

77

understood by travelers and fiction writers than by geographers who should have a special claim on such facts."[14]

The vast interior continent of the middlewestern United States produced a great number of the best writers of the early part of the twentieth century: Theodore Dreiser, Sherwood Anderson, Sinclair Lewis, F. Scott Fitzgerald, Willa Cather, Ernest Hemingway—and this list includes only the truly great ones. They begin with geography in common, and generally they also share some other characteristics which may derive from their somewhat similar environments. All are persuaded in part and at times to adopt a deterministic or naturalistic view of the world.[15] If Lewis, Fitzgerald, and Hemingway are hardly naturalists, they do create worlds of despair, cynicism, disbelief. Willa Cather's work is the least pessimistic of the group, but, strangely, a contrast between two novels with different settings seems to bear out the association between the Midwest and determinism: set in Nebraska, *My Ántonia* seems at times to have characters with determined lives; on the other hand, set in the Southwest, a land of greatly varied landscape, *Death Comes for the Archbishop* contains not a naturalistic word. Willa Cather's Virginia origins as well as her later residence in different places might be a cause of the difference. Not one prominent writer in the southern Renaissance, which generally came after the midwestern school of authors, created a town as sterile as *Main Street* or wrote fiction as naturalistic as Anderson's or Dreiser's.

Another trait these writers have in common is their not staying at home. All of them lived more in other regions and abroad than they did at home. Most of them settled into alien cultures and wrote more about their adopted countries than about the Midwest. Dreiser's novels which started in the Midwest wound up in the East. Neither Fitzgerald nor Hemingway ever wrote a major novel about his native region. Lewis created midwestern towns mainly to satirize and condemn. Willa Cather again (with Sherwood Anderson) is the exception. She moved her residence from her region but continued to write about it for more than half her productive years. Then she turned away from home for most of her later work.

Perhaps Cather's Nebraska and her fiction illustrate what she had in common with her fellow writers in the region and show how she was different from them.

Again writers from other regions provide meaningful contrasts. Many of the twentieth-century southern writers have stayed at home—Ellen Glasgow, James Dickey, Flannery O'Connor, Eudora Welty, William Faulkner. Those who have moved away have continued to write almost exclusively about southern settings—Tate, Ransom, Warren of the Fugitive-Agrarians, Carson McCullers. More than any other, Thomas Wolfe turned away, but even his last important book was set partly at home and used a southern town to provide perspective on other worlds. The South's older culture and tradition, its history, its defeat in war, and its geography may explain the reluctance of its writers to turn away from homeland. The greater writers of New England have also stayed at home and written about home—Hawthorne, Emerson, Thoreau, Dickinson, and later Robinson and Frost. Staying at home or leaving does not necessarily reveal a writer's love or hatred for his origins, but it does indicate the extent of his involvement with his native culture.[16]

Willa Cather was neither a sojourner nor a native. She moved from the South to the vast prairie landscape, almost as much an immigrant as the Bohemians were. She changed peoples almost as much as place and heard for the first time foreign languages (p. 6).

From her arrival in Nebraska Willa Cather's reactions to her new geographical and social world were complex. Her attitudes, loyalties, and rejections were inconsistent, inconstant, unpredictable. The progression seems generally to have been from early fear to love to arrogant youthful contempt (a stage in which she seems to have undergone quick shifts in attitude depending upon where she was and what she was doing at the moment) to a remembered love of the land with some ambivalence in *My Ántonia*. There is a general direction in her views—with many curves and sharp turns.

My Ántonia is Willa Cather's most intense study of the relationship between person and place. The diversity of the characters and of attitudes reveals almost the entire scope of her own feelings from the time she began to express them in writing in the 1890s until her last days. *My Ántonia* is of course self-contained, but the other literary works about Nebraska are a helpful background for the novel. They reveal the ardency of Willa Cather's passion about Nebraska. There are distinctions between her attitudes toward the land and those toward the people who lived on it and the others who lived off the workers of the land. She responded differently toward immigrant and Anglo-American, toward country people and town-lovers. Sometimes, however, in moments of extreme reaction she would wrap the entire state and its people up into one generalization.

After Willa Cather left high school and Red Cloud to become a student at the University of Nebraska and a reviewer and columnist for the Lincoln papers, she was hostile to her rural prairie world in the manner of many sophisticated youths when they first look at the country of their origins from the perspectives of a foreign land. In "Lou, the Prophet," a short story published in her college student newspaper, the religious fanaticism of the protagonist seems to spring from the adversities of his life on the prairies: he suffers homesickness for his native Denmark, long hours of hard labor, monotonous food, exhaustion, a routine "as uneventful as the life of his plow horses," the loss of a sweetheart to another man who has more money, and the prospects of a disastrous loss of his corn crop. And his life, Willa Cather generalizes, "was that of many another young man in our country."[17]

The early short stories reveal only antagonism toward the prairie country, but ambivalent attitudes are apparent in letters Willa Cather wrote back to Lincoln when she visited Red Cloud. She wrote in 1893 about an evening when she and a friend sat high on the tower of a windmill. They saw the horizon miles away. She thought the fields of wheat and corn were beautiful. The ugliness of the prairie world, she wrote to her friend Mariel Gere in 1894, was not revealed by moonlight—only the wonder. In July of the next summer she wrote Ellen and Francis Miner that the forests of cornfields were indescribably beautiful. Early in 1896 she again wrote of the association between suicide and what she called the

Province and asked a friend to think of her as dead and in a tomb. The next month she described the monotonousness and bitterness of her exile in Red Cloud, but she had enjoyed a wedding breakfast, card parties, and her happy associations with her brother Douglas. For a long time her responses to her homeland were vacillating and temperamental.

The short stories written about Nebraska before Willa Cather journeyed east to Pittsburgh in 1896 contain condemnations and little praise.[18] Youthful bitterness and animosity without relief cause the despair and anger of "On the Divide," first published in *Overland Monthly* in January 1896. The Divide lies between the Republican and the Platte rivers; when the Cather family first came from Virginia, they settled there near one of the flattest stretches of country in that section of Nebraska. Willa Cather links suicide and the place where she first lived on the prairies. "If it had not been for the few stunted cottonwoods and elms that grew along its banks [those of a "turbid, muddy little stream"] . . . , Canute would have shot himself years ago." The dominant effect is monotony. The protagonist has memorized "every individual clump of bunch grass in the miles of red shaggy prairie." Canute's nearly fatal melancholy and his madness are shared by many of his neighbors and are directly caused by the land and the weather: "Insanity and suicide are very common things on the Divide." Willa Cather writes with utter lack of sympathy, even disrespect; she becomes flippant and clever: "It causes no great sensation there when a Dane is found swinging to his own windmill tower, and most of the Poles after they have become too careless and discouraged to shave themselves keep their razors to cut their thoats with."

The country along Rattlesnake Creek is level, lonely, barren without trees; it has a "deceitful loveliness" in early summer, a "bitter barrenness" in the fall. Canute's place has been "smitten by all the plagues of Egypt. He had seen it parched by drought, and sogged by rain, beaten by hail, and swept by fire, and in the grasshopper years he had seen it eaten as bare and clean as bones that the vultures have left." In contradiction to the views of prairie dwellers who associate their land with freedom and faith, Willa

Cather attributes "faith and aspiration" to high altitudes: "All mountain people are religious." The people on the Divide are damned by the place where they live: "It was the cities of the plains that, because of their utter lack of spirituality and the mad caprice of their vice, were cursed of God."[19]

In June 1896 Willa Cather left the provinces and Nebraska for the lure of the glorious and shining cities of the East; she went to Pittsburgh. At Chicago she began to leave the curse of the prairies behind and her spirits soared as she saw trees and hills and streams which were clean. Ironically at the precise time of leaving home she wrote that she felt emotionally as if she were going home. As yet she did not know herself, and she was unaware of the fullness of her relationship with her homeland. "She did not then suspect," Mildred R. Bennett has written, "that she had been forever branded by the prairie, and that her life was to be a tug of war between East and West."[20]

For a time Willa Cather in Pittsburgh was kept busy by the *Home Monthly*, writing much of it, editing, supervising it through the press. Suddenly she became involved in a busy social life; she attended "picnics, boat rides, and excursions," meetings of women's clubs, parties, teas, concerts, and so on.[21] Very quickly, however, the thrills ended; she tired of Bohemian pleasures; and she began writing her friend Mariel Gere of her disaffection for Pittsburgh and her love of the very things she had been happy to tell good-by. She tired of the glittering lies and decided that she could not be happy as an exile far from Nebraska, which she now liked more than any other place in the world.

Some of the short stories published between 1900 and the first novel of the prairies, *O Pioneers!* (1913), continue the condemnations of "the inexorable ennui," the lack of levity, and the "toil and isolation" of the Divide. "Oh, those poor Northmen of the Divide!" Willa Cather exclaimed. "They are dead many a year before they are put to rest in the little graveyard on the windy hill where exiles of all nations grow akin."[22] A story published in 1901 began: "People who have been so unfortunate as to have traveled in western Kansas will remember the Solomon Valley for its unique and peculiar desolation."[23] The Lincoln *Courier* wrote that the story was "enraging the Kansas people," that she did not know the truth about her region, and that her "ignorance is . . . colossal."[24]

The abrupt changes in Willa Cather's attitudes toward her land, her condemnations in her short stories, and her dislike of exile are good indications of her lifetime of vacillation about the people and the land of her homeland. She would return to Red Cloud for many visits between her trip to Pittsburgh and 1931, when she came home the last time. In the later years she had friends but no close kinspeople in the town. Physically she was ever more removed from the prairies; much of her sardonic youthful bitterness disappeared by 1900, and she developed nostalgia and understanding of the land.

Between the time of Willa Cather's denunciatory short stories and her publication of *O Pioneers!* she moved from the attitude of a sojourner on the prairies more toward the views of one native born. This novel is not as good a work as *My Ántonia*, but the landscape is made from the same materials as those of the later book. By this time Willa Cather had developed her understanding of the difference between the virgin prairies and the land after it was settled for a time, and of the difference between the attitude of a newcomer and that of an old-timer. In an interview in 1913 she described her first impression when she came to the prairies as a child: "I felt a good deal as if we had come to the end of everything—it was a kind of erasure of personality." It was a country "as bare as a piece of sheet iron." But she began to change, decided that "life might not be so flat as it looked there," and learned to "care a lot more about the country and the people."[25]

In *O Pioneers!* Willa Cather for the first time creates a relationship between man and the land which is sufficiently complex to serve as the basis for excellent fiction. She describes the country with many lavish adjectives: the prairies are stern, vast, hard, bewildering, wild, unfriendly, destructive, monotonous. They are "like an iron country, and the spirit is oppressed by its rigor and melancholy."[26] It is a world of extremes and opposites. It is also beautiful, constant, wealthy, peaceful, "strong and glorious."[27]

Most of the early short stories of Willa Cather are oversimplifications because of her limited view of the characters and her shallow treatment of man's relationship with the land. In *O Pioneers!* she found the land to write about, and in *My Ántonia* she found the people to inhabit it.

The years shortly before and after *My Ántonia* seem to have been the time when Willa Cather and her midwestern country were most happily adjusted to each other. Twenty-five years after she published the novel she remembered that she had written one hundred pages of it in a tent on a farm outside her home town. While she was on an extended visit home in 1921 a reporter wrote that she said that "there is not any place in this world that is more interesting to her than Red Cloud."[28] She remembered her journey to Pittsburgh as being much different from the way she had described it at the time (see above). She had left because "she could not be contented to stay here and depend upon her parents for support. But the thought of leaving her family and friends who meant so much to her was almost too much."[29] During a visit to Red Cloud a few years later she told another reporter that "all the descriptions" of Nebraska in her fiction were written "with fondness, warmth and appreciation."[30] In 1922 she wrote to Carrie Sherwood that she had never loved the country east of the Missouri River. She had written of Nebraska, "not from any sense of duty," but from interest. She briefly spoke to the Old Settlers' picnic and "eulogized the climate of Nebraska."[31] How sweet are the fruits of forgetfulness! By this time Willa Cather's response had ranged over the whole emotional horizon. Her vacillations and her generally increasing fondness for her homeland form a typical pattern for an American author from a small town.

In 1923 Willa Cather published her longest essay about Nebraska.[32] Here she adds little to what she had created in her fiction, but she does describe an admirable prosperity of modern Nebraska as well as a new and "ugly crest of materialism."[33] Older times continued to fascinate her. On a visit to Omaha in 1929 she described again her coming to the frontier. "That shaggy grass country," she said, "had gripped me with a passion I have never been able to shake. It has been the happiness and the curse of my life."[34] Nebraska did not, however, remain Willa Cather's most beloved country until the end. After 1931 she lived elsewhere and cut nearly all her ties with Red Cloud, and the prairies did not remain her favorite kind of geographical world. About four years before her death she wrote a child who had written to her that she loved New Mexico better than any other country in the world. Willa Cather's native Virginia also lingered in her memory. A road near the small town of Gore, she wrote, was the loveliest of any that she had ever known. [35]

After all of Willa Cather's views of her prairie world are surveyed and after the possibilities of man's relationship to his place are studied, the major critical task still remains: to define the accomplishments of *My Ántonia* in telling a story of the way Cather's people live in their world. The book is about Ántonia Shimerda Cuzak, her response to the tragic defeat of her father by the land and the weather in the first winter of his immigrant life, her sufferings and labor in wresting a farm from the earth, the few years when she works as a servant in the small town of Black Hawk, a moment of utter defeat in the city, and finally her return to the country to build her own farm and to raise a family. She succeeds because of and in spite of the land. The scene of her children bursting out of the fruit cellar where the family has stored a great and various harvest is perhaps the image of the most unmitigated happiness of any family in American fiction. Conversely, *My Ántonia* is also a narrative of the failures of the characters who give up both their ancestral cultures and the land but never find a satisfactory way of life—Tiny Soderball, Lena Lingard, and Jim Burden.

In a frontier world one essential element in man's relationship to nature was change. The immigrant gave up nearly everything he owned in the world, sold almost everything and translated it into a little money, left his friends and his homeland, and isolated himself from the sources of all his ancestral tradition and culture—his language, occupation, folklore, music, art, foods, the institutions of his education and religion. Almost all of the past that he had known was brought to the strange world only in his memory. If the frontier where he arrived had a past of its own, it was not known to the immigrant. "Of all the bewildering things about a new country," Willa Cather wrote in *O Pioneers!*, "the absence of human landmarks is one of the most depressing and disheartening." [36] A country which had not been long lived in provided less material for the imagination and for the writer. "Generally speaking," Willa Cather told a group in Lincoln, "the older and more established the civilization, the better a subject it is for art. In an older community there has been time for associations to gather and for interesting types to develop."[37]

When Jim Burden arrives on the prairie almost nothing remains of any habitation prior to the immigrants of the 1870s. The Indians have left only a trace; after a snow Jim can see "beyond the pond, on the slope that climbed to the cornfield, . . . faintly marked in the grass, a great circle where the Indians used to ride" (p. 62), but this faint trail is all that survives of a native culture. The white man came to the prairies late in American history. Not until the 1860s was Nebraska opened for homesteaders to file claims. Before them were only white explorers, traders, trappers, and the migrants of a frontier. So few of the artifacts of Coronado and the old Conquistadors survived that Jim was "taught that he had not got so far north as Nebraska" (p. 243). But Jim knows that "a farmer in the country north of ours . . . had turned up a metal stirrup of fine workmanship, and a sword with a Spanish inscription on the blade" (p. 243). Jim and his friends, the hired girls, can only ponder questions about this relic from the past. It is not a symbol of their own inherited southern and Continental cultures.

The one story about earlier white explorers or passers-through is told to Jim by Otto Fuchs. He has heard that the persecuted Mormons threw sunflower seeds on the road as they were "crossing the Plains to Utah" so that other Mormons could follow that trail the next year (p. 28). This scanty folklore is the only remaining legend from historic times, and Jim has heard that it is not true. The only living survivor is the ancient rattlesnake which Jim kills and which he believes was "left on from buffalo and Indian times" (p. 47). Newcomers to the prairies were having to begin with little more of a human past than existed at the first creation.

After the "Introduction," the early narrative in *My Ántonia* creates the impact of the first shock of a journey to a new home on the prairies. Jim travels within the known world of the railroad train. He does not at first form a distinct impression of Nebraska except in thinking of the sameness, the monotony; he notices only that "it was still, all day long, Nebraska" (p. 5). The strangeness of another world first intrudes on his consciousness when he meets Otto Fuchs, a foreigner, an Austrian, and a new devotee of the Wild West. But the dominant impression is geographic. "There was nothing but land: not a country at all, but the material out of which countries are made" (p. 7). Jim is amazed at the vast horizon. The world is so changed from the mountain ridges he had known that he believes even the spirits of his dead father and mother have deserted him. In a wagon on the prairies he can now interpret: "I felt erased, blotted out. I did not say my prayers that night: here, I felt, what would be would be" (p. 8). One night in this new world and he has already given up his freedom and become a determinist.

The story of Book I, called "The Shimerdas," tells of their coming to the prairies. The new life is a tragedy for all of them, and the terrible loss of Mr. Shimerda tempers the tone of rosy sentimentalism which seems sometimes near in the novel. After one chapter in which Jim settles into the comfortable Burden home, he visits the primitive frontier world of the immigrant Bohemians. Utterly unprepared for the world to which they have come, they have brought virtually nothing to enable them to tear a living from the virgin prairies. Indeed, the things they do possess only emphasize the great disparity between the earth and the people who must try to live on it: "a little tin trunk" (p. 5), Bohemian clothes such as "an embroidered shawl with silk fringes" (p. 22), only one overcoat (p. 70), a fiddle "which would not be of much use here" (p. 20), mushrooms, and a gun, "a queer piece from the old country, short and heavy, with a stag's head on the cock" (p. 42). The gun is the only instrument they have brought which helps to cope with the environment, and Mr. Shimerda shoots nothing but rabbits and prairie dogs with it—and then himself. What they do not have is significant: a house (they live in a "hole in the bank" (p. 24), food (only "corncakes and sorghum molasses"), stock (except scrawny creatures bought from the cheating Krajiek), "no garden or chickenhouse," furniture (they have only one chair). The only native food besides rabbits is prairie dogs, which Otto Fuchs says are members of the rat family. The gentle Bohemian Shimerda has long hair,

Continental manners, "white and well-shaped" hands (p. 24)—and none of the stamina necessary at the vanguard of the frontier. He must die because, in the terms of anthropogeography, "Sometimes removal to strongly contrasted geographic conditions necessitates a reversion to a lower economic type of existence." In the "lower hunter stage of civilization" Mr. Shimerda can only shoot rabbits.[38]

Willa Cather has carefully created the intricacy of Mr. Shimerda's relationship with the prairie world and the patterns of images which help to reveal it. An ugly natural world surrounds his farm, and bad weather dictates the events of his life. Leaving the comforts of the Burden farm and riding toward the Shimerdas, Jim sees "only red grass like ours, and nothing else, though from the high wagon-seat one could look off a long way" (p. 19). Here is the dread monotony of horizon so oppressive to the prairie newcomer. The Shimerdas' own piece of prairie is ugly; Jim sees "nothing but red hillocks, and draws with shelving banks and long roots" (p. 21). They must deal with the prairie at its worst; their land is "rougher" than the Burdens', and a creek makes it "of little value for farming" (p. 21). The imagery does vary a little from despair. The cottonwood trees, an ironic reminder of the Old World, have "already turned, and the yellow leaves and shining white bark made them look like the gold and silver trees in [European] fairy tales" (p. 21).

Often Willa Cather makes an association between the land and its weather and the weak and the frail who are to be defeated or killed. Some must die with the world in the fall. Tony and Jim find "a little insect of the palest, frailest green" dying in "a shiver of coming winter," warm it, and take it home in Tony's hair. They meet Mr. Shimerda returning from a rabbit hunt. He hears the insect "chirp faintly" and listens "as if it were a beautiful sound" (p. 42). Thus Cather suggests an association between the beauty, the frailty, and the coming death of two beings facing a climate and a world they cannot survive. At the crucial moment she juxtaposes the man and his destroyer: "The old man's smile, as he listened, was so full of sadness, of pity for things, that I never afterward forgot it. As the sun sank there came a sudden coolness and the strong smell of earth and drying grass" (pp. 42–43).

The defeated Russians and Mr. Shimerda are similarly conjoined with a dying world: "While the autumn colour was growing pale on the grass and cornfields, things went badly with our friends the Russians. Peter told his troubles to Mr. Shimerda" (p. 50). One afternoon while Pavel is raving during his final illness, "a cold wind sprang up and moaned over the prairie," and the red sunset is "angry" (p. 52). The prairies and the skies are deterministic: Tony and Jim both believe that the stars "have their influence upon what is and what is not to be" (p. 52). At the times of death in Book I of *My Ántonia* nature hastens to participate actively in the killing. Cold kills the insect. As Pavel lies dying the wind shakes "the doors and windows impatiently" and the coyotes "howl . . . to tell us that winter was coming" (p. 53), and they remind Pavel of the wolves of his native Russia. After the death of Pavel, Mr. Shimerda sometimes sits in the Russians' "empty log house . . . , brooding" (p. 61). He is close to these two losers in culture, geography, and finally in death.

Storms remind Mr. Shimerda of his frailty and of the easier life he had lived in the old country. One storm comes shortly before Christmas day, when he spends some time with the Burdens, the last comfortable hours of his life. "The big storm of winter began on . . . the twentieth of January" (p. 92) and the snow "simply spilled out of heaven," and that very night, defeated by the cold world of the prairies, Mr. Shimerda shoots himself. For five days he lies frozen in the barn waiting for the coroner to come. The coldness of his world dictates all the details of his burial: the corpse is frozen "with his knees drawn up," the funeral procession moves "against the fine, icy snow which cut our faces like a sand-blast," and the grave-diggers have to chop "out the frozen earth with old axes." The "stranger come to a far country" (pp. 114–117) is buried in the cold and the earth which destroyed him.

The tragic and inevitable union between Mr. Shimerda and the earth which swallows him up is described in Willa Cather's most lyrical and elegiac language. Denied a tomb in a Catholic cemetery because he committed suicide, he is buried at the crossroads. The refusal of travelers to drive their wagons over his grave ironically preserves "a little island" of virgin prairie on the grave of the man who never was able to cope with his New World:

Years afterward, when the open-grazing days were over, and
the red grass had been ploughed under and under until it had
almost disappeared from the prairie; when all the fields were
under fence, and the roads no longer ran about like wild
things, but followed the surveyed section-lines, Mr. Shimerda's grave was still there, with a sagging wire fence around it,
and an unpainted wooden cross. (p. 118)

The world of the Burdens is more comfortable. Although they
are not born inhabitants of the prairies, they have had more time to
adjust themselves and to alter the land to make it livable. They
have built "the only wooden house west of Black Hawk—until you
came to the Norwegian settlement" (pp. 13–14). Even so, the imagery Jim uses to describe his first daytime impression of the farm
is unpleasant: "From the windmill the ground sloped westward,
down to the barns and granaries and *pig-yards*. This slope was
trampled hard and *bare*, and *washed out* in winding *gullies* by the
rain. Beyond the corncribs, at the bottom of the shallow draw, was
a *muddy little pond*, with *rusty* willow bushes growing about it" (p.
14; note particularly the words I have italicized). The trees are little
and "insignificant against the grass" (p. 15). In conjunction with
Jim's early feeling that he was "erased, blotted out," this imagery
makes *My Ántonia* anything but what one critic has called it, "one
long paean of praise to the joys of rural living."[39]
Although Jim's views of the prairie are ambivalent and increas-
ingly favorable, the determining and unattractive features continue
throughout his life. He always remembers the loneliness and
monotony of the prairies. Nature has provided few furnishings.
"Trees were so rare in that country, and they had to make such a
hard fight to grow, that we used to feel anxious about them, and
visit them as if they were persons. It must have been the scarcity of
detail in that tawny landscape that made detail so precious" (p. 29).
Lena Lingard studies Ole Benson's tattoos "for hours; there wasn't
much to look at out there. He was like a picture book" (p. 282).
Only the struggle for security alleviates the boredom of a
snowstorm. "Next to getting warm and keeping warm, dinner and
supper were the most interesting things we had to think about" (p.

66). In one instance monotony is the mother of Willa Cather's invention. The bleak reality of a winter evening causes "a hunger for colour" (p. 174), and Jim and his friends linger at the Methodist church watching the light shining from the painted glass window. (Actually, the windows of that church in Red Cloud have never been painted or stained.) Even spring is also unvaried. Again there is quantity without variety. "There were none of the signs of spring for which I used to watch in Virginia, no budding woods or blooming gardens. There was only—spring itself" (pp. 119–120). Toward the end of *My Ántonia* Willa Cather's ambivalence is embodied in opposing views of two characters. Ántonia tells Jim that she is never lonesome as she "used to be in town" (p. 343), and four pages later Jim thinks of "the loneliness of the farm-boy at evening, when the chores seem everlastingly the same, and the world so far away" (p. 347).

Nature never loses altogether its naturalistic control over man in *My Ántonia* despite Ántonia's triumphs and the successes of the immigrants as they wrest some comforts from the world. The winter's "bitter song says 'This is reality, whether you like it or not' " (p. 173). The adversity of farm work continues beyond the death of Mr. Shimerda, and even Ántonia is coarsened for a time by her field work. She has the "draught-horse neck" of "the peasant women in all old countries" (p. 122). Despite the optimistic ending of the novel when the two old friends, Jim and Ántonia, are together again Jim concludes that forces outside themselves have controlled much of their lives: "For Ántonia and for me, this had been the road of Destiny; had taken us to those early accidents of fortune which predetermined for us all that we can ever be" (p. 372). Here Cather writes almost as Dreiser did in those naturalistic asides which begin many of the chapters of *Sister Carrie*.

There are also many smiling aspects of life in the prairie country. As early as the end of the first day Jim spends in Nebraska, he sits "entirely happy" in the garden and thinks joyfully of the vast quantity of his new world. Happiness, he reflects, is "to be dissolved into something complete and great" (p. 18). In later years he "loves with a personal passion the great country through which his railway runs and branches" (p. 2). The triumphs of the characters in *My*

Ántonia and of the book itself spring from Willa Cather's writing about the land. It is at times a world of real and delicate beauty. At the end of Book IV Jim and Tony walk homeward in the evening as the sun sets and the moon rises. "In that singular light every little tree and shock of wheat, every sunflower stalk and clump of snow-on-the-mountain, drew itself up high and pointed; the very clods and furrows in the fields seemed to stand up sharply. I felt the old pull of the earth, the solemn magic that comes out of those fields at nightfall. I wished I could be a little boy again, and that my way could end there" (p. 322). The happiness of the people springs directly from the earth. Jim goes back to the country once soon after wheat harvest. The homes, the barns, and the orchards, he thinks, "meant happy children, contented women, and men who saw their lives coming to a fortunate issue" (p. 306). Most significant of all, Ántonia Cuzak's large and happy family spring from the midwestern landscape both in spite of and because of its quantities and adversities.

My Ántonia is as directly based on the lives of individual people and the immigrant cultures as it is on the prairie land. Willa Cather wrote fiction with almost as little invention of person and event as did Thomas Wolfe. Much of the novel comes out of the materials of her own life. "One must live the life," she said two years after writing *My Ántonia*, "without thought of a novel until suddenly in its living there comes to a person the understanding that here is a story worth writing down."[40] Many of the characters come straight from life to fiction: Jim Burden (from Willa Cather's own childhood and youth), the Burden grandparents, all of Ántonia's family, the Harlings, Wick Cutter and his wife, the blind piano player and the other traveling entertainers, and many others. The landscapes, homes, public buildings, events, and almost all other aspects of her fiction are drawn from reality. Mr. Shimerda's death, Ántonia's affair and illegitimate daughter, the murder-suicide of Wick Cutter and his wife, the lifestyle of the hired girls, Jim's years at the University of Nebraska, his later visits to Ántonia's family—all derive from Willa Cather's knowledge of events and people and places. Some of her characterizations caused distress; she depicted the hired girls, for example, as so wild that some people in Red Cloud still remember objections.

Like Wolfe again, Willa Cather was inconsistent from one statement to another about how closely she modeled her people on prototypes. All her characters, she said, were "drawn from life, but they are all composites of three or four persons."[41] She did not like gossips in Red Cloud who talked about the materials of her fiction. She said that she "had never drawn but one portrait of an actual person"—Mrs. Harling in *My Ántonia*. She "absolutely" denied creating "actual portraits," but she wrote a friend that she tried hard to create in a character the exact color of the prototype's eyes. On the other hand, she makes the most absolute statement possible about the impossibility of invention in fiction: "You can't write imaginary things. To have universal appeal, they must be true!"[42] She did make changes. The prototype of Wick Cutter, for example, did kill his wife and himself in a manner close to that in the story, but he had moved away from Red Cloud and was living in Arkansas at the time of his death. Wick's elaborate plan to die just after his wife does may be Willa Cather's invention also. The prototype "died without giving any statement," but his brother said that "he and his wife had been having trouble over money matters."[43] The statement gave Willa Cather at least a clue to the motive for the murder. His character as a usurer seems to have been based on reality, and citizens in Red Cloud remember other parallels.

Obviously nothing in fiction is measured by the extent to which an author creates his materials from reality. But the background of a novel may be helpful in interpretation. The changes an author makes may enable a reader to see an aspect of a work he had not previously noted. Knowledge of the origins may confirm something about the authenticity of fiction. "Imagination," Willa Cather told a reporter, "does not mean the ability to weave pretty stories out of nothing. In the right sense, imagination is a response to what is going on—a sensitiveness to which outside things appeal. It is a composition of sympathy and observation."[44] One who stands at a place Willa Cather wrote about and who reads the passage about that particular place discerns her skill even when her seeming artlessness remains so difficult to describe.

Willa Cather admitted that "the ideas for all her novels have come from things that happened around Red Cloud during her childhood."[45] In a lengthy chat with a writer for a local newspaper in 1921, she seemed pleased with the materials: "She declared that the average person has just as interesting emotions and experiences as public personages. . . . She found people here just as interesting as those she met in London and Paris, although in a different way. She summed up the matter by saying that if a person is wide awake and not self centered he can see these interesting things in the life of those about him."[46]

Although Willa Cather was herself an Anglo-American and a native-born southerner, she was most attracted to Scandinavian and Bohemian immigrants in Nebraska and most repelled by people of her own kind. When she was a young girl she moved from the comparative racial and cultural homogeneity of Virginia to the diversity of Nebraska. She rode over the countryside and talked with the neighbors. "I have never found any intellectual excitement more intense than I used to feel when I spent a morning with one of these pioneer women at her baking or butter-making," she remembered later. "I used to ride home in the most unreasonable state of excitement; I always felt as if they told me so much more than they said—as if I had got inside another person's skin."[47] She "particularly liked the old women, they understood my homesickness and were kind to me."[48]

Willa Cather's absorption of details of several European cultures shows up in the great variety of characters and nationalities in *My Ántonia*. The first book, of course, is dominated by Bohemians. Besides the Shimerdas, the Burdens also know Peter Krajiek and Anton Jelinek, who explains Catholicism to them and tells a story about his experiences during a cholera epidemic in a war with the Prussians (p. 106). A Bohemian who has written a book about her people in Nebraska writes that Willa Cather has grasped "entirely . . . the psychology of a foreign people."[49] Prominent also in the first book are the two Russian brothers; their pleasures in owning a cow and raising melons are offset by the terrors of their Old World tale of throwing a bride and groom from a sleigh to halt the pursuit of hungry wolves. The nearest neighbors to the south are Germans, and there is a Norwegian settlement nearby (pp. 110–111). Jim's closest friends, the Harlings, introduce him to many cultures. They are Norwegian, and they have a Danish cook. The three hired girls he knows best are Bohemian, Swedish, and Norwegian. Ole Benson, a Norwegian, has an English wife (p. 282). Three Italians bring a dancing pavilion to Black Hawk and teach dancing, and a blind Negro musician with a French name, D'Arnault, comes to the hotel to play the piano for the traveling salesmen. Lincoln adds to the cosmopolitanism of the characters. Lena lives in an apartment across the hall from a wild Polish violin teacher. Gaston Cleric introduces Jim to "the world of ideas," Virgil, and the classics. At the theater Jim sees a French play, *The Count of Monte Cristo*, and he and Lena watch *Camille* together.

Otto Fuchs adds to the variety of Jim's acquaintance with cultures which had been strange to him. He tells a comic story of escorting from Europe to America a woman who had two children and who gave birth to triplets during the trip. He spent some time in the West, wears western clothes, and sings songs like "For I am a Cowboy and Know I've Done Wrong" and "Bury Me Not on the Lone Prairie." While making Mr. Shimerda's coffin, he sings old German songs. He tells a story about mining in Colorado and making a coffin for an "Eyetalian" (p. 109).

One of the minor themes of *My Ántonia* is racial intolerance. If most of the foreign characters are attractive and admirable, they nevertheless are regarded with old hostilities. Otto will not advise the Shimerdas about buying horses because "Bohemians has a natural distrust of Austrians" (p. 21) because of "politics." After the quarrel between Jake and Otto about a horsecollar, Otto reveals his own prejudice: "You can't tell me anything new about a Czech; I'm an Austrian" (p. 131). Jake brings with him from Virginia a distrust of all non-Anglo-American peoples. When he first sees the Shimerdas, he tells Jim that "you were likely to get diseases from foreigners" (p. 5). After the fight with Ambrosch, he angrily tells Jim "these foreigners ain't the same. You can't trust 'em to be fair" (p. 130). The fight, of course, "typifies in a muted way some of the tensions implicit in American history."[50] Despite their prejudices Jake and Otto are admirable characters. That tramp who throws himself "head-first right into the threshing machine after the wheat" and who is "cut to pieces" is a despicable racist. " 'My God!' he says, 'so it's Norwegians now, is it? I thought this was Americy' " (p. 178). Except for the surly Ambrosch and his mother, it is not the foreigners, as they are called, who are violent.

The immigrants establish the tone of *My Ántonia* as happy. They sing "them queer Bohemian songs" (p. 308), dance, play the piano and the harmonica and the fiddle and the trombone, go to the circus, make their own beautiful clothes, tell stories, and, in general, live with a healthy merriment. Mrs. Harling, for example, is "quick to anger, quick to laughter, and jolly from the depths of her soul. . . . Her enthusiasm, and her violent likes and dislikes, asserted themselves in all the everyday occupations of life. Wash-day was interesting, never dreary, at the Harlings'. Preserving-time was a prolonged festival" (p. 148). Tony remembers how her friends talked about "music, and the woods, and about God, and when they were young"; it was "beautiful talk, like what I never hear in this country" (p. 236). The triumph of Ántonia springs in part from her immigrant ways. Despite the adversity and the hard labor she has preserved in her family "that something which fires the imagination, [she] could still stop one's breath for a moment by a look or gesture that somehow revealed the meaning in common things" (p. 353). While surrounded by her happy family, Jim hears the story of Wick Cutter's murder and suicide, and the contrast makes Bohemian happiness even more striking.

Mr. Shimerda's music and gentility and Ántonia's happiness and domestic accomplishments derive from Bohemian culture. Willa Cather in 1923 argued that political emigrants are superior to economic emigrants. Mr. Shimerda is of the class that emigrated because of revolution and political problems. In contrast, Mrs. Shimerda and Ambrosch, the most unattractive Bohemians in the novel, compel him to come to America purely to provide economic opportunity for Ambrosch. Other results of Continental immigration to America, as described by Cather in 1923, are a multilingual population, economic prosperity, happy companionship, good the-

ater, and excellent cooking, especially of pastry, and good literature.[51] "Knut Hamsun, the Norwegian writer who was awarded
the Nobel Prize for 1920, was a 'hired hand' on a Dakota farm to the
north of us."

With the land and his wife and family, Ántonia's husband,
Cuzak, can give up the Bohemian life and culture to which he was
so devoted. It does not seem to him that he has been away from
Czechoslovakia more than a quarter-century. The ending of the
novel is an idyll with the atmosphere of an older American farm
family in a simpler time. When Jim arrives for a visit he first sees a
touching scene of two little boys "bending over a dead dog" (p.
329). Ántonia's love is apparent in the way the older brother tries to
comfort the younger. They live among farm animals in "the
deepest peace" of an orchard and on land where Ántonia knows
"every stack and tree, and where all the ground is friendly" (p.
320). The children take great pride in the ample provisions they
have grown and stored for their large family. Leaving the fruit cellar, "Ántonia and I went up the stairs first," Jim says, "and the
children waited. We were standing outside talking, when they all
came running up the steps together, big and little, tow heads and
gold heads and brown, and flashing little naked legs; a veritable
explosion of life out of the dark cave into the sunlight. It made me
dizzy for a moment" (pp. 338–339). The images here are as un-
forgettable as Jim's earlier vision of the plow against the sun.

Those who leave the land fail. Jim and Lena and Tiny do not
succeed in acquiring another culture when they give up the country for the city. They acquire only wealth. Jim is "a wasteland
figure,"[52] sensitive but somewhat like Prufrock. He can create his
portrait of Ántonia mainly because she represents what he would
like to have been. He has no family, only an estranged wife and
association with Tony's family. Lena Lingard and Tiny Soderball
live in San Francisco, Lena with her pretty clothes and Tiny with
the money from her gold mine, and neither has roots or family or
the happiness of the Cuzaks. She is as materialistic as Wick Cutter,
and she admits "frankly that nothing interested her much now but
making money." Lena is her only living friend, and her ennui
seems to be as complete as Ántonia's fulfillment. Tiny is "like

someone in whom the faculty of becoming interested is worn out"
(pp. 301–302).

Southern social life and ways provided Willa Cather with some
lifelong attitudes. Her father was always regarded as first a gentleman, even a somewhat reserved and southern gentleman. Her
mother, according to her reputation among the women of Red
Cloud, never ceased being a snob, a Virginia snob. Willa Cather
"was well aware that her mother was behaving in the southern genteel tradition, and throughout her life shared something of her
mother's benevolent, if distant, desire to champion the under-
privileged or the misunderstood."[53] And she shared other southern
traits. Her air of acting like a Virginia aristocrat is still remembered
in Red Cloud. She appreciated the dress, the music, the dining,
the ways of gentility. Virginia manners in *My Ántonia* appear
mostly in the Burden family, in Grandmother Burden's "polite
Virginia way" (pp. 73–74) and in her pleading with Jake that he not
go West and that he stay "among kindly Christian people" (p. 144).
They preserve their old ways: Virginia foods when they can get
them, Grandfather's reading the Bible, their pleasant manners and
good neighborliness, Jim's reading classical stories to his grandmother, a gentlemanly tolerance of Mr. Shimerda's Catholicism
(despite Mrs. Burden's anxieties about her husband's possible
intolerance), the "country Christmas, without any help from town"
(p. 55).

Jake is also an admirable southerner, but Willa Cather's cultural
views seem to prohibit favorable characterizations of the other
Anglo-Americans in the town of Black Hawk. The musicians and
music-lovers (always admirable characters) are mainly not Anglo-
Americans.[54] Those who came from the East or South erected bar-
riers between themselves and the immigrants. New Englanders
remained "insulated," and "the incomers from the South—from
Missouri, Kentucky, the two Virginias—were provincial and utterly without curiosity. They were kind neighbors—lent a hand to
help a Swede when he was sick or in trouble. But I am quite sure
that Knut Hamsun might have worked a year for any one of our
Southern farmers, and his employer would never have discovered
that there was anything unusual about the Norwegian."[55] She did

not see the irony that she had sprung from the stock of southern farmers she wrote about.

This kind of inattention to the things appreciated by Continental culture causes a dullness in the Anglo-American town society which makes it resemble the Main Street Sinclair Lewis was to create two years later. The merchant's daughters try to be "refined" (p. 199); rather than do domestic work "they sat at home in poverty." Even the young have aspirations very much like those of Flem Snopes. "The respect for respectability was stronger than any desire in Black Hawk youth" (p. 202). Like Flem, Sylvester Lovett, who is much attracted to Lena Lingard, will give her up and marry a woman for money and position. This cashier of his father's bank, "daft about" Lena, "ran away with a widow six years older than himself, who owned a half-section. This remedy worked, apparently" (p. 204). Although Willa Cather was to say later in 1921 that the lives of common people are as interesting as those of anyone in Europe, she did not find them so in the town of Black Hawk. The fathers of Black Hawk are dull, and their thoughts and actions predictable. They are without culture and interest: they "had no personal habits outside their domestic ones; they paid the bills, pushed the baby-carriage after office hours, moved the sprinkler about over the lawn, and took the family driving on Sunday" (p. 57). Even the Burdens' Anglo-American puritanism and concern for social position prevent Jim's enjoying the immigrant saloons and stop his dancing with the immigrant girls; the most exciting diversions of the evening are hanging around the drugstore or the depot (p. 218).

Willa Cather's portrait of life in a midwestern small town is not nearly so adverse as Lewis's in *Main Street*, but her Jim Burden is like Carol Kennicott in his ennui and disgust with small-town life. Whether Black Hawk is a true representation of towns of its kind is a social question. As fiction, it is not so richly teeming with life as Faulkner's Jefferson or Wolfe's Altamont. Perhaps Willa Cather was not willing to acknowledge the richness that it had. Since the 1890s she had been willing to exaggerate its weaknesses. When she was sent as a reporter to describe the town of Brownsville and its attempts at self-improvement, she mussed up the inside of a

church before she asked her friend and photographer, Mariel
Gere, to take a picture of it. Years later Miss Gere remembered
that she had been "somewhat disturbed by the fact that only the
places in Brownsville which had deteriorated seemed to interest
Willa . . . [and] shocked when we went into a church . . . , and she
pulled the kneeling benches out from between the pews, carried
them down to the end of the church and piled them up so the
church looked like it was in ruins, and asked me to photograph the
pile."[56] She did not stack the pews so obviously in *My Ántonia*, but
she does view the town with some harshness. The wonder of Ántonia and the immigrants and Jim's childhood are offset by the barrenness of people who "sit around here and whittle store-boxes and
tell stories" all their lives (p. 224). "The growing piles of ashes and
cinders in the back yards were the only evidence that the wasteful,
consuming process of life went on at all" (pp. 219–220).

The worst Anglo-American evil and materialism unfolds in the
sketch of Wick Cutter, who is cunning and inhuman in the ways of
the Snopeses. The main difference is that Wick is "notoriously dissolute with women" (p. 210) rather than impotent like Flem. Like
I. O. Snopes, he is "full of moral maxims for boys" (p. 209), and he
often quotes *Poor Richard's Almanack* (p. 210). He is a usurer, and
those to whom he lends money do not understand how they become so deeply in debt. He would offer a boy a quarter for an
errand "and then drive off, saying he had no change and would 'fix
it up next time' " (p. 211). Childless, also like Flem Snopes, he
values money over any human attachment. He murders his wife
and then kills himself in such a fashion as to guarantee that none of
his money will go to her kin. Willa Cather creates him explicitly as
a religious, cultural, and social embodiment. His name and descent
and language are English-American: Wycliffe Cutter "liked to talk
about his pious bringing-up. He contributed regularly to the Protestant churches, 'for sentiment's sake,' as he said with a flourish of
the hand" (p. 209). Biographically, he is a portrait of the life and
death of M. R. Bentley in Red Cloud. Curiously, he has the same
nationality and occupation as Willa Cather's father, whom she admired a great deal, who lent money and wrote title abstracts, but
who had the reputation of a fair and honest man. As fiction, Wick

Cutter is something of a melodramatic oversimplification. Confirming Willa Cather's cultural generalizations in Wick Cutter is the brief portrait of another Anglo-American villain, Larry Donovan, who tricks Ántonia, fathers her child, and refuses to marry her.

My Ántonia seems to be a simple book, the story of a happy immigrant farm woman told by her friend, who left the Midwest to live in New York and to become a lawyer for a great western railroad. Actually, it is a simple book and sometimes also nearly melodramatic and nearly sentimental. A certain kind of simplicity in a narrative may contribute to the art of fiction. One of the best attributes of Willa Cather's greatest novel about the prairies is that it is a success story and also a happy one. It is, furthermore, peculiarly American—based directly on a specific time and place, an era of basic significance in national life and the history of the world.

6

The Enchanted Mesa. "On this . . . there had once been a village, but the stairway which had been the only access to it was broken off by a great storm many centuries ago, and its people had perished up there from hunger."

The St. Francis Cathedral in Santa Fe, New Mexico. It was built mainly because of the efforts of Archbishop John B. Lamy, prototype of Father Latour in Willa Cather's novel.

❦ SIX ❧

Death Comes for the Archbishop:
Worlds Old and New

Few narratives treat a greater diversity of cultures than Willa Cather's *Death Comes for the Archbishop*.[1] Set in Mexico, New Mexico, Arizona, and Colorado, this novel portrays to some extent the life of many kinds of peoples: the Spanish fathers of the early days, Pueblo and Navajo Indians, Mexican descendants of Spaniard and Indian, French missionary priests brought to the Southwest by Archbishop Jean Baptiste Lamy just after New Mexico became a territory of the United States, and Anglo-Americans who succeeded the Mexicans. Within these cultures, especially among the numerous pueblo villages of the Southwest, are infinite variations of language, legend, and folklore. In some situations several cultures intertwine in harmony or conflict, complexity or simplicity, retrospect or the present. A Jesuit French priest, for example, visits Taos and lives at the home of a Mexican priest, meets an expelled member of the flagellant Penitentes society, talks with and about Mexicans and the Taos Pueblo Indians, learns of the massacre of the Anglo-American governor of New Mexico by Indians with the probable collusion of the Mexican priest five years before, and hears about the great Indian rebellion of 1680. And most of the episodes of *Death Comes for the Archbishop* involve almost this much cultural and racial interchange.

Willa Cather was not native to the religions or the people of the Southwest. She was not herself Catholic; in 1922, five years before she published *Death Comes for the Archbishop*, she had become an Episcopalian; but she knew Catholic priests in the Southwest.[2] She first visited the country of *The Archbishop* in 1912, but she began her extended visits there in 1925. She spent summers in New Mexico, stayed for weeks in the places she wrote about (a month at Taos, more than a month the next summer), camped in the outdoors, traveled by wagon,[3] did research in Denver[4] and in general became an adopted southwesterner as much as she could.[5] She learned the fauna, the flora—primroses, fireweed, butterfly weed, rainbow flower (pp. 165, 233)—the history, and the people. She read numerous books about the region and studied history, archaeology, folklore, and anthropology. In *The Archbishop* she retold stories in a manner very close to that of the previous tellers of the tales. She followed the biography of one of her two priests so closely that the author "gently reminded" her that she had forgotten to acknowledge her indebtedness.[6] She paraphrased and briefly quoted historians and official documents and did not acknowledge using them either. Also, some of her episodes are invented.

The tones and the events in *The Archbishop* are as varied as the peoples. The history of the Southwest records violence, treachery, bloodshed, and trickery of Indians, Mexicans, Spaniards, and Anglo-Americans. But along with violence there are many other modes or manners: serenity, magnificence, benevolence. The book also is one of the most devout stories written in the twentieth century. It is sometimes meditative but never psychological in the manner of James or of Faulkner. Often the tone seems nearly sentimental or legendary. There are stories of elemental struggles: the necessity of taking refuge from marauders on a flat-tabled rock like the Enchanted Mesa, or the people of Ácoma carrying water almost straight up a cliff with only handholds and toeholds to cling to. Most of the time Willa Cather treats the violence somewhat generally and at a distance, but some of the episodes clearly represent the worst of the old West.

The tranquil mood of *The Archbishop* is impressive; it is much easier to describe it than it is to know how Willa Cather created it. Despite danger, vigorous exertion, and strenuous conflict with evil, the calmness and serenity of the Jesuit priests and some of their parishioners dominate the narrative. On the whole, the other cultures are more admirable than the Anglo-American. The lowly are more worthy than most of those in high places. "The Mexicans were always Mexicans, the Indians were always Indians. Santa Fé was a quiet backwater, with no natural wealth, no importance commercially" (p. 286). In contrast, those hunting gold under Pike's Peak, and by implication American frontiersmen, comprised "a great industrial expansion, where guile and trickery and honourable ambition all struggled together" (p. 286). Much of the mission of the two priests derives from hostility between peoples, and much of the interest of the book springs from the mingling of cultures.

The tone and the technique of *The Archbishop* are unusual for fiction in the twentieth century. Willa Cather was trying to create something like a martyrdom of a saint such as is found in *The Golden Legend* of Jacobus de Voragine. "The essence of such writing is not to hold the note," she explained, "not to use an incident for all there is in it—but to touch and pass on. . . . In this kind of writing the mood is all the thing—all the little figures and stories are mere improvisations that come out of it."[7] This kind of fiction is at the furthest extreme from the dramatic situation in fiction and from the psychological introspection of stream of consciousness. It is story and mood rather than dramatic enactment or mental analysis. In a legend "historical fact may either be developed or disfigured by popular imagination"[8] or by Willa Cather's creative imagination. The book is more legend than novel. Like traditional legends, *The Archbishop* mingles fact and fiction and narrates both as fact; many of the particular legends derive from an oral tradition; and Willa Cather's legend is a culmination of other legends which have grown by accretion.[9] There is little despair, anguish, anxiety, uncertainty. Both priests resemble the saint of an old legend, who "is the truly perfect man. He must have all the virtues, and be free of every fault. His wisdom must be such as exceeds human powers."[10] The episodes and situations have in common some of the following characteristics: religion, miracles, heroism, violence, death, love, simplicity. Many of the legendary stories in *The Archbishop* have typical folk situations—the death of a miser, the problems of a lady who refuses to tell her age, the saving of a good woman from a murderous husband, the miraculous appearance of the Virgin Mary to a poor neophyte.

These are unusual events and stories for a novel, a genre of literature which (in our time) has usually been philosophical, complicated, and analytical. *The Archbishop* goes just as far as modern fiction can in moral and religious example—indeed, further than some kinds of novels can. It has the directness of explicit folk wisdom. Legendary and exemplary, it retains plausibility by its use of diverse cultural characteristics and by depicting the evils confronted by the priests. It qualifies its portrait of saints by depicting one of the protagonist priests as a man of gentle humor and the other as reticent and even somewhat cold. *The Archbishop* is something like a romance, "an heroic fable, which treats of fabulous persons and things."[11] The actions of the two bishops are "marvelous," but they are themselves human beings. Northrop Frye's description of the romance is applicable to Willa Cather's book, but to apply it exactly would be an exaggeration. "The ordinary laws of nature," he writes, "are slightly suspended: prodigies of courage and endurance, unnatural to us are natural to the heroes of romances."[12] *The Archbishop* stands just a little closer to the form of a novel than that.

Although characters besides the two priests in *The Archbishop* are seen externally, the connections between God and nature, man and nature, and race and nature are intimate. The Catholic sees God in nature as the southwestern Indians have always seen the supernatural in the strange phenomena of the mesas, mountains, canyons, caves, deserts, springs, and rivers of the Southwest. Indeed the first section of Willa Cather's account of Father Latour's mission in America is called "The Cruciform Tree," and "living vegetation," the father thinks, "could not present more faithfully the form of the Cross" than the tree does (pp. 18–19). Father Latour and Father Vaillant have different views of nature. Father Latour sees God in nature, "but his dear Joseph must always have the miracle very direct and spectacular, not with Nature, but against it" (p. 29). Father Latour meditates on the meanings of natural phenomena and the implications to the Indian and to the Christian. When he sees the mesa of Ácoma, a great rock almost square in shape, he wonders why man first thought of "living on the top of naked rocks like these, hundreds of feet in the air, without soil or water" (p. 97). From other tribes of Indians and then from the Spaniard, the Ácoma Pueblo found sanctuary on the rock.

With human and religious understanding the bishop is able to turn immediately from the pagan meaning to the Christian: "The rock, when one came to think of it, was the utmost expression of human need; even mere feeling yearned for it; it was the highest comparison of loyalty in love and friendship. Christ Himself had used that comparison for the disciple to whom He gave the keys of His Church" (p. 97).

Nature in *The Archbishop* is not altogether benevolent and romantic. The two priests endure the terror and suffering of thirst in the desert, a blizzard that kills their mounts and drives them into a cave, and arduous travels over long spaces and high mountains. Nature in the Old World was "worn to the shape of human life," but the early Spanish missionaries in the New World "threw themselves naked upon the hard heart of a country that was calculated to try the endurance of giants" (pp. 277–278). One may step from adversity to safety and beauty in a moment. Father Latour stands on a "wavy ocean of sand" and looks down at "a green thread of verdure and a running stream" which his horse and mule have scented and discovered. "This ribbon in the desert . . . was greener than anything Latour had ever seen, even in his own greenest corner of the Old World" (p. 24). Adversity, safety, beauty—and mystery, especially in association with the Indians' "old road of fear and darkness" (p. 211). Caught in a snowstorm in the mysterious ceremonial cave of the Pecos Pueblo, Father Latour stoops to a narrow "fissure in the stone floor" and listens "to one of the oldest voices of the earth . . . , the sound of a great underground river, flowing through a resounding cavern" (p. 130). Such a natural wonder is not implausible in the Southwest; much of the course of the Cimarron River is underground in New Mexico.[13] But the river is a supernatural wonder also because of its association with the terrible storm outside the cave, the mysteries of the Pecos cave itself, the Indian guide Jacinto, and a Jesuit father.

The local colorist creates an exaggerated nature to emphasize the quaintness and strangeness of his characters and their remoteness; his descriptions of any ugliness in nature are melodramatic; the beauties of nature appear in a polysyllabic vocabulary and saccharine imagery. Willa Cather's nature, in contrast, is simple, somewhat biblical, somewhat pastoral, certainly in the mood of a legend. At Taos "there was a religious silence over the place" (pp. 150–151). Nature is associated with the character of a people and described from the perspective of the character who sees it. The tamarisk tree, the favorite of Father Joseph, has "feathery plumes of bluish green" (p. 202). It helps Willa Cather to create a Mexican homestead. "The family burro was tied to its trunk, the chickens scratched under it, the dogs slept in its shade, the washing was hung on its branches. Father Latour had often remarked that this tree seemed especially designed in shape and colour for the adobe village" (p. 202).

The lyrical meditations of Father Latour are one of Willa Cather's major accomplishments in the book. They establish his character, create a mood, and quietly reveal his sincere reverence. He and Willa Cather see the Southwest as a "brilliant blue world of stinging air and moving cloud. Even the mountains were mere ant-hills under it. Elsewhere the sky is the roof of the world; but here the earth was the floor of the sky" (p. 232). Nature for the father also has domesticity; and in his old age after he has retired as archbishop, his cottage, the place where he put it, and his garden reveal his serenity, his age, his joy in fruits, and his knowledge that the old may still be fruitful. He chooses a "place in the red hills spotted with juniper" (p. 266). The feature he likes most is an ancient "apricot tree of such great size as he had never seen before. . . . The apricots were large, beautifully coloured, and of superb flavour" (p. 266). The cottage and its surroundings are images of his declining years. He dies in the exile of New Mexico away from his native Auvergne because of the southwestern air, which "would disappear from the whole earth in time, perhaps; but long after his day" (p. 275). Thus Willa Cather has united the archibishop and his world.

The Archbishop is a religious book and more specifically a Catholic book. "The longer I stayed in the Southwest," Willa Cather wrote the year she published it, "the more I felt that the story of the Catholic Church in that country was the most interesting of all its stories." [14] The faith provided the form of the legend, the only two constantly reappearing characters, many of the episodes which fill out the action, and the standard for individuals and cultures. For some the Church furnishes a simple and optimistic world. One Mexican child believes that the priest is sent to her village directly by God as an answer to her father's prayers (p. 25). Willa Cather does best with her bishop and her vicar. The other characters have some of the generality and remoteness one would expect of an author foreign to the culture of her book. People and cultures are measured in terms of Jesuit Catholicism. Father Martínez of Taos is a vigorous man and a good creation for the legend, but to the extent that he contradicts Catholic ideals he is religiously wrong. A lack of harmony with Catholic or religious ideals also reveals a lack of harmony between peoples and cultures. The two Jesuit fathers follow their beliefs so much that they become ideal heroes of romance and legend. Such specific affirmation of human and religious values by ideal characters is extremely rare in our time. Their perfection is unique, but also a little flawed as fiction, a little sentimental, faintly suggestive of the ways of the local colorists.

Although Willa Cather could be a dust-covered camper in the Southwest, she seems always to have retained some preference for the niceties of European civilization. She admires the French urbanity of Father Latour, whose "manners, even when he was alone in the desert, were distinguished" (p. 19). Mexican art, Indian tradition, ancient stories of the Spanish Fathers, the aristocratic society of Santa Fé—several aspects of life in New Mexico provide some of the arts and refinements of the Old World, but the moments when the two French priests can dream of being at home in Auvergne are cherished. Thus the French meal worked on so hard by Father Joseph and described so much by Willa Cather is a little heady. In occasional lapses *The Archbishop* becomes somewhat patronizing to the characters usually admired. "Certainly it was a great piece of luck for Father Latour and Father Vaillant, who lived so much among peons and Indians and rough frontiersmen, to be able to converse in their tongue now and then with a cultivated woman" (p. 177) like Doña Isabella. Furthermore, Willa Cather is on occasion daintily aware of the foul body odors of a group of common New Mexicans (p. 193).

That moment of time when the design for *The Archbishop* flashed into the author's mind was governed by Catholicism. She was reading a biography of a bishop written by a bishop, W. J. Howlett's *Life of the Right Reverend Joseph P. Machebeuf, D.D.: Pioneer Priest of Ohio, Pioneer Priest of Colorado, Vicar Apostolic of Colorado and Utah, and First Bishop of Denver.*[15] In Willa Cather's workshop the materials of this old-fashioned biographical laudation were turned into her legend. Father Machebeuf became Father Vaillant, and Father Jean Baptiste Lamy became Father Latour. In the manner of a good artist she followed her source closely and still adapted it to her own purpose. Although the active and colorful Machebeuf is the central figure in the biography, Willa Cather chose the calmer and more meditative Lamy for the prototype of her main character. Machebeuf's biographer left Lamy and followed his subject into Colorado; Willa Cather stayed on in New Mexico, where Father Latour heard stories of his friend. For the account of Father Latour's death, she found only one paragraph in a history of the Church in the Southwest.[16] She closed her legend and impressively depicted the archbishop's retirement and death by creating his peaceful mental reflections. She describes him selecting a site for his cottage and puttering in his garden. After he becomes sick and returns to Santa Fé, he sits looking at the cathedral he has built, remembers the places and friends of his youth, instructs a younger priest about the Southwest, and recalls at length legends about Father Junipero, remembers the youth and the funeral of his friend Father Joseph, reflects on the sufferings of the Navajo Indians and their chief Manuelito.

On the whole Willa Cather makes few changes in the history by Salpointe and the biography of Machebeuf. The parallels are numerous: the bishop's trip to Santa Fé, the difficult journey through Texas, Machebeuf's missionary work in Colorado, the life in Ohio, the visit to the pope, Machebeuf-Vaillant's begging for the Church, especially the begging from Mexican women for the Anglo-Americans in Colorado, the relationship between Machebeuf-Vaillant and the sisters who are in a convent in France, the lives of the two priests in France, their departure to be missionaries, the physical appearance of the priests, the theory of "rest in action,"[17] the enlistment in the French military service, the acquiring of the white mules (actually bays),[18] and so on and so on. Willa Cather adapts her materials in many ways; she adds descriptions of places and emotions, creates her own style altogether, omits, invents, quotes, drops the strictly chronological approach and creates character through reminiscence, composes private prayers a biographer would never know, changes a factual sentence into a lengthy meditation, describes personal experience in great detail derived from a photograph, and in general does whatever she can to make the book a true legend of her Catholic priests and the Southwest. She was able to use fact and to sacrifice fact for her artistic designs.

The Catholicism of the two priests is best seen not merely in their characters but also in their confrontation of a wide variety of Catholics and Catholic legends, churches, painting, figures, stories, and factions. Only three episodes primarily involving Catholics and Catholicism are mainly invented. Imaginary events and real events are chosen for their religious and historical representativeness and for a variety of effects in the legend. The invented sections are the story "Hidden Water" very early, "The Legend of Fray Baltazar" of the pueblo of Ácoma, and most of the story of the miserliness of Padre Lucero.

"Hidden Water" (see above) presents early in the novel the terrors of thirst in a southwestern desert, the constrasting beauties of an oasis, the simplicity and reverence of the lowly and isolated Mexicans, and the ministrations of a good priest to them. Willa Cather's entire source is an objective statement in Howlett that Bishop Lamy made a journey of fifteen hundred miles to see the bishop of Durango. To begin her legend she chose the natural miracle of "The Cruciform Tree" and the account of the bishop's ministrations to his people: "This settlement was his Bishopric in miniature; hundreds of square miles of thirsty desert, then a spring, a village, old men trying to remember their catechism to teach their grandchildren. The Faith planted by the Spanish friars and watered with their blood was not dead; it awaited only the toil of the husbandman" (p. 32).

"The Legend of Fray Baltazar" tells of the relationship between a dissolute and tyrannical priest and his murmuring Indian parishioners at Ácoma. The "proud old Spaniard" prepares an extraordinary feast and invites padres from other pueblos. When an Indian serving-boy spills "rich brown gravy" on one of the diners, Baltazar hits the boy on the head with a pewter mug and kills him. The Ácomas "rid their rock of their tyrant" by throwing him over "the most precipitous cliff" (p. 113). Willa Cather has created her own individual legend of one kind of typical missionary-parish relationship in the Southwest. The priest who succeeds Baltazar Montoya is "a native Mexican, of unpretentious tastes," and a legend of the past has shown a change in history with the simplicity and violence of an old fairy tale. A padre was forced to leap from Ácoma.[19] But he survived with the aid of an umbrella.

When Bishop Lamy arrived in New Mexico the native Mexican priests resented him, denied his authority, and continued the practices the bishop condemned. Willa Cather selects three actual priests to represent the historical conflict. One of these is Father Marino Lucero (based on Father Mariano de Jesus Lucero), who appears only briefly in history and biography[20] and who is excommunicated "for irregularities and schismatical tendencies." He became an ally of Father Antonio José Martínez in setting up a separate church, which Willa Cather calls the Holy Catholic Church of Mexico (p. 159). She adds substantially to the story of Lucero. Probably she invents her additions to history, but some of the life of Lucero may be based on folklore. She provides him with a daughter, Conceptión Gonzales, to give flesh to his violation of his vow of celibacy; and she demonstrates his materialism by making him the most extreme of misers. Simple tales of particular types of men are common in folklore—the lazy man, the miser, the fighting man, and so on. Lucero prides himself on his avarice, "the one passion that grew stronger and sweeter in old age" (p. 161). When a robber tries to steal his money, the priest kills him and, "covered with blood" rushes out "to arouse the town" (p. 163). This legend ends with Lucero's melodramatic deathbed scene. He repents and sends for Father Joseph, but spends his thoughts on his money. He asks why God "did . . . not make some way for a man to protect his own after death" (p. 168). In the way of folk, watchers hope that at the moment of death he will see the world beyond and reveal something to them. His words in Spanish are addressed to his rival: "Eat your tail, Martínez, eat your tail!" (p. 171). The watchers believe that he has seen Martínez in hell. Lucero is a sorry piece of humanity, but the stark melodrama is qualified by the patience of the watching Mexican women.

Two other historical priests besides Lucero appear in *The Archbishop*. Howlett's biography presents a dramatic confrontation with Father Machebeuf facing the Reverend J. M. Gallegos and expelling him from his church in Albuquerque.[21] Willa Cather here describes the scandalous life of her gambling, hunting, dancing, drinking priest: "he would still dance the fandango five nights running, as if he could never have enough of it" (p. 82). Father Latour finds him "engaging . . . as a man" but "impossible" as a priest (p. 84). *The Archbishop* is on the whole a very happy book, and the merriment, even if it is a priest's, helps to establish that tone.

Willa Cather invents with Lucero, selects with Gallegos, and records and fills out history with Padre José Martínez of Taos. Father of a son after he became a priest, he argues against celibacy and for sin, eats and drinks "generously" (p. 145), feeds his cats "carelessly from his plate" (p. 144), keeps a disorderly house, foretells an early death for Latour if he begins a campaign of reforms, and establishes his own independent church when he is excommunicated. But he is not a simple villain; he is attractive, and he has admirable talents. "The Bishop had never heard the Mass more impressively sung than by Father Martínez. . . . Rightly guided, the Bishop reflected, this Mexican might have been a great man" (p. 150). But he is not rightly guided. He brings disorder into the Church, and that violates the entire mission of Latour. The men who selected him had said that the chosen bishop would have to be "a man to whom order is necessary—as dear as life" (p. 8). And in those terms the disorder in Martínez's house "was almost more than . . . [Father Latour's] fastidious taste could bear" (p. 144).

Although some writers have defended history's Father Martínez,[22] some historians paint his career almost as black as Willa

Cather does. "His power over his parishioners was absolute," a historian of the Southwest writes, "and his hatred of Americans and American institutions was recognized by all."[23] He had five children by his housekeeper, and they were "provided for in his will."[24] In general, Willa Cather adopts the worst political and religious view possible for Martínez, but makes him personally attractive in some ways. Certainly other admirable things in the Catholic Church in the Southwest offset her evil Mexican priests. Many invented details of the priest's personal life make him more real than Lucero or Gallegos. As Father Latour goes to his bed for the night, he is "annoyed . . . exceedingly" when he sees "a bunch of woman's hair that had been indolently tossed into a corner when some slovenly female toilet was made in this room" (p. 149). Besides the bishop's fastidious reaction, Willa Cather has created in this one image the lechery of Padre Martínez and the domestic disorder of his home.

Fiction can use rumor as fact even when defenders of the historical figure are annoyed at the certainty. In a notorious rebellion in Martínez's Taos in 1847 the Indians and Mexicans revolted against the new American government in New Mexico, killed Governor Bent of the territory and scalped him, and killed, as Willa Cather says, about a dozen other whites (p. 140).[25] Martínez's contemporaries and many historians believed that he was one of the principal instigators of the violent rebellion. Cather not only asserts his definite guilt but also invents additional villainy for her corrupt priest. He promises to save the lives of the rebellious Indians who were "sentenced to death . . . if they would deed him their lands, near the pueblo" (p. 140). He goes off on a visit, and "the seven Indians were hanged on the appointed day" (p. 140).

Willa Cather lightens the tone of her story of Martínez by creating a comic character who is involved in one of the most sensational societies in the Catholic Church in New Mexico—the Penitentes. The lecherous and gluttonous candidate for the priesthood, Trinidad Lucero, whose kinship in the Martínez household is left intentionally vague, has failed in his attempt to be one of the Penitentes. They are a flagellant order who have themselves scourged and subjected to many kinds of cruel and unusual punishments. Latour contemplates stopping the extravagances (p. 155), but neither Latour nor Lamy succeeded in stopping the flagellations. Rumors were that the crucifixions sometimes caused death.[26] Society members continued their secret practices into the twentieth century, and there may have been crucifixions when Willa Cather was visiting the Southwest.[27] Flagellations may be sexual in intent, perhaps, as well as religious. Trinidad regards the serving girl in a "greedy way" (p. 145), and he also "carries the heaviest crosses to the highest mountains, and takes more scourging than anyone" (pp. 148–149). Martínez, himself a native of Abiquiu, the center of the Penitentes society, describes Trinidad's sufferings with a humorous and degrading simile: "He comes back here with his back so full of cactus spines that the girls have to pick him like a chicken" (p. 149). And Trinidad's flagellant career comes to a farcical end. Tied to a cross with ropes, "he is so heavy that after he had hung there a few hours, the cross fell over with him, and he . . . said he would bear as many stripes as our Saviour—six thousand. . . . But before they had given him a hundred, he fainted" (p. 154).

Many religious things in the Catholic Church in New Mexico and Arizona in *The Archbishop* offset the evils of some of the priests. Besides the goodness of the Church in the portraits of Vaillant and Latour, there are the symbolic physical beauties of Church things, the accomplishments and the martyrdoms of the early Spanish missionaries, the love of God among some Indians and many Mexicans, and legends of miracles in the New World. The goodness of the Catholic Church in *The Archbishop* overshadows the evil and the violence. Indeed, it is in part the suffering which reveals the goodness. Shortly before his death, Father Latour recalls how "those early missionaries threw themselves naked upon the hard heart of a country that was calculated to try the endurance of giants" (p. 278).

Besides suffering deprivations and martyrdom, the early fathers were great builders, or at least they persuaded the Indians to erect magnificent churches. Father Latour is himself a master builder. Always Willa Cather succeeds in creating a sensitive relationship between the priest and the sensuous things in his life. The bishop rides over the "hills in every direction" before he finds "one yellow hill among all these green ones" (p. 241) to furnish the stone for his church. He selects a French architect to design "the first Romanesque church in the New World" (p. 243). Father Vaillant questions the building of a fine church "when everything is so poor" (p. 244). Father Latour, perhaps more contemplative and reverent and less charitable than his friend, replies, "The Cathedral is near my heart, for many reasons. I hope you do not think me worldly" (p. 245). The church is central in the bishop's meditations in his old age. He admires its close relationship to its place. It is "of the South" (p. 271), a part of the place where it is built, and "once that kinship is there, time will only make it stronger" (p. 272). Neither Willa Cather nor her bishop ever contemplates any cultural disparity between the Midi Romanesque architecture in a city of predominantly Mexican and Spanish origins. The character of the priest determined his choice of architecture. In Santa Fé there was some objection to the cathedral on cultural grounds. "I was very much distressed," Mary Austin wrote, "that she had given her allegiance to the French blood of the Archbishop; she had sympathized with his desire to build a French cathedral in a Spanish town. It was a calamity."[28]

An old bell found "in the basement of old San Miguel Church" brings one art of the Old World to the New. Its rich historical backgrounds and its "beautiful tone" as it rings the Ave Maria cause Father Latour to sense "something Eastern, with palm trees— Jerusalem, perhaps, though he had never been there" (p. 43). Father Vaillant tells a legend of how the people of a Spanish city besieged by the Moors pledged to St. Joseph to make a bell of "all their plate and silver and gold ornaments" (p. 44). The date on the bell, 1356, and all the other information about it Willa Cather found in Howlett's biography.[29] Indeed, Howlett's legend is more filled with details than Willa Cather's. Her accomplishment is the creation of the lyrical meditations of the bishop as he awakens to the sound of the bell.

The ancient history of the Catholic Church in the Southwest has provided not only martyrdoms but also miracles for Willa Cather's legend. Once Father Latour has gone to Mexico to establish proof of his authority, returned, and settled down in his home, Willa Cather writes of the bell and a miracle to establish the mood and the religious theme of *The Archbishop*. She tells the story of the appearance of the Virgin to Juan Diego, "a poor neophyte of the monastery of St. James" in 1531 (pp. 46–47). As proof of her appearance and her request that the bishop build a church where she appeared, she gives Juan roses at a time when roses are out of season, and miraculously she causes a painting of the Blessed Virgin to appear on his wretched *tilma*, "a mantle . . . of coarse vegetable fibre" (p. 48). One of the native priests has been to the shrine of Our Lady of Guadalupe, and he comes to tell Father Latour about it. Willa Cather presents without significant change the details of the story as she learned them from a source.[30]

The Archbishop ends as it began, with miracles. Three stories are told about Father Junipero Serra, a Spanish missionary to Mexico and California in the eighteenth century.[31] Once "a mysterious stranger appeared" and showed Father Serra how to ford a river; again a horseman saved him from thirst in the desert (Willa Cather changed a gift of a loaf of bread for hunger to a gift of pomegranates for hunger and thirst); and the Holy Family provides a home for an overnight stay in a desert. Cather adds dimensions to the character of her old archbishop as he recalls (in a tale of much greater length than that in the source) in his last days the warmth of Father Junipero's affections for the Christ Child: "from the moment he entered the house he had been strangely drawn to the child, and desired to take him in his arms. . . . After prayers . . . he did indeed stoop over the little boy in blessing; and the child had lifted his hand, and with his tiny finger made the cross upon Father Junipero's forehead" (p. 282).

The Mexicans in *The Archbishop* represent a wide variety of characters, classes, and religions. Two of the priests in the early days of the Church are Baltazar, the high-living, fleshly, courageous, corrupt priest, and Ramirez, the church builder. The Mexican group she admires are the primitive villagers, such as those at Agua Secreta. To portray the aristocratic and wealthy Mexicans of old Santa Fé, Willa Cather chose the Olivares family, who are probably a composite portrait of a number of people. The mysterious Doña Isabella Olivares is not unlike Kit Carson's Mexican wife, Josefa Jaramillo, sister to the wife of Governor Bent. Her musical accomplishments may be derived in part from Mrs. Julia Miner, who is also the source for Mrs. Harling in *My Ántonia*. In some ways Doña Isabella and her husband resemble Captain and Mrs. Forester in *A Lost Lady*. Doña Isabella gives a party, and Fathers Latour and Vaillant attend. They admire her Old World sophistication, her sexuality, beauty, mysterious past, musical accomplishments, entertaining, and her refusal to testify in court about her age until she has to do so to protect money her husband had willed to the Church. Certainly the Olivares party is a social and a narrative change of pace after the encounter with Martínez and the story of the death of Lucero.

The Mexican people are in many ways the most admirable culture described in *The Archbishop*. It is a happy and "a friendly world, where by every man's fireside a welcome awaited" the priests (p. 277). Unlike the Anglo-Americans especially, the Mexicans have a past like an Old World culture. The well at the village of Agua Secreta reminds Father Latour of an image of a Roman river goddess at a well-head where "later the Christian priests had planted a cross" (p. 32). The Mexicans enjoy rooster-pulls and cock-fighting and foods and wines. They forget their prayers because they cannot read, but they retain a simple faith. Father Joseph believes "it was people like them our Saviour bore in mind when He said, *Unless ye become as little children*. He was thinking of people who are not clever in the things of this world, whose minds are not upon gain and worldly advancement" (p. 206). The Mexicans are not thrifty and materialistic like the Anglo-Americans.[32]

In religion the Mexicans are "fickle" (p. 117) and narrow-minded (p. 27) and demonstrative. Women throw shawls in the path of the bishop and kiss the episcopal ring. In France that would be "highly distasteful. . . . Here, these demonstrations seemed a part of the high colour that was in landscape and gardens, in the flaming cactus and the gaudily decorated altars,—in the agonized Christs and dolorous Virgins and the very human figures of the saints. He had already learned that with this people religion was necessarily theatrical" (p. 142). The art in Mexican churches and homes expresses the individual relationship between the folk artist and the figures that he represents.[33] Father Latour is interested in "the wooden figures of the saints, found in even the poorest Mexican houses. . . . He had never yet seen two alike" (p. 28). Folk art is superior to the manufactured images of plaster which he remembers in American churches in Ohio. And the episcopal home shares with the images a handmade quality. "The thick clay walls had been finished on the inside by the deft palms of Indian women" (p. 33–34), and the furniture is handmade. In the village of Chimayo the people frequently make new boots for "a little equestrian image of Santiago" (p. 249), and the "little wooden figure" of the Virgin has been carried in a procession in her honor since two hundred years before the bishop's time. Willa Cather describes even a physical relationship between the Virgin and those who love her. "She was their doll and their queen, something to fondle and something to adore, as Mary's Son must have been to Her" (pp. 256–257). Willa Cather attributes to Mexican art the same qualities Ruskin admired in architecture: "every building of the Gothic period differs in some important respect from every other."[34] Strangely, the individuality of Mexican art is Christian in the same way as a Gothic cathedral. Christianity's "exhortation is: Do what you can, and confess frankly what you are unable to do" (p. 221). Even the imperfections that are shown "in every touch" create love and uniqueness.

To represent the violence latent in some of the passionate Mexicans, Willa Cather turned to history for the character of the swashbuckling Don Manuel Chavez. Except for the description of his appearance and his emotions at the Olivares' party, nothing in *The Archbishop* expands or contradicts history: his descent from Castilian knights, his fighting the Navajos, even the "seven arrow wounds, and one shaft clear through his body" (p. 185), and his escape as the sole survivor of fifty-one men (thirty-one according to one authority).[35] Willa Cather's account is close enough to one unacknowledged source to be termed paraphrase.[36] There is considerable ironic contrast between the good Father Latour's quiet reflections and the fierce warrior Chavez, between former Navajo-killing and a quiet parlor party, between Chavez and his rival Kit Carson at the same party, between Chavez and the uniformed American soldiers whom he hates.

The greatest diversity in culture of any one race or people of the Southwest is found among the Indians. There are families of tribes, legends, languages, and religions, but every tribe has its own cultural uniqueness. On the whole the Indians remain less known and more mysterious than the other peoples of *The Archbishop*. Probably their inscrutability is attributable not only to their secrecy and character but also to the difficulty of getting to know them. Willa Cather knew at least one Indian well,[37] but she was not an anthropologist like Elsie Clews Parsons, and many of the best anthropological studies of the Southwest like Miss Parsons's *Pueblo Indian Religion* had not been published when *The Archbishop* was written. Partly because of the form of the legend and also perhaps because she did not know Indians intimately, Willa Cather's treatment of Indian culture in *The Archbishop* is more general and less detailed than Scott Momaday's in *House Made of Dawn*. Eusabio taps a drum and sings a song. Navajo songs were available in writings of anthropologists before 1927, but Willa Cather did not quote Eusabio's. In a sense it is convenient for her that Indian ways are comparatively unknown to her bishop. She has a plausible reason for being general or vague in her account of Indian life.

"The Mass of Ácoma," Book III of *The Archbishop*, is really a cultural tour of the pueblos between Santa Fé and Ácoma, and parts of the next two books are stories of southwestern Indians. Father Latour's visit to Ácoma shows how the Indians who lived on mesas "had found the hope of all suffering and tormented creatures—safety" (p. 97). The story of Fray Baltazar Montoya at Ácoma not only recounts the story of a corrupt priest who exploits the Indians but also depicts the suffering and the great patience of the Indians before they are at last provoked to violence. The narrative of the conflict between the pueblos of Laguna and Ácoma over a worn-out religious painting of Saint Joseph shows a blend of ancient superstition and Christian reverence. The Pecos tribe in *The Archbishop* as in history preserves the mysteriousness, the occult, and even the evil of ancient Indian religions. A story of the Pimas, on the other hand, shows the adaptability to Catholicism of southwestern Indians and their reverence. The Taos Pueblo Indians accept the Catholicism of Padre Martínez but also revolt as so many tribes did against the Spanish in 1680 and then again revolt against American rule in the 1840s. Martínez' account of Popé's planning the Indian rebellion against the Mexicans in 1680 in Taos is accurate history. Willa Cather's assertion that he "sealed himself up for four years and never saw the light of day" (p. 151) is, I believe, an invention to add atmosphere and make the story more sinister. Father Latour's journey to visit his Navajo friend Eusabio and his memories of his talk with the Navajo chief Manuelito represent the pastoralism of the Navajo shepherds and their sufferings when the Americans forced them to live for a time on a reservation.

Father Latour does not know the Indian as well as he knows the other cultures of his people. His many and conflicting views of the Indians[38] derive from his encounters with different kinds of tribes, but his interpretations of Indian culture also vary according to his moods. At one time he is "convinced that neither the white man nor the Mexicans in Santa Fé understood anything about Indian beliefs or the workings of the Indian mind" (p. 133). When he is going through one of his "periods of coldness and doubt," he feels that the Indians in his territory will travel "their old road of fear and darkness, battling with evil omens and ancient shadows" (p. 211). During mass at Ácoma he thinks of the Indians as "antediluvian creatures . . . types of life so old, so hardened, so shut within their shells, that the sacrifice on Calvary could hardly reach back so far" (p. 100; see also pp. 92, 103). Father Latour also admires Indian qualities. He thinks of "how kind the Indian voice could be when it was kind at all; a slight inflection made one feel that one had received a great compliment" (p. 91). He admires the Indians' adjustment to nature. When Navajos leave a campsite they are "careful to obliterate every trace of their temporary occupation" (p. 233). They wish to live with the "great country," to respect it, not to "disturb the landscape."[39] White men wish to " 'master' nature, to arrange and re-create" (p. 234). Instead of having the Indian's "caution and respect" for nature, the white man wishes "to assert himself in any landscape" for his ego and for materialistic exploitation (p. 233). Father Latour seems to regard most whites as guilty of the kind of aggrandizement Willa Cather associates with Anglo-Americans like Buck Scales, the southern Smiths who have made a peon of the poor woman Sada, and Wick Cutter of *My Ántonia*.

Without exception Willa Cather's narratives about particular tribes are based on actual geography, history, and culture. She selects carefully, makes no attempt to give a full account, occasionally fills out a character or a story with invention, and changes however she wishes. One of the most intriguing legends of the Indians of the Southwest is the story of the Enchanted Mesa. Its inhabitants climbed up and down a stairway until a great storm destroyed their access while the people were working their fields on the plain below. The legend is that two women who were sick and could not go to the fields were left to starve on top of the Mesa.[40] In Willa Cather's brief paragraph she writes that the "people had perished up there from hunger" (p. 96). She omits the anguish of the survivors who watched the women from the plain below and creates a story of the death of an entire people.

The patient Indians of Ácoma build an elaborate church for Padre Ramirez, carry dirt for the cemetery, and labor in the rich garden of Fray Baltazar Montoya. Willa Cather tells how Fray Baltazar "was never done with having earth carried up from the plain in baskets" for his "deep garden" (p. 104). Within the invented story of Baltazar (see above) Willa Cather describes the picture of St. Joseph, a gift from the King of Spain. Ácoma has had no drought since the portrait came. The pueblo at Laguna wishes to borrow it, "but Friar Baltazar had warned them never to let it go" (p. 107). In fact, the Ácomas did lend the picture, probably later than Willa Cather's story, and they were able to get the picture back from Laguna only after they had won a lawsuit. Willa Cather has worked a part of the actual story into her invented story to create religious reverence to offset the corruption of Baltazar. Also the story indicates how the Indian temperament, like the Mexican, attached itself to things, especially to sacred objects and painting or art.

Willa Cather chose the Pecos tribe to represent the mysteries of Pueblo Indian religion. Father Latour visits the Pecos Pueblo although, as Willa Cather indicates in a footnote, "the dying pueblo was abandoned" several years before the bishop came to New Mexico. Apparently she wished the advantages of the well-known historical and anthropological backgrounds of the Pecos Indians and did not wish to use an invented name with their lore. She was thus trapped into her curious and rather pedantic documentation. Caught in a storm, Jacinto takes the priest to the Pecos cave. Incidentally, admitting the priest is an indication of great trust. These are the same people who come to the Jemez Pueblo in *House Made of Dawn*. Momaday calls them by their Indian name, Bahkyush. Father Latour is confronted with the Pecos mysteries but in such a confusing way that he hardly knows what he is seeing. He has heard that the tribe "guarded an enormous serpent which they brought to the pueblo for certain feasts. It was said that they sacrificed young babies to the great snake" (p. 123). In the cave he smells "a fetid odour, not very strong but highly disagreeable" (p. 127). The clue is slight, but unmistakably the priest is in the presence of the snake.[41] A "fetid smell" also comes from the enormous rattlesnake Jim kills in *My Ántonia* (p. 47). Later the trader Zeb Orchard tells of a Pecos girl who came to his house for safety because of her fears that the men "were going to feed her baby to the snake" (p. 136). Anthropologists believe that the Pecos did keep such a snake, and there were stories of human sacrifice.[42] Willa Cather was familiar with Charles F. Lummis's debunking of the story by pointing out that the "very grandfather of all rattlesnakes could no more swallow the smallest baby than he could fly,"[43] but she preferred legend and imagination to reality. Also, there are fossils of extinct rattlesnakes which were large enough to swallow a baby.

The story in *The Archbishop* about the ceremonial fire which had "never been allowed to go out, and had never been revealed to white men" is authentic anthropology (p. 122).[44] Serving the fire, Willa Cather writes, "sapped the strength of the young men appointed to serve it,—always the best of the tribe" (p. 122). Like the tone of her writing about many of the Indians, her account of the tribe of Pecos Indians is elegiac here. Jacinto's actions in the cave are ceremonial and inscrutable. He moves sticks from one place to another without building a fire, gathers stones and puts them in "a hole . . . about as large as a very big watermelon" (p. 128), closes up the hole with stones, then builds a fire, and shows Father Latour a crack where he can hear "the sound of a great under- ground river" (p. 130). The cache anthropologically derives from sacred and ceremonial objects which were kept both in a wall niche of the kiva and in a cave.[45] The association of the mystery of the river with the Pecos is, I believe, Willa Cather's own invention used to magnify the supernatural mysteries with a natural wonder. In the story of the bishop's visit to Agua Secreta and this sound of the underground river she represents the awe of desert people at oases and water and seemingly miraculous events associated with water.

The Navajos, one of the tribes written about most in *The Arch- bishop*, are sheepherders; they live a more pastoral life than the agricultural Pueblo Indians. Father Latour visits his Navajo friend Eusabio and stays in a "solitary hogan" for three days of "reflec- tion" before he calls home his friend Father Vaillant. At the end of the novel Willa Cather describes Father Latour's death from the point of view of a physician and Father Latour's Catholic friends. Immediately before that, the last section of the archbishop's medi- tations recreated his memories of the persecution of the Navajos, "when they were being hunted down and driven by thousands from their own reservation to the Bosque Redondo, three hundred miles away" (pp. 292–293). The bishop's "misguided friend, Kit Carson, . . . finally subdued the last unconquered remnant of that people" (p. 293). Willa Cather stresses the peace, the suffering, and the traditions of the Navajo. She establishes a friendship be- tween Father Latour and Manuelito, one of the Navajo chiefs. The last thought of the archbishop is that "God has been very good to let me live to see a happy issue to those old wrongs. I do not be- lieve, as I once did, that the Indian will perish. I believe that God will preserve him" (p. 297).

Willa Cather's Navajos are not merely a representation of history but also a particular interpretation of history. One historian re- garded the Navajos as deceitful and more troublesome to the American government "between 1850 and 1860 than all the other

New Mexico Indians combined."[46] On the other hand, a distinguished commission appointed in 1867 to study the Indian problems said, "Our wars . . . with Indians had been almost constant, and they unhesitatingly affirmed that the government had been uniformly unjust toward the Indian."[47] The destruction of the crops and livestock is agreed on by Willa Cather and all the historians. The chief Manuelito "brought in his stock; there were about 50 horses and 40 sheep. He said—'Here is all I have in the world. See what a trifling amount. You see how poor they are. My children are eating roots.' "[48] Willa Cather condenses and quotes: "Two years ago I could not count my flocks; now I have thirty sheep and a few starving horses. My children are eating roots" (p. 296). History's Manuelito was ruined by alcoholism.[49] Willa Cather's remains heroic to the end. *The Archbishop* presents a noble Manuelito as an image of Father Latour's accomplishments in his southwestern world.

The Indian's association between tradition and religion and place in *The Archbishop* is embodied in the Canyon de Chelly, the dwelling place of the Navajo gods (p. 294). The canyon was a traditional residence, and until the coming of the Americans it was "inviolate" (p. 293). Edward A. Bloom and Lillian D. Bloom have asserted that "no authoritative work on the religion and mythology of the Navajos supports her proposition that their gods dwelt in the canyon."[50] One contemporary of the Navajo conflicts, however, has said that they lost "several places traditionally sacred" to them.[51] But perhaps little it matters. Willa Cather has created a place in the spirit of the Indians and of her characters. Besides adding religious dimensions by making the canyon the home of the gods, Willa Cather adds the Indian origin myth associated with Shiprock, which she places north of the Canyon de Chelly. The rock looks like "a one-masted fishing-boat. . . . Ages ago . . . that crag had moved through the air, bearing upon its summit the parents of the Navajo race from the place in the far north where all peoples were made,—and wherever it sank to earth was to be their land" (p. 295). There is a Ship Rock in Arizona, but the legend is not associated with it, and it is not close to the Canyon de Chelly. She strengthens the Navajo tradition by moving a legend associated with Shiprock in New Mexico and a rock in that shape to Arizona and by having Manuelito tell the story to the bishop.[52]

On the whole Willa Cather's portrait of her Indians is idealized and romanticized. She shares the twentieth-century social concern about the long and violent abuse of a people. But the Indians of *The Archbishop* are not the traditional noble savages of some nineteenth-century American fiction. They are mysterious, inscrutable at times, more civilized than the Indians of Cooper's forests and prairie. And they are themselves violent. Willa Cather does not create as much blood and gore as there was in some nineteenth-century writings about Indians and the frontier. Nor does she present as much killing as there was in the Bent Rebellion or in Popé's great Indian rebellion of 1680. She does describe how Fray Baltazar recalls how "the old Padre at Jamez had been stripped naked and driven on all fours about the plaza all night, with drunken Indians straddling his back, until he rolled over dead from exhaustion" (p. 112). The priest at Jemez was killed in this fashion but first the Indians tied him naked to the back of a hog and sent him careening through the pueblo before they rode him with spurs until his death.[53] Comparisons of *The Archbishop* with historical accounts show usually more selection than invention. Use of more details might have created distractions, ruined the form of the legend, and lost the focus upon the story of the two central priests. Essentially and finally the things in the legend are used to create the character of the two missionaries more than the priests are used to provide a cultural tour of the Southwest. That is not, however, to diminish the importance of the cultures in the least.

The Anglo-Americans of *The Archbishop*, like some of those in *My Ántonia*, are presented in the least depth of any people, with the poorest cultural backgrounds, and with some of the most intense melodrama. Indeed, the design of *The Archbishop* may derive from Willa Cather's interest in the ancient and multiracial cultures of the Old World (like those of the immigrants in *My Ántonia*) and of one of the oldest parts of the New World. There are some good Anglo-Americans in *The Archbishop*. Zeb Orchard is "honest and truthful, a good friend to the Indians." But his mother's anti-Indian racism has almost destroyed him. She would not agree to his marrying a Pecos girl, and so he "remained a single man and a recluse" (p. 134). The American soldiers and the Yankee traders do good things. When the bishop first arrives in New Mexico, they send "generous contributions of bedding and blankets and odd pieces of furniture" (p. 33).

Although Kit Carson "did a soldier's brutal work" (p. 294) in his war against the Navajos, he is a good Anglo-American but not a very well realized character. Willa Cather's Kit is genteel, "pure and noble," as he had been characterized by "a series of biographers."[54] Her old Indian fighter has "a capacity for tenderness," and Father Latour feels a quick glow of pleasure in looking at the man" (p. 75). Kit's wife has "lustrous black eyes and hair"— symbolizing all the passion of a Latin or Mexican lover—and she greets the priest with "quiet but unabashed hospitality"(p. 154)— symbolizing all the purity of a maidenly wife. Although the Carsons are walk-on characters, their perfections make them unbelievable.

Most of the Anglo-Americans in *The Archbishop* are as bad as the Carsons are perfect. The "degenerate murderer, Buck Scales," attempts to kill Fathers Latour and Vaillant. Magdalena married him because "to Mexican girls, marriage with an American meant coming up in the world" (p. 72). He is so depraved that he murders his own three children "a few days after birth, by ways so horrible that she could not relate it." (p. 72). The Mexican woman Sada comes at night to pray "in the deep doorway of the sacristy" (p. 212); she "was slave in an American family. They were Protestants, very hostile to the Roman Church, and they did not allow her to go to Mass or to receive the visits of a priest" (p. 212). A Yankee trader deceives Father Vaillant in a horse trade (p. 54). Americans have poor taste in architecture. The churches in Ohio are "horrible structures" (p. 242), and indeed Father Latour remembers "ugly conditions of life in Ohio, . . . the hideous houses and churches, the ill-kept farms and gardens, the slovenly, sordid aspect of the towns and country-side" (p. 228). A murder that follows a cockfight enables Willa Cather to make two adverse comments about Anglo-Americans. Ramón Armajillo kills the owner of the defeated bird because he had killed Ramón's rooster. Ramón's "American judge was a very stupid man, who disliked Mexicans and hoped to wipe out cock-fighting" (p. 250). Ramón is himself Mexican and a religious craftsman who makes "tiny buckskin boots . . . for the little Santiago in the church at home" (p. 250). Father Vaillant pursues Willa Cather's prejudices when he reflects on the Anglo-Americans he will meet as a missionary to the gold miners of Colorado. The "criminals would hardly be" like the lovable Ramón (p. 250).

And later they are not. They are materialistic, and they save their money to invest in sawmills and mines, not to give to the church. On the contrary, the Mexicans give if they have "anything at all" (p. 259). They contribute money "to pay for windows in the Denver church" of the Anglo-Americans. The greedy Americans are so busy searching for gold that they will not even plant gardens (p. 260). In *The Archbishop* Americans on the whole are a sorry class; they are the weakest aspect of the book, stick figures whose creator has denied them their humanity.

Willa Cather's failure with the characters of her own race and culture is a minor flaw in a book that is a remarkable accomplishment in part because she richly portrays the lives and cultures of other peoples. She has created a credible and rich world for her bishop, and despite occasional sentimentality and melodrama, she has written in *The Archbishop* a genuinely religious fiction in an age with little belief, especially in fiction. Although the novel is episodic in its treatment of the people and the events in the lives of the priests, the episodes come together in the unity of a geographic region, the Southwest. The lives and the moods of the two priests form a unity even in the diversity of events and cultures. *Death Comes for the Archbishop* is not only different from Willa Cather's other works, but it is also unique as a devout legend in twentieth-century fiction.

7

Museum of New Mexico

"The Valle Grande . . ., the right eye of the earth. . . . The clouds were always there, huge, sharply described, and shining in the pure air."

Jemez Pueblo, 1879–1880

SEVEN

Culture versus Anonymity in
House Made of Dawn

Dypaloh. Or, in the lore of the Jemez Indians, thus begins the story. So, without even translation, Scott Momaday begins *House Made of Dawn*, a novel about a young Indian's struggles to adapt himself to the world of the white man or the red, to the pueblo or the city. *Dypaloh* introduces a prologue which seems to consist of mysterious and aimless running, and then the first chapter begins with "The Longhair" (an old-fashioned and traditional Indian who wears long braids of hair wrapped up in cloth at the back of his head), with "Walatowa" (meaning in the unwritten Jemez language the people who live in Jemez Pueblo on a reservation fifty miles north of Albuquerque), and with "Cañon de San Diego, 1945" (the geographical setting of Jemez Pueblo—also called the Jemez Canyon but not identified on the usual road maps).

Thus in the mysteries of unexplanation and untranslation begins one of the finest recent novels in America, a study in fiction of the cultures of two of the major races in North America—red and white. In the first chapter Momaday drops his alien reader into an ancient world not made simple by the loss of detail (as in Frost's "Directive"), but made almost incomprehensible by a profusion of elaborate cultural, mythical, and ritualistic detail. The opening paragraph, a beautiful introduction of mood and setting, starts the novel simply in a fashion reminiscent of the first paragraph of *A Farewell to Arms*. The pueblo is built over a river which "lies in a valley of hills and fields." The canyon is furnished with natural things like snow and "great angles of geese [which] fly through the valley." Man has built a town, and in the past Indians (usually fleeing from the Spaniards) left "ruins of other towns." The realms of man, beauty, nature, and the supernatural are represented in the townsmen's esteem for "feathers of blue and yellow birds,"[1] which are used to make prayer plumes.

The longhair Francisco journeys in his wagon on the old dirt road to the highway where he will meet his grandson returning from World War II. He sets a snare to catch a beautiful bird for a prayer plume, remembers how he raced over the road as a young man, sings and talks to himself about his late-arriving grandson Abel (using the diminutive, Abelito), and wears a new shirt for the welcome. Arriving at the place where the bus will stop, he hears the whine of tires, that "strange sound" of the other world; "it began at a high and descending pitch, passed, and rose again to become at last inaudible" (p. 8). Back from the war and the other world comes Abel—drunk. Francisco laughs to hide his tears and loads his grandson into the bed of the wagon. Abel will leave again and attempt to come home again; and later in the novel two other prominent Indian characters will try to resolve their own conflicts and Abel's over the differences between two utterly dissimilar cultures, between the old world of the Indian and the anonymity of the city.

From a narrow perspective *House Made of Dawn* is the story of a poor Indian who cannot find a place for himself. In broader terms, the novel is about man's loss of traditions, past, community, nature, fellow man, religion, even meaning. In particular the displaced Indian longs for the vitality of the earth, for the old people living with each other in familial and community groups. A rootless world provides little place, order, or ceremony for any man. Customs, stories, and legends which gave a perspective on the communal life are forgotten. The twentieth century is a time of disappearance of cultures without adequate substitutes. The wasteland of actuality stimulates the imagination to remember and preserve the richness of cultures not found in an anonymous world.

More than any other people in America, the Pueblo Indian is still living in his own culture. The appearance of Momaday's novel may signal, as such things have before, change and the approaching end of a way of life. The Pueblo Indian's groups, his culture, even his religion promise to be destroyed by modernity rather than violence, and that is a theme of this novel. The Indian relocated in the city is a different kind of invisible man from the black man and even the displaced southern white. Whether America will ever have a substantial body of great fiction about the older and more traditional Indian and Negro is a question to ponder.

Change has been significant in Jemez Pueblo, the nonfictional setting of much of *House Made of Dawn*. In 1964 Momaday described the modernization he had seen in the previous eighteen years: "the mode of transportation has changed from the horse and wagon to the automobile; electricity has replaced the old kerosene lamps and the flatirons and has introduced refrigeration; and only in the last year a sewage system has been constructed." And problems accompanied changes: alcoholism, juvenile delinquency, gloom and lethargy after failures in the city and returns to the pueblo. Momaday describes the pueblos as "the most anachronistic clusters of humanity in this country." But he does not mean *anachronistic* to be pejorative. These Indian peoples live in sanctuaries from "cultural extinction," and when the ways of the pueblo have been forgotten, the "sense of timelessness and peace" at Jemez will also vanish. "No one who has watched the winter solstice ceremonies at Jemez can have failed to perceive the great spiritual harmonies which culminate in those ancient rites."[2]

Some Pueblo Indians do not reveal their culture. With great secrecy they seek to preserve it. The Jemez, a secretive people, are not open like the Zunis or the Hopis. Jemez were among those who resisted Spanish explorers and settlers with determination, and they still oppose "penetration by White people."[3] About ordinary matters they are smiling and cordial. In Spanish Catholic ceremonies "and other less sacred aspects of the native system"[4] anyone may participate; but one who wishes to ask about Jemez traditions must first get the permission of their pueblo governor. In the 1920s the anthropologist Elsie Clews Parsons learned much that she was not supposed to know from an informant and published the secrets in *The Pueblo of Jemez*. Gossip still flourishes about Mrs. Parsons's book. The identity of her informant, it is said, was discovered, and he was punished, perhaps expelled from the pueblo. The Jemez people reportedly have stolen many copies from New Mexico libraries and destroyed them to prevent the spread of their secrets.

It is a merry time when the people gather for races or a rooster-pull or even to have their dogs vaccinated when the veterinarian comes. But when an outsider intrudes upon secret things, the faces of the Jemez people freeze, and it is chilling to be told that a subject like the Eagle Watchers Society is touchy and that indeed it is touchy to have to say that it is. The governor and his council turned down the large sums of money that would have been paid into the village if moviemakers had been allowed to film *House Made of Dawn* there.

Secrecy was strengthened by conflict, especially with the aggressive Spaniards. At the risk of their lives, defeated natives concealed their most sacred religious rites and beliefs. "Their very lives depended on how well they concealed them." [5] When a white man or even an Indian from another pueblo learns a secret, the power of the ritual or the ceremony is diminished or lost. Momaday himself was never permitted to enter the kiva and to witness the most sacred ceremonies. His father, Al Momaday, a Kiowa Indian, taught for many years in the school in the reservation and lived among the Jemez. Once the governor gave him permission to enter the kiva, but the council vetoed the privilege. Through hearsay during many years of living in the pueblo and through his scholarly study of the writings of anthropologists (his Ph.D. in English was good preparation for writing this novel), Scott Momaday knows many of the mysteries of Jemez beliefs. But time and again in the novel he stops short of explanations of touchy things, and some he cannot explain because he does not know. "It is good that the Jemez preserve the secrecy of the kivas," he says and adds that he would not write about them even if he knew them. He chuckled with some delight when I remarked that possibly *House Made of Dawn* is too difficult for a white man to understand without much study and explanation.

One of the most sacred symbols in Jemez beliefs is the eagle. A secret society catches eagles and keeps them in a semidomesticated captivity. In 1971 there was one eagle kept in the pueblo. It belonged to Pablo Gachupin. When I asked him as he worked at the Yahtay Industries whether I might see his eagle, he said, "Yes." When I asked the governor whether I might take pictures in the pueblo, he said, "No." When I asked whether I might take a picture of the eagle if Pablo Gachupin gave his permission, the governor said, "Yes." When I told Mr. Gachupin that the governor said I could take a picture of the eagle, he said nothing. When I went to see the eagle, Mr. Gachupin answered only direct questions. Respect and perhaps embarrassment prevented my asking questions any more meaningful than an inquiry about what the eagle eats. I did not ask about what an eagle symbolizes, how he is caught, or what ceremonies are associated with him. Still on the literal level, Mr. Gachupin said, when asked, that he did not know whether his eagle was male or female. The Eagle Watchers Society derives from the Pecos people. As Momaday writes in the novel (without explaining that Bahkyush is the Indian name for the people known by white men as Pecos), they were reduced by marauders and a plague to "fewer than twenty survivors in all" (p. 15). They joined their "distant relatives," the Jemez. When I asked Pablo Gachupin whether he was Pecos, he said, "Yes."

Early in *House Made of Dawn* Abel remembers when he saw "golden eagles, a male and a female, in their mating flight." She carried a rattlesnake and then dropped it. "He hit the snake in the head, with not the slightest deflection of his course or speed, cracking its long body like a whip." To Abel, the eagle flying with the snake was "an awful, holy sight, full of magic and meaning" (p. 15). He tells old Patiestewa what he has seen, and he is allowed to go eagle-hunting with the society. After a rabbit hunt to catch bait, Abel washes his head in the river "in order to purify himself." He catches a female eagle, and another hunter catches an aged male. To the leg of the male they fix "a prayer plume and let it go." Abel's eyes fill with tears. "Bound and helpless, his eagle seemed drab and shapeless in the moonlight, too large and ungainly for flight. The sight of it filled him with shame and disgust. He took hold of its throat in the darkness and cut off its breath" (p. 22).

These memories of eagle-hunting come to Abel shortly after he returns home on the bus and wakes from his drunk. They arouse a sense of mystery and of the supernatural in the reader, but Momaday leaves them unexplained despite the great traditions of eagle-watching which even the author did not know. He does suggest depth: "In their uttermost peril long ago, the Bahkyush had been fashioned into seers and soothsayers. They had acquired a tragic sense, which gave to them as a race so much dignity and bearing. They were medicine men; they were rainmakers and eagle hunters" (p. 16).

The detailed procedure of catching the eagles by luring them into pits matches that described by the anthropologists except that the fictional hunters do not tie a live eagle as a decoy to lure the wild eagle to the bait. Probably Momaday added scholarly study to what he had heard at Jemez. But he has precisely adapted tradition to character. Abel's choking of the eagle is not merely the result of his shame and disgust. It is also ritualistic. Those eagles which were not to be kept in cages were trapped for their feathers. "Their bodies are hung up for four days before they are skinned, and then buried."[6] And the manner of killing is traditional. Small birds caught so that their feathers might be used as prayer plumes are choked.

Eagle-catching is a religious ritual as indicated by the "shrine, a stone shelf in which there was a slight depression" (p. 20), and Abel's prayer offering at the shrine. An eagle is like the eye of God: "all things" in the land "are related simply by having existence in the perfect vision of a bird" (p. 57). Jemez tradition interprets the meaning of eagles much more specifically than the novel, which benefits from mystery rather than specificity. A Jemez dancer in a performance at Coronado National Monument (June 1971) explained that eagles, the closest of all birds to heaven, bring the truths of God to man. And the anthropologist Hewett explains that the eagle "was supposed to have direct intercourse with sky powers and was much venerated."[7]

The eagle, furthermore, is even more sacred in conjunction with the snake. Perhaps the holiness derives from a tradition among the Pecos, who, it is said, "venerated," "harbored," and "adored" an extremely large rattlesnake.[8] The horned serpent, *wanakyudy'a*, has an important role in some ceremonies in the spring. But it is more likely that the serpent in *House Made of Dawn* is a thing of evil; at least evil corresponds appropriately with a central motif in the novel—witchcraft. Abel is sent to prison for killing a man, a witch who apparently threatened to turn himself into a snake and bite Abel. Abel has a vision of himself as an agent of God, like the eagle, killing a witch who is like the rattlesnake. The book is not merely "about" a poor lost Indian moving between two worlds; it treats an older scheme of things, an ancient natural and super- natural vision of evil, good, and the world. The white man, his courts, due process of the law have nothing to do with this Indian cosmic view and cannot even take it into account. The Jemez In- dians (and implicitly all men of their race) "after four centuries of Christianity" "still pray . . . to the old deities of the earth and sky" (p. 58). The characters in *House Made of Dawn* live in an order not to be comprehended by man, civilization, the Bureau of Indian Affairs, even by the somewhat studied reader of the novel. As the eagle, a natural symbol of the divine, destroys the snake, a natural symbol of supernatural evils, Abel makes himself a symbol of good and destroys the white man, an albino, a witch. Thus the eagle- catching essentially is a symbolic representation of the basic conflicts and actions of the novel.

Witchcraft in the space age seems impossible to a modern who has lost his sense of nature and of mystery (the two go together). But it is still believed and practiced in twentieth-century America. In modern times Pueblo Indians regarded witches as "the greatest of all dangers."[9] Execution of witches in recent times seems im- possible. That foolishness, we think, vanished in Salem. But the Sandia Pueblo, it was reported late in the nineteenth century, "has been so decimated by the official killing-off of witches that it bids fair soon to become extinct; and these executions still continue."[10] Jemez still believe in witchcraft. *House Made of Dawn* is based directly on a case of homicide in Jemez Pueblo. Momaday's use of an actual source indicates the authenticity and credibility of the novel. More important, the belief in witchcraft shows the great chasm which divides Abel's primitive world from the city to which he tried to move. The ancient traditions of Jemez Indians are perhaps incomprehensible and mysterious to civilized men, possibly even to the novelist, Momaday, himself.

On November 30, 1958, in Jemez Pueblo, Juan L. Chinana shot Rafael Toya because, Chinana said later, "Toya threatened to turn himself into a snake and 'bite me.' "[11] Toya died about a week later. New Mexico lawyers speculated about how civilized mores may deal with primitive beliefs. The case raised "interesting questions about the laws of self-defense." Assistant U.S. Attorney Joseph Ryan said "the case poses interesting legal questions. If the man actually believed that Toya could turn himself into a snake, Ryan said, it might be self-defense if he shot Toya."[12] White man's law, however, did not pursue the case in the interest of truth. The task is left to the novelist. Without any known reason, Chinana changed his plea to "guilty to a voluntary manslaughter charge."[13] Perhaps he had been persuaded to submit without protest to the system of civilized law.

Momaday knew nothing of the crime or of subsequent events except what he read in the paper. It is a passing curiosity that the name of the murderer stuck in his mind, perhaps subconsciously, and that it appears in the novel. Perhaps it is coincidence that the character in the novel is associated with Catholicism rather than "superstition." Juan Chinana is sacristan to the priest in *House Made of Dawn*.

In the actual event there was no trial, only a plea and a sentence. But the novel attempts a confrontation between primitive and modern man. Abel does not plead guilty, and there is testimony by Father Olguin. The mysteries of Catholicism enable the religious mind to deal with the primitive occult better than the legal mind can. "In his own mind it was not a man he killed," the father says. "It was something else." The Indian Abel's mind represents "a psychology about which we know very little." The father explains that "homicide is a legal term, but the law is not my context; and certainly it isn't his" (pp. 101–102). Momaday rephrased it in an interview: "Due process is a limited remedy for snakebite." What Abel's terms are, the courts cannot be told. Father Meldon Hickey, formerly pastor of the Catholic mission in Jemez Pueblo, tells me that he knows little about the Jemez belief in witchcraft, and they do not discuss the subject with outsiders. Priests have testified, Father Meldon says, that Indians committed crimes because witches made them think they had to do it. "Not a person at Jemez," Momaday told me, "would have held Abel liable."

Momaday created the trial as a vehicle, in part, for conveying the Indian's sense of mystery. Another significant variation from the real crime is that the murdered man is a white Indian, an albino. Jemez Pueblo provides precedent. For some reason the incidence of albinism is extraordinarily high. At almost any given time several albinos live in this little village, which has never been as large as two thousand people. Three were living in the pueblo when Parsons made her study, and I saw two at a religious festival in the summer of 1971. Pueblo Indians regard albinism as an unnatural and abnormal state; treachery may cause it. Often it results from some act which should be avoided. "Eating the inner whitish leaf of the cornhusk," "making white prayer sticks," eating egg yolk during pregnancy are considered causes. Albino women are believed to have magical powers.[14] The birth of an albino to Manuelito and Diego Fragua—recorded in the journal of the priest—emphasizes the significance of albinism in the novel. Momaday made his victim an albino, he says, in order to suggest that the man was abnormal and unnatural. The white man is described as "something out of place, some flaw in proportion or design, some unnatural thing" (p. 43). By Abel's killing an unnatural thing, the novelist suggests the possibility that his protagonist is potentially in harmony with the good and the natural forces of his world.

Witchcraft is mentioned only briefly in scattered places in the novel. Even a fairly careful reading might not indicate that the occult is a major theme. Francisco's dying ramblings in Spanish include the term *Sawish*, which means "witches" in the unwritten Jemez language.[15] But the word is not translated in the novel. Nicolás *teah-whau* is said to be a witch. In Jemez *teah-whau* means having face whiskers. A woman with this characteristic, it is believed, may be a witch. Francisco on his deathbed remembers a "Pecos woman . . . whom everyone feared because she had long white hair about her mouth" (p. 204). Abel's Navajo friend Benally

141

reports how the Kiowa Indian Tosamah described Abel's trial, "making fun of things." Momaday, incidentally, says that Tosamah's interpretation of Abel is the best in the novel. This talk about the trial implies witchcraft but does not state it directly or explain.

> A *snake*, he said. He killed a goddam *snake!* The *corpus delicti*, see, *he threatened to turn himself into a snake*, for crissake, and rattle around a little bit. Now ain't that something, though? Can you *imagine* what went on at the trial? . . . Think of it! *What's-His-Name v. United States.* I mean, where's the legal precedent man? When you stop to think about it, due process is a hell of a remedy for snakebite. (p. 149)

That the novelist himself may lend some credibility to the existence of witches is shown in the characterization of the albino. Hoeing in his fields, the good Francisco feels the ominous presence of the albino, the witch, though he does not identify him. He is something "not quite absorbed into the ordinary silence: an excitement of breathing in the instant just past." Francisco feels "a dull, intrinsic sadness, a vague desire to weep." After the old man leaves the field, the author himself describes the thing: "Above the open mouth, the nearly sightless eyes followed the old man out of the cornfield, and the barren lids fluttered helplessly behind the colored glass" (pp. 66–67).

Witchcraft and albinism explain the otherwise inexplicable even in the murder scene itself. The imagery seems to suggest the physical intimacy of sex, perhaps homosexuality. In the clutches of their fighting, the white man "closed his hands upon Abel and drew him close. Abel heard the strange excitement of the white man's breath, and the quick, uneven blowing at his ear, and felt the blue shivering lips upon him, felt even the scales of the lips and the hot slippery point of the tongue, writhing" (p. 82). The scales, the extended tongue, the writhing—all suggest the physical traits of a snake, and Abel reacts with the revulsion one might feel toward snake or witch. When he feels the lips, he fears a bite. After death, the white man's arm resembles a lower vertebrate: "The white, hairless arm shone like the underside of a fish." Even the hand suggests, perhaps, the skin of a serpent: "the dark nails of the hand seemed a string of great black beads" (p. 84). With many details in this obscure characterization and elaborate but secretive theme of the occult, Momaday has suggested Abel's respect and fear for the natural and the supernatural, for a world the white man may believe science has explained and partly conquered. To the poor Indian Abel, his world remains mysterious and unknown. Perhaps Benally's conjecture best describes Abel's fears:

> You grow up in the night, and there are a lot of funny things going on, things you don't know how to talk about. A baby dies, or a good horse. You get sick, or the corn dries up for no good reason. . . . And then you *know*. . . . Maybe your aunt or your grandmother was a witch. Maybe you knew she was, because she was always going around at night, around the corrals; maybe you saw her sometimes, like she was talking to the dogs or the sheep, and when you looked again she wasn't there. (p. 150)

Witchcraft, civilized law, Abel's military service and jail sentence, the rootlessness of life in the city, the bureaucracy of those supposed to help Indians relocate in the city, the tug of the old way, Abel's own sensitivities and weaknesses—all sorts of instruments and forces are significant in Abel's struggles. The only sharply delineated and attractive cultures in the book are traditional and Indian. Innumerable myths, legends, customs, rituals, ceremonies, and religious beliefs help the Indian to hunt, to raise his crops, to define his own identity, to relate himself to the divine, to fit into the natural world around him, and to live among his people and in his community. The richness of *House Made of Dawn* is hardly comprehensible to one outside the Indian culture. A major problem is for one who has no myth or folklore of his own to grasp the alien ways. For the older American, especially the Indian, time and progress surround a deeply primitive people with a vast and civilized world.

In Indian culture and in *House Made of Dawn*, the more mysterious and secretive the custom, the more meaningful and significant it is. Momaday often provides only the image of the thing happening and leaves the reader to guess the meaning. Without glosses of the ceremonial, *House Made of Dawn* might seem to be a book about damnfool Indians running constantly in many directions. The novel begins and ends with Abel running. In the prologue he runs alone, "naked to the waist, and his arms and shoulders had been marked with burnt wood and ashes" (p. 1). At the end he leaves the house of his grandfather, Francisco, just after the old man has died. He takes off his shirt and goes to the oven in a neighbor's yard. "He reached inside and placed his hands in the frozen crust and rubbed his arms and chest with ashes" (p. 210). Seeing runners "standing away in the distance," he runs after them. The last words of the novel depict Abel "running on the rise of the song. House made of pollen, house made of dawn." The race that begins and ends the novel is the same, as indicated by the coldness of the day, his taking off his shirt and rubbing his upper body with ashes, presumably in grief for the dead grandfather. In between the two accounts of the same race, Abel has returned from the war, killed a man, served a prison sentence, failed in Los Angeles, and returned to Jemez Pueblo. His future is uncertain, undetermined. The racing in ceremonial grief indicates at least that the pull of the old ways is still strong to him—whether strong enough to enable him to return to live in his traditional community will never be known.

For the Pueblo Indian, racing may be athletic, religious, ceremonial, agricultural. For the Jemez Indian, as for the Hopi, a man who races devoutly is "relieved of all heaviness of heart, all sadness is dispelled, his flesh is made good, his health is renewed."[16] Juan Toya, a sort of gay Indian blade, says, "All races are happy races," somewhat in the spirit, I suppose, of one Jemez man who complained to Father Meldon because there were no dances for Easter. Ceremony, however, does not diminish the physical accomplishment of the Pueblo runner. Some modern Jemez Indians are reported to have run eighteen miles to a sawmill and then eighteen miles on the return trip after a hard day's physical labor. And "the Tarahumares are said to cover as much as a hundred miles a day."[17]

In Jemez Pueblo alone, according to Parsons, "there are sunrise foot-races the morning of a dance, and in the spring before the irrigation ditches are opened there are kick-stick races. And there is the winter race in which Black-paint-all-over smears with paint the runner he overtakes, for good luck in hunting."[18] Ceremonial racing precedes the Hopi dance in Jemez and involves elaborate rituals. A society goes into retreat and invites one man to take the lead in the race. "Every one of the four nights of the retreat this man will practice running, starting from the society room in one of the four directions, the usual order, north, west, south, and east, being followed. At the start of the sunrise race, he carries an ear of corn and a piece of buckskin, which the other racers try to get. Whoever succeeds in bringing these things into the plaza keeps them and wins the race."[19] In the spring the racers "deposit prayer-sticks in the ditch before the water runs in," a rite which connects racing, religion, and fertility. Momaday calls this "the long race of the black men at dawn," and in an article on Indian-hating he says this race is "symbolic of the cultural spirit, . . . an expression of the soul."[20]

Momaday's racers just run and run and never stop to philosophize, because running is a secrecy too. One Jemez Indian who is much involved in Pecos ritualism did not wish to discuss racing with me. Anthropology provides needed explanations. As Francisco travels the old wagon road going to welcome Abel, he remembers how once he ran in "the race for good hunting and harvests." Covered with soot, he pursued and finally overtook the great "Mariano, who was everywhere supposed to be the best of the long-race runners." Passing him, Francisco strikes him, "leaving a black smear across the mouth and jaw," and he says "Se dío por vencido," (p. 8), meaning "You gave up." Momaday says that the action and the statement means that the defeated racer "threw in the towel."

In Jemez Pueblo, the Eagle Society has a four-day retreat in January. The personage şumihowa overtakes a runner and "stretches his arm out in front of the runner to stop him. Then he rubs him over with black paint, for good luck in hunting deer and rabbits."[21] In some races in Jemez the lead runner carries corn, which is taken away by anyone who passes him,[22] but there are similar customs which are more hostile and violent, like that followed by Francisco. In one legend the overtaker defeats "T'aiowa in a race, cuts open his chest and takes out his heart to cut it up into small pieces and mix with sand and throw in every direction."[23] And in some races a kachina who overtakes a runner whips him, "cutting his hair or pretending to gouge out his eyes or blacking his face."[24] Francisco's own victory and his slap are less violent, but he has been triumphant in intricate tradition.

Mysterious "runners after evil" in *House Made of Dawn* preserve "perspective, proportion, design in the universe. . . . Evil was. Evil was abroad in the night; they must venture out to the confrontation" (p. 104). Francisco on his deathbed remembers how he carried his grandson Vidal to a "round red rock" (many of the races in Jemez begin two miles north of the pueblo at such a place) and told him to listen. "It was faint at first and far away, but it rose and drew near, steadily, a hundred men running, two hundred, three, not fast, but running easily and forever, the one sound of a hundred men running. 'Listen,' he said. 'It is the race of the dead, and it happens here' " (p. 206). In Jemez no one would discuss this kind of race with me, and I have found no account of it in folklore or anthropology. Momaday, however, tells me that these are the Pueblo Indians who fought the conquering Spanish in the Jemez rebellion of 1680. "They say you can still hear the footsteps of the runners coming together as an army against the Spanish." History, then, continues to live in the physical racing of the Jemez Indian.

House Made of Dawn creates in action the ritual of racing; in an essay Momaday himself has best stated the meaning of the fertility race and, indeed, of the Jemez world view: "To wach [sic] those runners is to know that they draw with every step some elemental power which resides at the core of the earth and which, for all our civilized ways, is lost upon us who have lost the art of going in the flow of things. In the tempo of that race there is time to ponder morality and demoralization, hungry wolves and falling stars."[25]

As much or more than racing, hunting brings man into intimate contact with the various realms of the world—nature, the land, God. God grows things; man harvests. *Piñones*, edible nuts from a

146

low-growing pine, and deer are "the gift of God." The Jemez in *House Made of Dawn* hunt eagles, rabbits, deer, bear; and often the hunt is communal, carried out in groups, as in Faulkner's "The Bear." During his confusion immediately after the war, Abel remembers the religious hunt for the eagle. But the heroic hunt in the book belongs to Francisco: he remembers his solitary stalking of a bear "beyond the white cliffs and the plain, beyond the hills and the mesas, the canyons and the caves" (p. 198). Momaday has derived the terrain from stories told him by his father, who once made an extended hunt to and behind the Blue Mountain west of the pueblo to territories he did not believe existed.

Francisco sees deer, "tracks of wolves and mountain lions." At night wolves surround his campfire. Friendly, they bid "only welcome and wild good will"; they are "like a litter of pups, full of shyness and wonder and delight" (pp. 200–201). The search for the bear is ceremonial. The bear knows of the presence of the man but does not hasten. Hunted animals, an anthropologist says, are "considered friendly" by the Indians.[26] The relationship between bear and hunter is almost serene rather than violent; Francisco and the bear communicate much as did Faulkner's Isaac McCaslin and Old Ben. Francisco "did not want to break the stillness of the night, for it was holy and profound; it was rest and restoration, the hunter's offering of death and the sad watch of the hunted." The bear even broods "around at last to forgiveness and consent" (p. 201). Rules prescribe the conduct of the hunter. Even when the bear is close, "he must make no sound of hurry." When Francisco and the animal meet, they face each other much as did Ike and Ben in their famous confrontation after Ike had at last given up the watch and the compass: "the timber stood around a pool of light, and the bear was standing still and small at the far side of the brake, careless, unheeding. He brought the rifle up, and the bear raised and turned its head and made no sound of fear." After a long and deliberate pause, almost meditation, "The bullet slammed into the flesh and jarred the whole black body once, but the head remained motionless and the eyes level upon him. Then, and for one instant only, there was a sad and meaningless haste" (pp. 202–203).

Only when the hunt is finished is the hunter allowed to hurry.

Francisco follows custom when he makes "yellow streaks above the bear's eyes" with pollen.[27] Then he disembowels his kill and immediately eats some of the raw liver. The custom is still observed, but the hunter now has the patience to wait until the liver is cooked—or tradition means less to him. Symbolism seems more important to the Jemez killer of a bear than the craving for raw meat. This consummation of the hunt represents, I believe, some sort of transmigration of spirit. The hunter attempts to avail himself of the qualities of the spirit of the dead natural thing. In a sense the animal is still friendly even in death, and perhaps it continues to live in the spirit of the man.

In many ways the hunting and the killing of the bear in *House Made of Dawn* are like the events of Faulkner's "The Bear." In both the traditions of an older America and of the wilderness are embodied in an old and dying man, Sam Fathers and Francisco. Community and communal traditions are dominant in the hunt in Faulkner and in the rituals following the hunt in Momaday. A loss of a great man and of a world order follows the death of the old one. But that Faulkner's Isaac McCaslin and Sam Fathers and Momaday's Francisco follow the patterns of man hunting animal in a primordial natural world is far more important than any likeness of Momaday's fiction to Faulkner's. That the Pueblo Indian and America are still close enough to nature and the past for a young novelist to write convincingly of the great patterns of relationships between man and animal is one optimistic note in a depressed and depressing age.

The killing and the eating of the liver are simple compared to the activities after the death. Francisco rides into town. "He was a man then, and smeared with the blood of the bear." When men come to meet him with rifles, he gives "them strips of the bear's flesh, which they wrapped around the barrels of their guns. And soon the women came with switches, and they spoke to the bear and laid the switches to its hide" (p. 204). Francisco's memory and the fiction stop with this simple detail. Mrs. Parsons reports that each man wraps bear meat around his rifle barrel, but she does not explain the custom.[28] It could mean that a man of the village has triumphed over an adversary. Women in Jemez Pueblo still whip the dead bear. The anthropologist Reagan tells a Jemez legend about how a bear imprisoned a mother and son. After they were rescued, two brothers became the morning star and the evening star. Since then, "the bear and his descendants have been enemies of the moon, our mother-god, and we, her children, and ever since it has been the women's privilege, the woman's duty to destroy the bear every chance she can, to avenge the wrong done the moon-mother in the long ago. Her sons capture or kill them, and she takes revenge on the living animal or upon its lifeless hide."[29] More simple and more effective perhaps is the interpretation of Father Meldon Hickey, who says that the bear is evil, a symbol of harm to children.[30] Consequently, in Catholic terms the women beat the devil out of it.

Fiction is not anthropology. Momaday uses just enough of the ritual for it to be appropriate to Francisco's dying memories. The actual ceremony is so elaborate that the Jemez kill only one or two bears a year. Killing more would involve too much ceremony and work. "The chiefs of the Arrowhead society and the Fire society" take four days to bathe and prepare the bear. And on the fifth day they give the legs to "a member of the society who has set up the altar. The recipient becomes the younger brother of the slayer."[31] But these matters are less important than the character of Francisco, his memories of the hunt, the significance of killing a bear in his life (the next year he became a healer and healed a child), and the sensitive brief suggestions of the character of the Jemez world.

Francisco's dying as he dreams of the bear hunt suggests change in the Jemez culture, especially for Abel. After the grandfather's memories, only a brief three-page chapter brings the novel to a conclusion. Abel wakes to discover that the old man is dead and decides that "there was no need for the singers to come; it made no difference, and he knew what had to be done" (p. 209). Momaday has described this as a moment of "unadulterated grief. Abel has nothing at stake in such ceremonies"; he is "apart from his conventional world" and has "nothing to gain." Yet he makes the "gesture" of going back to the grandather's world when he joins the races. It was "a gesture of respect toward his grandfather. There was nothing else to do."[32] Many have asked the author what hap-

149

pens to Abel at last, but he says only that he simply does not know. The uncertainty about Abel's future is shown by his use of some traditional ceremonies and his disregard for others. He does not call in the traditional singers; he does race. Every action in his treatment of the corpse of his grandfather is just as confused or contradictory. He washes the hair and sprinkles the pollen and dresses "the body in bright ceremonial colors" according to custom. Then he wraps "the body in a blanket" (pp. 209–210). That Francisco's body is laid out by his own kin, wrapped up, and hidden even from the eyes of the priest who will bury him may seem strange only to civilized men accustomed to commercial modern funerals. Apparently Abel does not flex the body, as is the Jemez practice. Either Momaday deliberately omits this detail, or he suggests that in this way Abel does not follow tradition. The immediacy of Abel's preparations for burial is traditional rather than a reflection of disrespect. After death among the Pueblo Indians, "a corpse is buried as soon as it can be prepared for the grave."[33]

After preparing Francisco for burial, Abel goes before dawn to the Catholic mission and tells the priest, "My grandfather is dead. . . . You must bury him." Burial by the priest breaks with Jemez custom. Possibly it is another instance of Abel's turning his back on the old ways. On the other hand, Momaday told me that he does not remember whether priests attend Jemez funerals.

Not all Jemez ceremonies and festivities are restricted. The days of the saints of the Catholic Church are publicly celebrated, and Anglo-Americans may participate even though Jemez traditions mingle with the Christian. Abel first comes into conflict with the albino on July 25, Santiago's day, at a rooster-pull; and he kills him on August 1, the day before ceremonies in honor of Porcingula, Our Lady of the Angels, the Virgin Mary. In New Mexico "the Feast of Santiago used to be celebrated in every village as a sort of traditional national holiday. Races and games on horseback were the chief nonreligious features."[34] Santiago is "a sort of patron saint of horses. . . . Sometimes Santiago helps poor people, making it possible for them to attain success and wealth."[35] The gallo, or rooster-pull, derives from a legend of Santiago in Mexico. Father Olguin tells the legend. Momaday has taken the priest's version almost directly from the legend as collected by the anthropologist Leslie White in the Santa Ana Pueblo, with only one change in the order of words and with only a few omissions. The versions of the novelist and of the anthropologist are given in parallel lines below:

WHITE: Santiago . . . is journeying in the guise of a plain,
MOMADAY: *Santiago   rode dressed in the guise of a peon*
common man, to Old Mexico from the Pueblo country.
       into   Mexico   southward.
He stops   at the house of an old man and his wife.
He stopped to rest at the house of an old man and his wife.
They are extremely poor,   but they make
They were poor and miserable people, . . . and they bade
Santiago welcome.   They have no food to offer him
Santiago welcome. . . . There was nothing in the house to eat;
save a   lone rooster.
but a single, aged rooster strutted back and forth in the yard.
Though this is all they have in the world,   they
The rooster was their only possession of value, but the old man
cheerfully   kill   the fowl and feed their guest.
and woman killed and cooked it   for their guest.
    They also give him their bed while they sleep outdoors.
That night they gave him their bed while they slept on the cold
       In the morning   Santiago reveals his true self to
ground. When morning came, Santiago told them who he was.
his hosts, gives them ianyi (blessing) and departs.
    He gave them his blessing   and continued on his
Santiago arrives at the city where El Rey lives in Mexico.
way. He rode on for many days, and at last came to the royal
    The King is going to have a great rodeo: wild horses are
city. That day the king proclaimed that there should be a great
to be ridden,   savage bulls killed.
celebration and many games, dangerous contests of skill and
       Santiago enters   the contest. Although derided at
strength. Santiago entered the games.   He was derided at
first as a weakling and an incompetent,   Santiago
first for everyone supposed him to be a peon and a fool. But he

151

. . . eventually triumphs and wins first prize: his choice of
was victorious,   and as a   prize he was allowed to
                    one of the king's daughters. . . . Santiago
choose and marry one of the king's daughters. He chose a girl
receives the girl   and   prepares
with almond-shaped eyes and long black hair, and he made
            to return   to his home (which, apparently, is the
ready to return with her to the north.
Pueblo country.)   The King is very angry with Santiago but
                    The king was filled with resentment to
manages to conceal it.
think that a peon should carry his daughter away, and he
                                He gives Santiago a
concealed a plan to kill the saint. Publicly he ordered a
guard   of soldiers to "protect" him on his journey.
company of soldiers to escort   the travelers safely on their
journey home. [36]

This is about half of each version of the legend. In the rest the
soldiers turn on Santiago as they were directed to do. Then Santiago is miraculously saved by the rooster which he had eaten at the
home of the poor people and which comes back to life. Then he
kills his horse and the rooster, tears the rooster apart, and strews it
on the ground. "The blood and feathers," Momaday uncharac-
teristically interprets, "became cultivated plants and domestic
animals, enough for all the Pueblo people." The anthropologist did
not explain in this fashion because his informant knew the interpretation and assumed his listener would know it. On the whole, the
novelist follows his source in the latter part of the story almost as
carefully as in the part quoted above.

Many times in *House Made of Dawn* Momaday follows a source
just as he did in the legend of Santiago. When I showed him this
comparison of his work and the legend, he did not remember seeing the version of White. He has no reluctance to admit his use of
sources. In fact, he told me where to find the originals he followed
for a Navajo song (see pp. 168–170) and for Tosamah's peyote ceremony (pp. 162–163).

Any technical and legal questions of plagiarism here are artistically unimportant. A credit to sources would not change the art of the book in any fashion whatsoever. Artists before Shakespeare and after Faulkner have always taken what they could get and used it as best they could. Momaday has just followed more sources more carefully than any other modern writer I know. But he has good reasons, and many. *House Made of Dawn* is culturally as exact and true as the work of any modern novelist, including Faulkner and Eudora Welty. A folk tale or poem carefully transcribed by an accurate anthropologist contains an authenticity and simplicity which can seldom (perhaps never) be reproduced in an invented or imagined story or poem. The very lack of elaborate details or the embroidery of a single artist, the stark factual statements of events in folk art, are better rendered in transcription than in imaginative invention. A modern ballad with a known author, similarly, shows the marks of not having been communally composed and sung. Momaday's sources are at the very cultural heart of his novel just as they are deeply involved in the cultural traditions of the three Indian peoples he writes about (Jemez, Kiowa, Navajo).

Probably Momaday has followed his own experience in the novel as much as he has his sources. When asked to identify the prototype for a character, he is the least hesitant writer I have ever known. He told me that Francisco and Benally especially derive from single models. Abel is based on several persons.

Like other ceremonies and festivals of American Indians, rooster-pulls or gallos are in decline. One may occur on any saint's day. My wife and I attended one on Saint John's day, June 24, 1971. Old-timers say interest in rooster-pulls is declining: fewer roosters are brought, more men stay on their jobs instead of taking the day off, boys participate rather than men, and there are fewer horses to ride. The Johns, the men who are celebrating their "name-day," bring roosters to the small arbor where the saints are kept in the middle of the pueblo. Women and the young people sprinkle water, saying "We want rain," and then playfully douse each other in water fights. Late in the afternoon the first rooster is buried to his neck. Men ride by, lean from their saddles, and attempt to pull the rooster from the ground. The game is much like

the southern gander-pulling described in Augustus Baldwin
Longstreet's *Georgia Scenes*. When someone pulls the rooster
from the ground, he holds the bird by the neck and strikes another
man with him as hard as he can. All the men on horseback struggle
to get the rooster and to hit the others with him. There is no win-
ning or losing in the game; the object is simply to tear the rooster
apart. That accomplished, the rooster is tossed aside, and the game
begins with another rooster.

Momaday has made several adaptations of the rooster-pull in the
novel. Part of it is seen from the point of view of the white woman,
Angela St. John, perhaps because she shares the reader's attitude
toward the strangeness of the ceremony and the cruelty to the
animal. She is a part of that outside world in which Abel will live
for a time. Although a rooster-pull involves the destruction of several roosters by many men, Momaday describes only one; and the
fight involves only the albino and Abel. The riders watch the white
man "to see whom he would choose, respectful, wary, and on
edge" (p. 44). In the usual gallo, I believe, no choice is made.
Whatever man can get the rooster flails whatever man he can hit.
The adaptation in the novel makes the antagonism between Abel
and the white man a personal matter. It supplies additional motive
for the killing later.

After the bird is destroyed and "scattered about on the ground,"
the women of the pueblo throw "water to finish it in sacrifice" (p.
45). Thus Momaday suggests the ancient symbolism of the practice. "When the rooster is buried," plants and domestic animals
"are magically and symbolically buried." "When the horseman
pulls the fowl out of the ground," plants and animals burst forth
and assure that the people "will have 'good luck,' rain, abundant
crops, and thriving herds."[37] Blessings are bestowed on animals
which walk over the spot where the rooster's remains were scattered. The personal attack by the white man on Abel may be, then,
a profaning of a religious ceremony. A man linked by a total com-
mitment to the forces of evil, at least in the mind of Abel, has used
his powers in a religious ceremony and has sinned as well against
the fertility of plants, animals, nature.

One week later on the first and second of August comes the feast for Porcingula, Our Lady of the Angels, when the Pecos bull, a mask, appears and joins black-faced children and clowns and dancers of the clans, the squash and the turquoise. The little horse is "an ancient likeness, like the black Arabian of the Moors, its head too small and finely wrought and the arch of its throat too severe" (p. 79). A long sheet worn by the rider almost hides the fact that the horse has no legs and a man does the dancing.[38] The horse is beautiful, but the bull is "a sad and unlikely thing, a crude and makeshift totem of revelry and delight. There was no holiness to it, none of the centaur's sacred mien and motion, but only the look of evil" (p. 80). When the small remnant of the Pecos people, the Bahkyush, made their sad journey to Jemez, "they carried four things that should serve thereafter to signal who they were: a sacred flute; the bull and horse masks of Pecos; and the little wooden statue of their patroness María de los Angeles, whom they called Porcingula" (p. 16). Thus the most saintly of Christians, the Virgin Mary, is mingled in pueblo ceremony with ancient Indian figures, and neither seems to suffer in the union. Momaday's description of the festivities resembles the descriptions of scholars, but it does not, I think, derive directly from any of them.

For the sake of contrast, perhaps, the transitions are sharp and mysterious after this description of the most elaborate Catholic and Indian ceremonies in the novel. Immediately after the end of the first day of the festival, the scene switches to a bar, where Abel and the white man drink together. After one paragraph, the two go "out into the darkness and the rain" (p. 82), and Abel kills him. A chapter hardly longer than a page describes Francisco's going to the fields, missing the dance for the first time in his life. Twice he says, "Abelito," as he had before at the time of Abel's drunken return. "The long afternoon went on around him, and he was alone in the fields. He knew only that he was alone again." Next Abel is seen in Los Angeles; he has finished that void in his life and the novel, the six-year or so prison term. Abel and the novel do not return from the city to the culture of Walatowa until very near the end of the novel and the death of Francisco.

The sections about Abel's and Francisco's lives amid the culture and the people of the pueblo is the best part of the book in many ways. The furniture of that world is described fully and correctly. I have found no errors. The food, the ovens, the quill brush, the wagon camps, the Mexican and the Tanoan language—the large and small details of the fiction ring true. Authenticity, I believe, is generally apparent even to those who do not know a culture.

When the culture is obscure, Momaday has allowed the mystery to stand unexplained. *"Dypaloh"* the novel begins. Jemez Indians begin a tale with the word *"dypaloh*, dy, arrow-head, paloh, still or standing water, i.e., pond or lake. The closing word is *qtsedaba*, meaning stop. *Ahöh*, is said at the conclusion by the listeners."[39] *Dypaloh* must figuratively represent the launching of the arrow, the story, into the pool, the silence or the group of listeners. Momaday says he used these words because they "appeal. They're authentic." But he did not really think about the obscurity without translation. Similarly, the word *sawish*, or "witches," is buried among the Spanish Francisco speaks on his deathbed, and the untranslated term provides no clue to the general reader even about a central motif in the novel.

Geography, the love of place, the intimate connection between people and the earth, the relationship between earth and the heavens, man's awareness of the changes of nature—the culture of the Jemez Indians and the art of *House Made of Dawn* are based on the most fundamental and admirable aspects of a primitive world. Jemez Pueblo observes "an old and solar calendar, upon which were fixed the advents and passion-tides of all deities, the last, least whisper of all oracles, the certain days and years of all damnation and deliverance" (p. 71). When Francisco's grandsons were old enough, he told them how they must live by the sun. The places on the horizon where the sun rises and sets during the seasons of the year mark the important recurring events of man's life—the times to plant and to harvest, to worship, and to dance. In short, Francisco explains, only if they know the sun can they "reckon where they were, where all things were, in time." Already the grandsons can interpret "the larger motion of the sun and of all the suns that were and were to come" (pp. 197–198). At the end in the glimpse of the eternity of all suns, Momaday's language turns religious if not biblical. If Abel's failure in the outer world is to be significant, the novel has to portray effectively the beauty of man's relationship to all of nature when he is in the pueblo. And it does so triumphantly. Momaday picked a place of much beauty and variety and described it poetically and precisely. Jemez Pueblo lies in a fertile valley of intensely green irrigated fields, and the people look westward to the mysteries of a large black mesa. The Jemez River flows boldly through its channel and the irrigation ditches. One who moves up the canyon sees the great walls come closer and closer together. Changes in light as the sun moves cause the many colors and their hues to change. Men see figures in the rocks and give them names such as the Praying Nun. The upper parts of the canyon provide the hot springs which attracted Angela St. John from California. The cottonwoods of the valley give way to the great pines of the Santa Fe National Forest. Jemez Canyon, or Cañon de San de Diego, provides richness and variety in geography for the Walatowa, and the characters move within its terrain in spirit as in action.

Momaday writes about the places he has known and where he has lived. The name of a place may be obscure, as Walatowa is, but nothing about a place is invented or changed. The novel is a map to Sandoval County. Abel journeys up the canyon to the springs to cut wood for Angela St. John, and his trek can be followed precisely on Highway 4. The old copper mine is fact. Angela's house, Momaday and his parents say, is the house where the parents live in Jemez Springs. Francisco and his grandsons ride out to the "round red rock" where many of the races begin or end. The most magnificent setting in the novel, the Valle Grande, appropriately forms the background for one of the most magnificent incidents in the novel—the eagle-catching episode. "Valle Grande is actually a giant caldera," the highway marker says, "formed a millon [sic] years ago when a whole series of volcanoes spewed forth ash flow and gases. The magma chambers under the volcanoes collapsed, and whole mountains were engulfed and formed the great valley below." Fiction, of course, must be different from a highway marker. Precise description, effective images, and Abel's responses to the scene make the terrain a vital part of the novel. The valley is "the right eye of the earth, held open to the sun." After Abel sees it and thinks of it as "scooped out of the dark peaks like the well of a great, gathering storm," he turns to the clouds, which "were always there, huge, sharply described, and shining in the pure air" (pp. 16–17). Then he sees the mating in the air of the golden eagles. When Abel hides behind a rock to watch, when he washes his head in the river "to purify himself," hides in the "shrine" of the eagle hunt house on the mountain, man is deeply involved ceremonially with both the earth and the supernatural. An experience of this sort creates nobility in man. By contrast, Abel's life in Los Angeles is a great emptiness.

Momaday never invented a placename. Paliza and Vallecitos are lumber camps; Seytokwa is a ruined Indian pueblo; San Ysidro is a small town near Jemez Pueblo and on the Cuba and Bloomfield road. Love of place and of the human things associated with places and of the character of things molded by place seems to be strong in *House Made of Dawn*, very strong as in most good American fiction. Indeed, the tragedy of the book is that for Abel, as for modern Americans, place and culture are vanishing from their ken.

Nearly halfway through the novel the setting, characters, perspective, and almost everything change. During the first part much of the novel is presented from Abel's perspective. The latter part presents less Abel's mind and more the points of view of others, especially the Navajo Benally and the Kiowa Tosamah (pronounced "Toé suh muh," though some Kiowas differ with Momaday's pronunciation, give the *T* the sound of *Ch*, and make other changes which I can hear but not imitate). When Abel's mind does provide the perspective, usually he is waking from a drunken brawl and a beating. His life is now like the time he spent in the military service, the "days and years without meaning."

The poverty of the culture of the displaced Indian in Los Angeles is revealed by impersonal and stupid questions asked by bureaucrats, who draw absurd social and psychological conclusions from inadequate information. Abel has an affair with a poor little white girl who lives in a flat which was "dingy and cheaply done" (p. 107). Her strength and love are admirable but not enough to save Abel. Wild and drunken parties do not suffice as replacements for the rituals of the pueblo. Despite the pathos, the novel is not as good when Abel comes to the standardized culture of Los Angeles. Places, like cultures and to some extent even people, in Los Angeles are indistinguishable. Abel loses his job, drinks much of the time, starts begging money, stops even looking for a job, finally becomes "always drunk," suffers a terrible beating which puts him in the hospital, and at last returns to Walatowa just before the death of Francisco.

Through this section of the book the experiences of others give complex perspectives on Abel's failure. On one occasion, his lover, Milly, tells the story of her life. Her father was completely destroyed by the land and his life on an arid farm where "every day before dawn he went to the fields without hope" (p. 123). He succeeds only in helping his daughter to leave. In the city she marries and has a baby, but her husband deserts her. Her four-year-old child dies with "a look of infinite wisdom and old age on her little face" (pp. 124–125). Her past indicates that the novel is not merely a nostalgic lamenting for the land and the past. Her father's relationship with the earth was pitiful and demeaning.

Tosamah and Benally do find ways to live with the city. Both remember the past but make no plans to return to it. Ironically, Abel is from the richest Indian culture described in the novel. Whether his tradition is the cause of his failure is never indicated. Whether the Kiowa culture of Tosamah and the Navajo background of Benally may permit their urban adjustment I do not know. The Kiowas were plains Indians, moving about, engaging in almost constant warfare. Navajos traditionally have absorbed the experiences and trades of other peoples quickly and easily. The Jemez have been stable, peaceful, and deeply secretive. These backgrounds may show generally in the careers of Momaday's three Indians, but his interest, on the other hand, may be personal and not tribally or socially speculative.

In the broadest terms, the urban Indian's adaptation to city life is the most typical and fundamental cultural experience in modern American life. Between 1945, when Abel came home from the war, and 1968, when *House Made of Dawn* was published, tens of millions of Americans moved to the city. This migration has been called "the greatest movement of human beings in history."[40] The change in the life of each migrant has been as great as that involved in going to America in the seventeenth century. "You have to change," as Benally puts it. "That's the only way you can live in a place like this. You have to forget about the way it was, how you grew up and all" (p. 148). And you can't go home. "You know that if you went home there would be nothing there, just the empty land and a lot of old people, going noplace and dying off" (p. 159).

The second part continues with a sermon preached by "Rev. J.B.B. Tosamah, Pastor & Priest of the Sun," "son of the Hummingbird" ("A prominent Kiowa family is called Hummingbird").[41] His establishment is the Holiness Pan-Indian Rescue Mission. That kind of emotional and fundamentalist sect has had some success among the Indians: there is an Indian holiness church at San Ysidro, near Jemez Pueblo. The shouting and jerking and speaking in unknown tongues may substitute for the old rituals and ceremonies. Tosamah's sermon belongs to a tradition of folk sermons in American literature. The best, perhaps, is the Reverend Shegog's sermon in *The Sound and the Fury*. Tosamah preaches on "The Gospel According to John" and the Word. John "imposed his idea of God upon the Everlasting Truth. 'In the beginning was the Word. . . .' " John was white, and the white man deals with the Word and "subtracts the Truth" (pp. 93–94). The sermon is Momaday's distinction between the two cultures, Indian and white; between time past and the present; between country or primitive and city; between Abel at Jemez and Abel in L.A. The creation as shown in John stands adjacent to the story of the coming of the Tai-me, a divine thing, to the Kiowas. And he ends the sermon comically: " 'Good night,' he said, at last, 'and get yours.' " Thus irreligiousness and near absurdity mingle with the mighty rhetoric. Tosamah, Momaday told me, is a clown. Like Shakespeare's clowns, he has an intelligible mind. He "sees into Abel more than anyone else does." Even he is a shallow cynic who cannot go far into the oracle.

Tosamah's second sermon is "The Way to Rainy Mountain," the same title as that of the book which Momaday has written about his family and the Kiowas. The introduction to that book is Tosamah's sermon, used almost exactly as it is written in the novel. Momaday referred me to Mr. Frank Kodaseet, of Anadarko, Oklahoma, as one who would know the stories and legends of *The Way to Rainy Mountain*. There is no difference at all between the way Momaday wrote the old stories, Mr. Kodaseet says, and the way he remembers them.

House Made of Dawn has many of the qualities of fact and history. The places, the mountains and rivers, are true; the history of the Kiowas is sound; and the people do not vary from the fact. Momaday's grandmother as well as Tosamah's "lived in a house near the place where Rainy Mountain Creek runs into the Washita River" (p. 134). Like Abel and Momaday, Tosamah remembers the lore of his people. Like the Jemez, the Kiowas have a kinship with nature and with the heavens. "Things in nature . . . engender an awful quiet in the heart of man. . . . Man must account for it" (p. 131). The Kiowas have done it with a legend. Momaday says he has no written source here, but his story is taken from the oral tradition: Among eight playing children a boy, "struck Dumb," runs on his all fours, turns into a bear, and chases his sisters. A tree carries the girls into the sky away from the bear, and they turn into the Big Dipper. [42] The great accomplishment of the use of a myth like this lies in its representation of the primitive world view of any Indian tribe and, indeed, of any traditional community. Bears for the Kiowa are evil. They are, as Mrs. Ella Poolaw says, taboo. Hostile to children and to man and even to the natural world, the bear is involved with the occult, with magical powers. The bear for the Kiowa Tosamah is equivalent to the witch for the Jemez Abel. Nature, the tree in the story, is involved with supernatural good. It rescues the sisters. In a version told by Mrs. Ella Poolaw scratches on a rock are a sign left to man that he is threatened by evil and may be saved. Symbolically, the meaning of the myth is unavailable either to Tosamah or to Abel. Tosamah—clown, priest, and cynic—is capable of surviving without the tradition. Abel is not, yet he also does not have the strength and the wisdom to return in time to the older ways.

After this legend, Tosamah tells of his grandmother, who "had a

161

reverence for the sun, a certain holy regard which now is all but gone out of mankind." She became Christian, but "she never forgot her birthright." She witnessed the end of the "living sun dance culture" when soldiers dispersed the Kiowas on "July 20, 1890, at the great bend of the Washita. My grandmother was there. Without bitterness, and for as long as she lived, she bore a vision of deicide" (pp. 132–133). Mr. and Mrs. Jimmie Wolf, Kiowas from Anadarko, Oklahoma, praise Momaday for his treatment of Kiowa history and of the spirit of the novel. Momaday's view is like that of the historians of the Kiowas. After the Sun Dance was prevented, the Kiowas' "culture was all gone—no horse, no buffalo, no Sun Dance. This undermined their faith and destroyed their religion. They were broken in spirit. Actually, the Sun Dance was harmless; behind it were their beliefs in good medicine for the health and future of the tribe."[43]

In addition to delivering the two sermons, Tosamah engages in another ceremony. He and his followers chew peyote, a drug which is "a symbol of the spirits being worshipped and . . . a sacrament."[44] The ceremonies and the trappings accompanying them are numerous and elaborate. Tosamah's rite in *House Made of Dawn* progresses from description of the peyote cactus through the ceremonies to the eating of the buttons. The effects are "a terrible restlessness, a sheer wave of exhilaration in the room. . . . Everyone wanted to shout that he was hale and playful and everlastingly alive . . ." (p. 112). When the joy is gone, feelings of grief and death are followed by "a deadly depression" and nausea and pain. Then a vision of color and fire and the sounds of the gourd and the drum. Religious testimonials and prayers are given.

The prayers seem to indicate the inadequacies of those who pray and of their prayers. But the great needs are still there, although peyote is a poor substitute for the culture which once provided definition and satisfaction. The consequences of the peyote religion, the needs for something greater, and the effects of the ceremony may be shown in what immediately follows: "Abel's face was cut and broken, and there was a burning at his eyes, a terrible irritation at the corners of his eyes, and he wanted to bring his hands to them" (p. 114). But the hands are broken. Abel is waking from a drunk and a beating. Either he does not know who beat him, or his confusion is so great that he never thinks about the fight. How different from the physical condition of the ceremonial racers at Jemez Pueblo!

If Tosamah interprets Abel best, Benally loves him most. He tells part three of the novel, "The Night Chanter," with an unwavering sympathy. Abel leaves to go home to Walatowa, and Benally tries to reach an understanding of why Abel killed a man for witchcraft, was beaten terribly, failed at his job, wound up in the hospital, and then had to go home as an Indian the bureaucrats could not relocate. Benally remembers Abel's failures and his relationships with Milly and Angela St. John. He describes dances, bars, the factory where he works, and the culturally vague city world where he can adjust himself and where Abel fails to survive. But Abel's problems are beyond the urbane Benally's poor power to perceive. He concludes at first only that "he was too damn dumb to be civilized" (p. 148). Later he explains something of the mystery of the failure: "You can see what it's like," that is, the way of life. "But you don't know how to get into it; there's too much of it and it's all around you and you can't get hold of it because it's going on too fast" (p. 158).

Besides the attempt to explain Abel directly, Benally recounts some incidents which implicitly help in interpretation. The lives of white characters show that it is not merely the poor Indian in the ghetto who fails. Old Carlozini, who lives in the same building with Abel and Benally, has a guinea pig named Vincenzo. When he dies, she continues to talk of him as if he were living. Told that the animal is dead, she sits "there on the stairs, holding that little dead animal real close to her, and she looked awful small and alone" (p. 180). She never speaks to Abel and Benally again. Her guinea pig had been her last real contact with another being, her only relationship to the natural world. The contrast with man's association with animals and nature and other men in the pueblo makes old Carlozini's world even more appalling.

As Abel journeys back to Walatowa, Benally's mind moves over the southwestern geography and goes with him past Williams and Flagstaff and the Painted Desert in Arizona. It stops at Chambers and turns off what is now Interstate 40 and goes out into Navajo country at Wide Ruins and the northern part of Arizona—where Benally, and as usual Scott Momaday, had lived. His father, Al Momaday, was principal of the school there for fifteen years. Like Tosamah, Benally looks constantly back and forth from his old world to his new place in the city. All the cultural details are described as precisely and sensitively as were those in the lives of the Jemez and the Kiowas. Benally remembers witchcraft among the Navajos, the coziness of his life in the hogan when he could see snow *"outside through the smoke hole, swirling around in the black sky,"* and his grandfather *"was there stirring the fire to keep it going, and you knew that everything was all right"* (p. 154).

As Abel had returned drunk from the white man's world on the bus to be met by Francisco, Benally remembers a trip back to his reservation on a bus. He got off *"at Chambers and walked all the way to the trading post at Wide Ruins"*—a distance in fact of twenty miles (p. 167). His talk of a beautiful ketch, jewelry which an uncle may give him, enables him to wrangle from the trader the use of a horse to go to a squaw dance. There, a beautiful girl wears the customary blue velveteen blouse of a Navajo woman (I saw two elderly women wearing such blouses and standing together when I made one trip to the trading post in 1971). At squaw dances girls traditionally invite the men to dance, and the girl of the *"dark blue velvet"* asks Benally to dance. As expected, he held her blanket "open to her and she stepped inside of it" and they danced. Benally probably is not the sort of Indian to meditate on the cultural topic of the decline of the squaw dance, but the subject is there implicitly in Indian culture even if Momaday did not have it in mind at the time of the writing of the novel. Squaw dances once were three-day ceremonials which revolved "around the healing of one or more sick persons."[45] Now many Navajos think that they have become drunken brawls since World War II and that nice girls should not go to them.

Benally knows well the legends, traditions, and songs of his people, the Navajos. When he participates in the Kiowa peyote ritual, he describes his climactic vision or prayer in terms of Navajo lore. He sees "blue and purple horses . . . a house made of dawn" (p.

114). When he and Abel get drunk, the Navajo Indian tells the Jemez of "those old ways, the stories and the sings, Beautyway and Night Chant," and these are names of specific rituals and ceremonies and songs. He also told Abel the meaning, "what I thought they were about" (p. 146). Once Abel thinks of these things as he listens to a sermon by Tosamah, and the traditions of the three Indians and their tribes have in some fashion come together perhaps. At one of the drunken brawls Benally sings the old songs while the others sing "the wrong kind of thing," and he wishes to pray. Thus the older myths return to haunt the relocated Indian Benally and even to inspire him with moments of reverence in surroundings of meaningless tumult.

When Angela St. John visits Abel in the hospital, Benally is there. She has talked to her son Peter about Indians and told him "a story about a young Indian brave. He was born of a bear and a maiden, she said, and he was noble and wise" (p. 187).

Benally's reaction to Angela's story is startling: "Ei yei! A bear! A bear and a maiden. And she was a white woman and she thought it up, you know, made it up out of her own mind, and it was like that old grandfather talking to me, telling me about *Esdzá shash nadle*, or *Dzil quigi*, yes, just like that" (p. 187). In itself Angela's story has little background or significant meaning, but she hit upon the archetypal pattern for a Navajo legend. Angela possibly seeks to tell such a story for the same reason that she came to Jemez Springs and took Abel: she apparently is engaged in an almost maddening search for meaning. Within a primitive culture, she would have been provided with a form for her story. In her own culture, if it can be called that, she can only tell a brief and inferior tale she has invented herself.

Angela's story provokes Benally to recall one of the legends of his tribe. Much condensed, the story tells how twelve brothers had two sisters. "It was time for the sisters to marry." They met "two old men, the Bear and the Snake." After sleeping and waking, the sisters know that "they had lain with a bear and a snake, and they were afraid." The elder sister bears a girl with "tufts of hair in back of its ears and down on its arms and legs. And then the Yei told the people to sing the Mountain Chant" (p. 188). The woman who lay

with the snake is heard of no more. The elder sister, the Bear
Maiden, apparently is the legendary origin of Navajo chants.
Another child, a male, marries a woman and has a child by her
sister. Through him, the Bear Maiden is the progenitress of a system of Navajo stories and songs, Beautyway. At the end of this
legend Momaday gives a version of a Navajo song:

> With beauty before me,
> With beauty behind me,
> With beauty above me,
> With beauty below me,
> With beauty all around me. (p. 189)

The chant at the end of the story is similar to the ending of the
prayer about a house made of dawn and also similar to the ending
of Navajo prayers. "It is finished in beauty" spoken four times "is
analogous to the Christian Amen." [46]

Significantly, Abel goes home to Walatowa in less than a page
after the legend of the Bear Maiden. Whether he takes advantage
of the Beautyway prayer is up to him, but at least he has heard the
"songs to help people cure their problems." Bright Path, which
Benally told Abel about, is "what lies ahead of you," [47] and it can be
sprinkled with the holy pollen (as with holy water). The Path of
Pollen is blessed.

Abel never fully participates in the joys of his people, their songs
and ceremonies. Benally does. On the way to the squaw dance at
Cornfields he sings:

> I am the Turquoise Woman's son.
> On top of Belted Mountain,
> Beautiful horse—slim like a weasel.
> My horse has a hoof like striped agate;
> His fetlock is like a fine eagle plume.

Then the similes turn into metaphors:

> His mane is made of short rainbows.
> My horse's ears are made of round corn.
> My horse's eyes are made of big stars.

166

The poem ends with the world pervaded by peace in all the conventional Navajo directions:

> Before me peaceful,
> Behind me peaceful,
> Under me peaceful,
> Over me peaceful,
> All around me peaceful—
> Peaceful voice when he neighs.
> I am Everlasting and Peaceful.
> I stand for my horse. (pp. 170–171)

In the Navajo origin legend the leaders of the Navajos found a "small turquoise image of a woman." All of the people but four have been devoured by monsters or "alien gods." *H*astséyal*ti*, the Talking God, orders the four to bring the turquoise image to the top of a mountain, where it becomes Estsánatlehi, the Bear Maiden, the woman of rejuvenation.[48] With a horse, among his own people, going to a squaw dance, Benally seems to be closer to happiness than Abel or even Tosamah can ever be. The turquoise woman is central in Navajo song and legend, but the mystery seems to be too difficult to translate into English. Helen Daw, a Navajo woman, tried to describe it for me as a prayer of imagination. All the images are imagined, entirely metaphoric, in the chant. Is that poetic or religious? Or both? The turquoise woman is a living thing, a thing in a dream to be imagined as real.

> My horse's head is made of mixed waters—
> From the holy waters—he never knows thirst.
> My horse's teeth are made of white shell.

I have found numerous parallels to Benally's song in Navajo poetry but no close source.

"House made of dawn," Benally quotes from Navajo legend and then says that he told Abel "about those old ways, the stories and the sings, Beautyway and Night Chant." This is as close as Momaday comes to giving credit to a source. The reference is to Washington Matthews, *The Night Chant: A Navajo Ceremony*.[49] Only the incredible intricacy of a chant like this can truly represent the extent of the Indian's lore about his relationship to his fellows, nature, and the divine. The Night Chant is one of seventeen Navajo ceremonies which last nine days, and during that period in the old days almost all of a man's time was given to the ceremony. The Navajos, "like other bodies of North American Indians, devote their winters to religion, mysticism, and symbolism, by which their whole lives and thoughts are imbued to an extent difficult to realize in modern civilization." [50] The amount of memory work required of an "unlettered shaman" in the Night Chant was staggering. Two lists of songs include a total of 324 songs, besides other "sets of songs" and "single songs for special occasions." [51] And all of them contained "meaningless vocables" and archaic words which the modern singer did not understand—these also to be memorized. [52] Further, the songs all had a proper place, and the shaman had "to remember the proper order." [53] "Sometimes, pertaining to a single rite, there are two hundred songs or more which may not be sung at other rites." And the songs demanded a severe exactness, "for an error made in singing a song may be fatal to the efficacy of a ceremony." [54] In a time when much of man's entertainment is provided by television and motion pictures, media which allow absolutely no opportunity for participation, it is hardly possible to imagine the old Navajo Indian's dedication to his ceremonies. Yet only after participating in the Night Chant and understanding it could a modern grasp some concept of what ceremony, community, mankind, nature, the divine, and the interrelationships of these things must have meant to the old people.

The title and a central image of *House Made of Dawn* come from the Navajo Night Chant. It is part of a ceremony which attempts to cure a patient. After the sprinkling of meal and the sacrificing of cigarettes, "the priest prays a long prayer to each god, which the patient repeats after him, sentence by sentence. . . . The four prayers are alike in all respects, except in the mention of certain attributes of the gods." The prayer from which Momaday derives the poem or prayer used in the novel is a prayer "to the dark bird who is the chief of pollen," [55] "a mythic thunder-bird . . . spoken of as a male divinity." It dwells with other supernatural beings in Tse'gíhi, the untranslated first word of the prayer. I asked Momaday what the literal meaning of the words "house made of dawn" is, and he said, "the earth." The Navajo words for happily and beautiful are similar (*hozógo* and *hozóna*), and both refer to an earthly beauty or happiness.[56] The Navajo chant is one hundred lines long; Momaday cuts it down to forty-five. Matthews's and Momaday's lines alternate below, with Matthews's appearing first each time. (After the clear pattern of differences is established, I omit Matthews's except where the pattern varies.)

> MATTHEWS: In Tse'gíhi.[57]
> MOMADAY: *Tségihi.*
> In the house made of the dawn,
> > *House made of   dawn*
> In the house made of the evening twilight,
> > *House made of   evening   light*
> > *House made of dark cloud,*
> > > *he-rain,*
> > *House made of   male rain,*
> > *House made of   dark mist,*
> > > *she-rain,*
> > *House made of   female rain,*
> > *House made of pollen*
> > *House made of grasshoppers,*
> Where the dark mist curtains the doorway,
> > *Dark cloud is at the door.*
> The path to which is on the rainbow,
> *The trail out of it is dark cloud.*
> Where the zigzag lightning stands high on top
> > *The zigzag lightning stands high upon it.*
> Oh, male divinity!
> *Male deity!*

The lines provide a good example of Momaday's version of the prayer. He has followed the content very closely except in the line where he has changed a rainbow to a dark cloud. The other changes seem to be in style and diction. By leaving out prepositions and articles Momaday gains an effect of the starkness of a primitive language like Anglo-Saxon.

After the address to "Male deity," Momaday omits twenty-two lines which tell how the deity should "come to us" in different kinds of clouds. In the entire poem the sure hand of a poet is apparent in the way he improves the style of Matthews's translation, changes some images, and cuts out much of the repetition. The effect of a changed ceremony is greatly different, of course, from that of a quiet reading of fiction. During the prayer, "the dancers keep up a constant motion, bending and straightening the left knee and swaying the head from side to side." Momaday, I believe, has changed the chant as little as he could and still maintain the interest. Ironically, for a traditional Navajo, Momaday's version is a sacrilege. Matthews describes a song which follows this one. "Although it consists mostly of meaningless syllables, . . . if a single syllable is omitted or misplaced, the ceremony terminates at once; all the preceding work of nine days is considered valueless and the participators and spectators may return, at once, to their homes."

Abel suffers because of forces which are not even intentionally hostile to him and his culture. Indeed, those who wish to relocate the Indians and other men in a metropolitan world act in the names of education and progress. Ultimately they destroy art and culture and literature. So far Jemez Pueblo remains almost altogether intact. The streets are still unpaved, and the automobiles hold down their speed to ten and fifteen miles an hour. Photographs, perhaps symbolic of some kind of ownership by alien tourists, still are not taken in the village. But unless the course of American civilization is changed, eventually the pueblos will be doomed, and only anthropology and fiction can attempt to bring them back. In these times, fiction can do better than anthropology. It can select, enact as well as describe and quote, create a living Indian instead of providing a scientific description. Momaday's novel, I believe, is the fullest and best representation in art of Indian culture that has yet been presented to the white man in all American history. He had available to him his own great talent and the scholarly equipment of a Ph.D. to enable him to tap the great wealth of anthropological studies of the American Indian. He knows the Indian, I believe, better than any novelist who has ever written about him. *Qtsedaba*.

8

From Richard Aubrey McLemore, *A History of Mississippi*.
Hattiesburg: University & College Press of Mississippi, 1973.

A dogtrot house in Mississippi like the Bundren home.
On hot nights Darl would lie in the doorless hallway and enjoy the cool wind.

William C. Connell, Jr., Historical Graphics, Oxford, Mississippi

The Yocona River, here shown in serenity, is noted for wild floods. The small inset of a blank receipt shows

EIGHT

As I Lay Dying:
The Dignity of Earth

Some of William Faulkner's sophisticated readers argue that he is not writing about the South but all the great concerns of mankind. And he is. But such a view unnecessarily separates vehicle and meaning. Over and over Faulkner said that he was writing just about people, and those who live in this fictional Yoknapatawpha County are unmistakably southern no matter what deep readers of the world take them to mean. The opposite kind of reading to that which does not see a southern vehicle stresses the regionalism excessively. In *As I Lay Dying*, for example, some readers do not see the people for the poverty and the absurdity. Thus they miss the point.

Faulkner depicts country life in Yoknapatawpha with accuracy and precision of details. Jewel has a haircut which leaves hair, a row of white, and a row of dirt or tan. The image of a ragged and energetic little country boy on the day of the first haircut after a long winter provokes a response belonging to the mores of a definite place and time, yet the little boy need not be just southern. Children in Yugoslavia or Ireland and even in some ghetto areas may have funny haircuts too, perhaps clean but perhaps not and possibly trimmed off around the edges of something like a bowl. Or with the jags that come from scissors used without clippers. Nevertheless it is possible that in the future readers will not understand the details of southern life that Faulkner uses. With the advent of the mechanized farm, for example, few people will be able to imagine the extent to which animals participated in the lives of men in Faulkner's world.

The surface details of *As I Lay Dying*—and not all of them are entirely rural—are becoming more inaccessible daily: Darl's spy-glass, the passenger train, the graphophone (a phonograph), the

buffalo nickel. In a few decades Faulkner's world may be less comprehensible than Shakespeare's. Indeed, judging by the errors of
some critics he may already be more obscure. A strange language
and an outmoded world are expected in Shakespeare, but Faulkner
on the surface may not even seem to be American, or what is
thought of as standard American. One who spends days studying
the background of the death of a hero in an epic may assume igno-
rantly that the death and the funeral of *As I Lay Dying* exist in a
vacuum among people who have no rituals, no ceremonies, no culture. And the surface seems so strange that a reader ignorant of
Yoknapatawpha may mistake a strange custom for a contorted symbol. Cash's name, for example, has been read as a symbol indicating that he is a materialistic, commercial character.[1] Cash is a
selfless character; the critic's symbol does not fit. His name derives
simply from Cassius as Faulkner said Darl's does from Darrell.[2]

Economically and culturally the world of *As I Lay Dying* may
seem absurd or even crazy. A woman dies, floods come, the corpse
rots before the family can get through the flood to the cemetery
where she has demanded to be buried, one son is sent raving and
laughing to the insane asylum, the illicitly pregnant daughter sub-
mits to seduction by a soda jerk who gives her talcum powder in
capsules supposed to induce abortion, and the father marries before he gets home from the cemetery. Surely these people cannot
belong to human actuality. But they do. Ludicrous as they seem to
be, Faulkner makes them deeply human. Anthropologically and
culturally their world is real and true. People like the Bundrens
lived their kind of life in the South from the beginning of the twentieth century until World War II. A country family had to establish
a self-sufficient existence in relationship with the all-providing
land. They made what they could, and they grew cotton to buy the
few necessities they could not raise. The wife kept chickens to
provide barter and egg-money. A family in that time established
a household with a wood stove, a few utensils, and homemade
furniture. They lived on an income of a hundred or so dollars a
year. Yet economic deprivation did not prevent intelligence, sensitivity, cleanliness, complex human interrelationships.

The Bundrens do not know that their world is unusual, deprived, or even very poor. Their only real social awareness is that there is a conflict between country people and those in town. Their opposition to the town is both economic and cultural. Townsmen have more money than country people. Dewey Dell is from the country; her lover, Lafe, is from the town. "I don't see why he didn't stay in town. We are country people, not as good as town people." The town which provided her pregnancy will not provide an abortion. A town lady changes her mind and refuses the cakes she had agreed to buy from Cora Tull. Her daughter Kate says, "Those rich town ladies can change their minds. Poor folks cant."[3] The town men, Anse says, do "no sweating, living off of them that sweats" (p. 104). For Vardaman, the town contains the promise of magical wonder and a threat. Dewey Dell promises him that the toy train will "be there come Christmas, she says, shining on the track. She says he wont sell it to no town boys" (p. 96). More than any other element in the novel, the town reminds the countryman of the adversities of his way of life.

The country needs things from the town, but it is so economically limited that it must select what it buys with great care. The farmer has to be self-sufficient so that he can make a few necessary purchases—wagons, hardware, sometimes the services of a doctor. Then he wishes for luxuries—bananas, a toy train, maybe false teeth. Anse gets the teeth, but the children must be satisfied with bananas. Significantly, the chief luxury they do come home with, the graphophone, is brought to them by the woman of the town who marries Anse.

Most of the mores and customs of the country world of *As I Lay Dying* are explained clearly by the speakers, to whom they are everyday events; most are therefore clear. But the culture of Yoknapatawpha nevertheless requires careful examination. No social or economic term precisely fits the Bundrens. Some people call them *rednecks* and *crackers*, but these words suggest a maliciousness like that associated with the words *Polack* and *nigger*. They are not sharecroppers because they own their own land. *Yeoman* seems an appropriate term if its associations with old worlds and cultures can be largely disregarded, but the Bundrens would not know what the word means. They just regard themselves as folks or country folks without any social or economic designations, people confronting the problems of being human in the terms of their own world.

Everything in *As I Lay Dying* begins with the death of Addie Bundren and continues with her controlling influence on her family at least until the time of her burial. Her father once told her that "the reason for living was to get ready to stay dead a long time." One of her ways of staying dead is to impress her will on the Bundrens so much that they continue to live according to her wishes long after she dies. That is her immortality, and it is virtually the same thing that Thomas Sutpen wishes to achieve by establishing a dynasty. When Addie asks Anse to bury her in Jefferson, she commits him, a man of inaction, to action.

The time and the manner of Addie's death may derive from this wish to make the family act according to her will. Medically, the little specific evidence about her physical condition does not indicate a particular disease. She might have pellagra or tuberculosis. But there is substantial evidence that her death is a psychic suicide. She wills her death and decides that it should come at a particular time. She is determined that Dr. Peabody shall not interfere with her design by healing her. He thinks that she wishes to "drive [him] from the room" (p. 44). He says that he "can feel her eyes. It's like she was shoving at me with them" (p. 44). She says that she has "laid down" her life; that is, she has given it for others, her family. She wishes to start the funeral journey at this particular moment. She has cleaned her house and is ready to die; all of the children are still at home, and all will be committed by Anse's promise to act in family unity as they go to the cemetery. Just before she dies she looks at the coffin and sees Cash gesture "in pantomime the finished box" (p. 47). She is then ready to die.

Committing suicide by resolving to die is not merely a modern psychological aberration; it has a long tradition in folklore. Thomas Wolfe's mountaineer Joyner family has members who go to bed and decide to die. *As I Lay Dying* plants several clues that Addie dies by suicide. Like Addie, Vernon Tull's mother made up her mind to die: "never a sick day since her last chap was born until one day she kind of looked around her and then she went and taken that lace-trimmed night gown she had had forty-five years and never wore out of the chest and put it on and laid down on the bed and pulled the covers up and shut her eyes. 'You all will have to look out for pa the best you can,' she said. 'I'm tired' " (p. 29). Tull says that Addie will "hold on" until the coffin is finished and then die in "her own good time" (p. 18). Anse speaks of her waiting and says that her mind "is set on it" (pp. 29, 31, 44). Dewey Dell tells Anse that Addie would not "go," that is, die "until you promised" (p. 109). Dr. Peabody describes death as "a function of the mind" although he adds the mysterious statement that it is "of the minds of the ones who suffer the bereavement" (p. 42). Addie dies, then, of her own will according to the beliefs of her own culture.

Poverty is not merely deprivation, but for a family like the Bundrens it is also a stimulus to independence. They have to survive with little of the world's goods even though they own their own farm, and their economic life controls their culture, even their manner of dealing with death. Cash's building his mother's coffin perhaps seems to some peculiarly unfeeling, but it too conforms to the mores of the time. Neighbors often built coffins for the dead and charged no fee. Many an independent farmer made his own coffin before his death to avoid trouble and squabbles among the children.[4] Most country people did not use an embalmer, "a regular man," as Samson puts it (p. 108). Relatives and friends washed and dressed, "laid out," the corpse. Often the body began rotting before the family could rush it to the cemetery, and the church might be filled with the terrible odor of decaying flesh. The buzzards flying over Addie's corpse, therefore, have a basis in grim reality. The wakes of the country dead were customarily social occasions, and out of respect for the corpse someone always sat up throughout the night, watching over the dead. Anse says that he "can set up with her. I dont begrudge her it" (p. 110).

The home funeral for Addie combines rural mores and punctilious formality. When Tull arrives, Anse has dressed in a white shirt and Sunday pants. "He looks folks in the eye now, dignified, his face tragic and composed, shaking us by the hand as we walk up onto the porch and scrape our shoes, a little stiff in our Sunday clothes, our Sunday clothes rustling, not looking full at him as he

179

meets us" (p. 81). Just before the service Tull listens to the men's talk of the flood and the crops being washed out of the ground. One says that he would not *"mind seeing it washed up if he could just turn on the rain himself."* Then Tull hears one of the men comment in biblical terms on the relationship between God, man, and nature or the land. *"Who is that man can do that? Where is the color of his eyes?"* (p. 85). The echo is of the Lord's question to Job: "Who hath divided a watercourse for the overflowing of waters . . . to cause it to rain on the earth?" The seemingly unintelligible question about the eyes adds to the mystery of death by suggesting the *ubi sunt* motif. Then the women start singing, and the men remove their hats and throw away their chews of tobacco. The singing, the dignity of the men, and Whitfield's voice, which "is bigger than him" (p. 86) compose a funeral as impressive as the Reverend Shegog's Easter sermon in *The Sound and the Fury*.

Poverty does not necessarily destroy culture as many sociological studies seem to contend; instead, poverty requires a different kind of culture. Those without material abundance often must develop a much more intimate relationship with nature and the land than those who have money to buy and who do not face the necessity of creating. Poverty determines the culture of the Bundrens and their kind, but they respond to their deprivations with a remarkable self-sufficiency. Their woes, as opposed to those of characters in primarily social fiction such as *The Grapes of Wrath*, spring not at all from their deprivations. In their moral, psychological and spiritual lives they confront the kinds of problems shared by all men, perhaps even particularly modern man.

Indeed, part of the humanity of the Bundrens is apparent because of their poverty. Jewel clears forty acres of new ground— terribly difficult if not impossible work—in five months at night as payment for a horse. Surely this episode is exaggerated, but perhaps not inordinately. It shows how little was actually paid for labor and how much a horse cost. Men worked in the South during the depression for as little as fifty cents for a ten- or twelve-hour day—sunup to sundown. But the social accuracy is not as important in the novel as Jewel's fundamental heroism. The incident does not necessarily indicate that Jewel had an unfair employer. The farmer and the region were caught in such poverty that perhaps it cannot now be believed.

In the Bundren family there are three unmarried sons older than their seventeen-year-old sister, Dewey Dell. One would usually expect early marriage in an uneducated country culture, but the economic system and its effects weigh against that. Families were large in the rural South, and a father could not scratch a living from the soil without help from his children. Younger children and girls hoed; boys about twelve and older plowed. Girls could marry young because they were not economic mainstays. After Anse trades Jewel's horse as part payment for a team, Armstid makes a comment which reflects the authority and even ownership of the father. Not knowing the circumstances of Jewel's buying the horse, Armstid says, "I be durn, if a man cant keep the upper hand of his sons, he ought to run them away from home, no matter how big they are" (p. 181). Jewel's working for himself at night to earn the horse reflects a belief characteristic of the southern past that a son owed his working time to his father. Sons were expected to labor for the father until they were twenty-one. It may be some such custom Eula Tull has in mind when she hopefully says, "I reckon Cash and Darl can get married now" (p. 32). And Kate hopes that Jewel may also. Addie's death perhaps would diminish their responsibility and loosen family ties. Even if this system is not responsible for the sons' failure to marry, Anse's dependence on them is a comic treatment of a country father's use of the benefits of the labor of his children. Child labor in yeoman families of the farming South was cruel but unavoidable among families who did not and perhaps could not easily practice birth control. It took every member of the family in country metaphor "to keep the sifter going."

Although Anse's not sending for Dr. Peabody sooner than he did may appear to be another aspect of his crass inhumanity, it again reflects the customs of the people. Anse is extreme but representative. The distance the doctor had to travel to get to the patient, the general distrust of townspeople by country folk, the practice of folk medicine, the cost of a physician, the general ineffectiveness of medical treatment at the time (a real doctor could do little more than a folk doctor)—many factors caused country people to delay in calling a physician. The setting of Cash's leg by the veterinarian Will Varner is a little more sophisticated than some medical practice of the time; sometimes a father reset a dislocated bone without taking a child to a doctor or even a veterinarian. The pharmacists in Mottson and Jefferson are called "doctor." They prescribe on their own and fit within the medical systems of the time. Use of patent medicines avoided a doctor's fee.

Dr. Peabody's eating supper with the Bundrens is also traditional. Doctors on their rounds ate with country people because the journey with horse and buggy was often a long one, and there were no restaurants. Often a family even paid the doctor his fee with some kind of barter. Peabody's fare, the greens without meat, was not unusual for an evening meal. The yeoman farmer ate fried meats for breakfast and boiled meat for lunch, which he called dinner. Then at supper he ate cold cornbread and vegetables, usually with milk.

Even the comical and sad fabliau about Dewey Dell's search for an abortion is a traditional situation or story. Always there have been folktales about pills which induce abortion, and in the time of *As I Lay Dying* ergot and quinine were used by betrayed country girls. But Dewey Dell's quest was futile; no medicine will cause the abortion of a healthy pregnancy. The unavailability of abortion in her time may seem incredible in recent years. The extent of her distress and of the potential disgrace may also seem exaggerated to those unfamiliar with the morality of the Bundrens' time and place.

Economic deprivation and the necessity of improvisation determine the kinds of things man is associated with in the world of the yeoman in Faulkner's fiction. One of the most pathetic toys in the world is the little wagon with wheels made of the tops of snuff cans which Mink Snopes's child carries with him as he leaves his father's home.[5] That Mink had made the toy shows a tenderness in him which is not often apparent. Vardaman lived in a similar world, and the child's love of the homemade toy may reveal the extent of Vardaman's desire for the red train and the shining track.

With a genius for identifying the telling cultural detail, Faulkner scatters richly through *As I Lay Dying* those sometimes ingenious, sometimes pathetic, sometimes comic objects that country people had to improvise. Jewel wears a "soaked towsack" to cover his shoulders in the rain (p. 51). The Bundrens drink warm water from a cedar bucket with a gourd dipper, sleep in the summer on a pallet in the cool of the hallway of a dogtrot house, or sleep under a quilt on a shuck mattress, wear homemade shoes, use a lantern for light, keep their milk cool in a spring (p. 132), and generally live in ways unimaginable to urban people.

Faulkner clearly knows the things of their world extensively and precisely. His characterization intimately involves the relationship between the person and the thing. Darl's sensitivity is created in his description of drinking water from a gourd and a cedar bucket. Mrs. Tull's self-deceit and materialism are apparent in her saying that the loss from not selling the cakes is not great because the eggs did not cost her anything. She is somewhat like the Snopeses. To her, hens are to make money, and they are eaten by possums and snakes. She buys a good breed because it pays, but she never tells their color or kind. In short, she is insensitive. Tull is different from his wife, more deliberative, meditative. He thinks of the weather: "It's fixing to rain this night. Yes, sir. A rattling wagon is mighty dry weather, for a Birdsell. But that'll be cured. It will for a fact" (p. 33). In dry weather the lumber of a wagon shrank and caused it to rattle. It would be an especially dry time when a good wagon like Tull's, a Birdsell, rattled. Not only are the tradename and the anthropology of the wagon accurate, but the kind of wagon shows the kind of man. Sometimes the metal rims of the wheel would become loose in a dry spell, and a farmer would pour water on the wooden spokes to expand them and stop the rattling. Often after a long dry spell a wagon was left out in the rain. A man knew the natural world so well that he lived according to its rhythms. "Lon Quick could look even at a cloudy sky and tell the time to ten minutes" (p. 154). One farmer who lived in north Georgia at about the same time as Lon set his watch by the sun and then accused his neighbors of keeping the wrong time. In a sense his natural time might have been truer than any other.

Tull's pride in his wagon indicates an attitude toward property that was characteristic of his culture. A good man who earns his living, who makes many of his possessions himself, and who takes care of what he has usually develops a strong sense of the right of property. Even the lazy Anse has "a house and a good farm" (p. 163). Jewel's horse, on the psychological level of the novel, is a mother surrogate, but first and foremost it is a horse, Jewel's horse. The man-horse relationship is more important than the man-mother symbol. It must be understood before the symbol can have any artistic significance. Also, the horse is more than a mother surrogate; to Jewel it represents his labor, his freedom, and his selfhood.

Cash has the same pride in the coffin he makes as Tull has in his wagon. Cash finds artistic pleasure in making and in well-made things. In the mores of the yeoman farmer the right to own property is fundamental because it involves survival on the most elemental level. Consequently, Darl's burning of Gillespie's barn to destroy the rotting corpse is a terrible violation of human rights; it destroys what Gillespie had taken from the earth and his tools which enabled him to work with the earth. Cash has constructed in his mind an ethical system which involves economics, property, and work. He lives by "the olden right teaching that says to drive the nails down and trim the edges well" (p. 224). But his way of life does not give him an adequate medium. It provides scrap slabs from a sawmill to build chicken coops with. Some have the chance to work with the materials to build a courthouse. But Cash's philosophy is that "it's better to build a tight chicken coop than a shoddy courthouse, and when they both build shoddy or build well, neither because it's one or tother is going to make a man feel the better nor the worse" (p. 224).

The country people in Faulkner's book do not know city manners, but their social relationships with other people in some ways are as elaborate as those of the aristocratic De Spains or the Compsons. If a formal society is one in which there are many forms and customs for doing things, then the yeomen of Yoknapatawpha live in a formal world with elaborate ethics and conventions and proprieties. Despite all the humor it is a solemn and even a gracious world. Faulkner sees precisely how the forms and conventions fulfill the intentions of the society and of the individual and recognize the worth of the person—poor man or not.

Cora Tull's addressing her husband as Mr. Tull seems strangely formal, but some country wives did (and perhaps still do) so address their husbands. Eliza Gant in *Look Homeward, Angel* similarly called her husband Mr. Gant. Cora's formality may also suggest some of her insensitivity in her relationships with others. Custom requires the Bundrens to feed and entertain Dr. Peabody. Manners demand that people who live on the road to Jefferson offer the Bundrens all the hospitality at their disposal, not only bed and food for the family but stables and food for the animals. It is the same custom as that of Thomas Jefferson entertaining hosts of people at Monticello. Samson says, "When folks stop with us at meal time and wont come to the table, my wife takes it as a insult" (p. 109). Jewel offers to pay Samson for extra feed, "a bait," for his horse. But Samson tells him he can't buy feed: "If he can eat that loft clean, I'll help you load the barn onto the wagon in the morning" (p. 110). But there is almost a contradiction between the manners required of host and the independence prescribed for the guest. Anse constantly reiterates that he is independent, that he does not wish to be "beholden." He refuses meals and says, "We got a little something in the basket" (p. 109). Addie wished her coffin to be made "by her own blood"; as Anse says, "She was ever one to clean up after herself" (p. 19). And the self-reliant Jewel tells Samson that his horse "aint never been beholden to no man" (p. 110). Peabody and Armstid and the future Mrs. Bundren who lends the shovels to Anse—many follow the system of manners which requires generosity.

Steeped in the manners of his region and time, Faulkner recognized that an elaborate system of conventions governed the mores of calling or not calling a man a son of a bitch. As the Bundren wagon with its stinking burden passes three Negroes, one says, "Great God, . . . what they got in that wagon?" Jewel says, "Son of a bitches." Either they did not hear him, or the relationship between the races deterred them from taking it up. But the wagon is moving, and Jewel's invective is uttered as he passes a white man.

Darl has to intervene to prevent a fight. Jewel does call the man a "goddamn town fellow. . . . Son of a bitch" (pp. 219–220). In order, Darl agrees that Jewel will take it back, the man has to put up his knife before Jewel will take it back, Jewel says he did not mean it, the man continues threatening, Darl asks whether he thinks Jewel is afraid to call him a son of a bitch, he says that he did not say that Jewel was afraid, and Jewel says for him not to think it. The whole process is as complicated as the ground rules for a nineteenth-century duel of honor.[6]

In a mechanized world it is difficult to understand the complex relationship a farmer of the past had with his animals. How can a modern reader who does not know the difference between the commands *gee* and *haw* know what goes on between Jewel and his horse? Watching Secretariat on television provides no indication. Farm people know their animals. The Bundrens can tell who owns a pig by its breed. That spotted shoat floating down the river, they say, belongs to Lon Quick; he grows pigs like that. The barn-burning in *As I Lay Dying* is not clear unless the reader knows, as Faulkner did, how farm animals act in a fire. When the fire is discovered, Jewel is the first to spring to action, and he wrestles a horse out of the barn. The contest is so furious that to Darl "they sound like an interminable train crossing an endless trestle" (p. 209). A horse is so determined to remain in his stable during the excitement of a burning barn that no man can get him out without covering his head. That Faulkner has Jewel to get the first horse out without a cover is a high tribute to his strength and determination. Knowing the nature of horses and mules in regard to fire, Gillespie uses his nightshirt and "stark-naked, his nightshirt wrapped about the mule's head, . . . beats the maddened horse on out of the door" (p. 209). When Jewel and Darl knock a hole in the wall, the cow "rushes . . . through the gap . . . , her tail erect and rigid as a broom nailed upright to the end of her spine" (p. 211). The comic simile accurately describes a romping cow, and she rushes from the burning barn true to the nature of cows. Darl sets the fire and does almost nothing to get the animals out of the barn. He is a man of words, willing to act only to thwart the journey to the cemetery. The episode is crucial in the lives of the Bundrens, but there is nothing deeply symbolic in the naked capers of the men in the barn.

Without knowledge of the seats on an old-fashioned passenger train and of a buffalo nickel, now rarely seen, a reader could miss completely the method in Darl's madness when he is taken to the insane asylum in Jackson. He is the most cosmopolitan Bundren. He has fought in Europe in World War I, but the outer world seems not to have made much of an impression on him. At the end of the journey to Jefferson he goes again into another world when he is sent to Jackson. Beginning his trip on the train, he encounters or recalls several things foreign to his culture. He crazily laughs and talks to himself as both "you" and "I."

> "What are you laughing at?" I said.
> "Yes yes yes yes yes." (p. 243)

The two men who escort him to Jackson put him on a train and arrange two of the seats so that they face each other. The guards sit on the outside with Darl next to the window. The imagery of this entire speech deals with a variety of couples facing or not facing each other in sexual terms. Probably the two seats facing each other are in traditional terms making the beast with two backs. One of the two men "had to ride backward because the state's money had a face to each backside and a backside to each face" (p. 244). He is referring to the heads and tails on coins, again in sexual terms. Many off-color jokes derive from the anatomy of a coin. Flipping a coin to see who will come first, for example, one man says, "You take heads; I'll take tail." As Darl progresses from one sexual image to another, they constantly become more explicit, more obscene, more perverted. The men's "riding on the state's money is incest." Darl means that they are riding on their own tax money as one engaged in incest may "ride" on his own relative. A nickel has a woman on one side and a buffalo on the other; two faces and no back. Many explanations have been given for this error, but none of them consistent with the character of Darl, the imagery of the passage, and the facts of a nickel. All buffalo nickels have an Indian man on the other side, Senator-Chief John Big Tree—in English, Isaac Johnny John—who sat for the portrait in 1912. Why does

187

Darl say that a nickel has a woman on the back? Uneducated, unfamiliar with the American past, he sees the feathers and the long
plaited hair of the Indian, and he is reminded of the hair and the
features of the country women he knows. The nickel, Darl says,
has "two faces and no back. I don't know what that is." Sexually, it
is nothing because there can be no sexual relationship between two
people or creatures who are standing back to back as on the coin.
Then he recalls "a little spy-glass he got in France at the war. In it
it had a woman and a pig with two backs and no face. I know what
that is." (p. 244). Obviously, it is sodomy between a woman and a
pig.

All the sexual imagery reflects Darl's insanity and its increasing
intensity. Darl desires love, his mother's most of all. And of course
sexual love is the most complete physical expression of love. The
novel provides no indication that Darl desires his mother in-
cestuously, but he thinks in incestuous and perverted terms because of his madness. He believes that the love he has known is
diseased. He knows of Dewey Dell's illicit pregnancy and of his
mother's having an affair with another man. He knows that Jewel is
the result of the affair. Worst of all, he knows that his mother loves
Jewel most and has too little love for Darl. Left without a mother,
rejected by his family, deeply troubled by his own sensitive bril-
liance, Darl at the end is destroyed.

Distinctive personalities though they are, the Bundrens represent certain definite types of folk characters. Darl is the crazy man;
Jewel, the silent man; Dewey Dell, the anxious illicitly pregnant
girl; Cash, the genuine plodder, the patient sufferer; Vardaman,
the sensitive but confused child; Anse, the lazy man. Anse is the
most typical folk character of all. He is the world's laziest man,
henpecked, selfish.[7] Anse is the farmer who does not go to town for
twelve years; despising going to town was a common attitude in the
South. In some ways Anse is the stupid man. Overimpressed by his
dominant wife, he believes that after she dies she will be upset and
impatient to get to the cemetery. Of all these kinds of people, most
rural people know funny stories about every one of them. The
wonder of the characterization of Anse and his family is that they
are not only humorous and representative but particular and real.

Many novels and some cultural studies describe well the life of the poor whites in the South, but no single work by Faulkner or anyone else attributes so much psychological and spiritual depths to them as does *As I Lay Dying*. The details of their lives are used thematically, dramatically, and poetically. And their profundities derive in part from their customs and manners and the things of their lives. No book shows more understanding of the social class of the small, independent white farmer and the virtual irrelevance of class to his daily living and associations with his community. Of more aristocratic origins himself, Faulkner had none of the contempt that is often found among city people, sociologists, and lesser novelists.

9

The Boyhood Home of Sinclair Lewis

The Main Street of Sauk Centre, Minnesota, c. 1906

NINE

Main Street: Culture
Through the Periscope of Ego

History and literature in America have evolved from the character
of the land, the cultural origins of the settlers, the developing control of the land by the people, and society's slowly establishing
itself into patterns of relationships between people and people,
people and land. Permanent settlement seems to have moved
westward, but it was also moving always from the fringes to the
inland. America seems to have begun in the area from Jamestown
up the northeast coast to Plymouth Rock, but Santa Fé was a white
settlement before any English colony in America. The movement
was not only relentlessly to the West but also to the inland, the
prairies, the great valley. Explorers, adventurers, and mad seekers
for gold rushed through the prairies without a thought of stopping
to grow anything, and bloody killers of buffalo cleared the earth of
its wild meat before anyone thought of raising grain, domesticated
stock, and vegetables. The agriculturally rich heartland of America
remained only a pattern of trails while the white man was digging
up the West. Not until after the Civil War did the steady-working
farmer begin to break much of the prairie soil. In a way, then,
Carol Kennicott in Sinclair Lewis's *Main Street* came to a country
not a great deal older than Nebraska had been when Jim Burden
moved there about thirty years earlier in the 1880s. The old
settlers and their children were completing their labors and looking up to find out what to do between chores.

Carol settled in Gopher Prairie with her new husband, Dr. Will
Kennicott, in 1912.[1] In the prototypal town, Sauk Centre, there
had been only a dam, a blacksmith shop, and a general store six
years before.[2] Historically Gopher Prairie had been built in little
more than a day. If Carol had not come as early as Lewis's departure for Oberlin in 1902, she still came too soon for the town to

know many of the beginnings of the cultural uniformity and sophistication which began to develop after World War I. She had come
to a "smug in-between town"[3]—between frontier and budding
modernism. And she hated it. Comparatively the old primitive
world had been good even to the jaundiced eyes of Lewis and
Carol. There was not much of a past in Gopher Prairie, not many
people to remember what there had been, and not the kind of
attitude to preserve it.

The author and his characters in *Main Street* were interested in
the immediate now; characters lived in the present and talked of
the future. Nostalgia and history do not become strong until some
remoteness of time has made less recoverable the spirit and symbols of history and antiquities. Almost despite the author and the
characters, a little of the old does survive: north of the town in this
headlands of the drainage basin of the Mississippi is Lac-qui-
Meurt, "in the Big Woods" (p. 106), a frontier territory with the
very name that William Faulkner was to make famous in the lower
Mississippi, the country of *Go Down, Moses*, published more than
twenty years after *Main Street*. Carol's hearty husband, Will Kennicott, springs immediately from this old stock; his mother lives at
the Lac near the Chippewa Indian reservation. She has the natural
virtues of the old people like Sam Fathers; she has "a hushed and
delicate breeding" and a "child's miraculous power of wonder. She
asked questions about books and cities" (p. 106), a contradiction to
the nature of Sam Fathers, who does not wish to know. But essentially she is a minor and incidental foil to the dull and lusterless life
of Carol's and Dr. Will's everyday smalltown world. The Chip-
pewas are nearby, but Carol and Will do not know them at all and
are not influenced by their heritage. All but their names have
passed away forever from the world of Gopher Prairie. The wilderness and the Indian have gone, as Walter Lippman wrote, and the
people of Gopher Prairie live in an already established world.
"They have houses and sanitation and incomes. They have the leisure to be troubled; for they really have very little to do. They have
nothing to do which exhausts them sufficiently to distract them
when they ask themselves: What is it all about? Is is [*sic*] worth
while?"[4]

The frontier by this time could be experienced only vicariously. Carol reads of the old grasshopper plagues, the blizzards, the dangers of the Indians, the packs of wolves; and she wants those trials if she cannot have "ballrooms of gray and rose and crystal" (p. 151). The human artifacts of the older ways symbolize only feebly their ancient heroisms. In a funeral procession Carol sees "the eleven people left out of the Grand Army and the Territorial Pioneers, old men and women, very old and weak, who a few decades ago had been boys and girls of the frontier, riding broncos through the rank windy grass of this prairie" (p. 411). Now even they live in a shabby and monotonous present. To the outsider at least, they have so far created "no dignity" in their homeland "nor any hope of greatness" (p. 26). It is a "frontier camp" to Carol, but only because she has never known what a true frontier camp really is (p. 27).

Carol in Gopher Prairie, then, is treading on what Schorer has called a "thin and sullen historical soil." [5] On the surface there is no history, no traditional culture. To expect the town to create a past so quickly is in a sense unfair. No one or two generations can provide the rich sense of the past of the older European countries or even of the eastern seaboard, which had been in the process of settlement and acculturation for three hundred years. To expect a sophisticated culture in Carol's small-town Minnesota is rather like expecting Shakespeare's or even Chaucer's London to take a couple of decades to install garbage disposal and a sewage system or to ask the medieval theater to produce a *Doctor Faustus* or a *King Lear*. A new world must be given decades or centuries for cultural as well as physical development. Those towns like nearby Mankato which had the "garden-sheltered streets and aisles of elms" typical of a "white and green New England reborn" (p. 6) had merely succeeded in arrogantly transplanting a superficial and inferior version of an older and remembered culture. Truly they were no more creative than Gopher Prairie.

Some of the people and the labors of the countryside around Gopher Prairie provide surviving vestiges of the old arduous tasks and inherent dreams of the frontier. The early settlers standing on a rise and staring at the ocean of grass looked with wild surmise at a world of some of the richest agricultural land on earth, all kinds of forests but pines, game that rivaled the wonders of the herds of Africa, lakes and dam sites and building rock and rivers. The world was all before them to do with as they might in the long decades required to turn an untouched natural world to subdued land on which man lives in communities. The Minnesota country may be the best of the prairie. A native of South Dakota who had moved to Sauk Centre was shocked by my reference to Sauk Centre as prairie country; the terrain was so different and variable, she thought that she had moved to a different geographical world. The prairie "rolls and dips and curves," Lewis wrote; "it lures the motorist like the English roads and Broad Highway fiction. Along the skyline the cumulus clouds forever belly and, with our dry air, nothing is more spectacular than the crimson chaos of our sunsets. But our most obvious beauty is the lakes."[6] *Main Street* itself still retains much of the original beauty: in a "hollow of the rolling prairie" Carol and Will Kennicott lose "sight even of the country road. It was warm and placid. Locusts trilled among the dry wheat stalks, and brilliant flies hurtled across the buggy. A buzz of content filled the air. Crows loitered and gossiped in the sky" (p. 55; see also p. 148). The land has "dignity and greatness" (p. 58). But Lewis's views of his native land are as changeable as the weather and the seasons. He was no naturalist or woodsman or lover of nature. Talk about fishing bores Carol and seems boring to Lewis (p. 52). Roads become muddy or powdery with "lozenges of black sleek earth like cracked patent leather" (p. 141). Winter can be simply dismal (p. 405) with daily snow and temperatures at twenty and thirty below (p. 81). A Wisconsin village is "hill-smothered" (p. 250). Between the trials of winter and the labor of heat and summer there is only "one week of authentic spring, one rare sweet week of May, one tranquil moment between the blast of winter and the charge of summer" (p. 145). Man adds some beauty to the landscape, works ambivalent changes, and pollutes with human disorder and nastiness that is the ultimate ideological antagonist in Lewis's prairie fiction. At first even Carol's spirits are "expanded" (p. 25), but soon she is frightened and the vast spaces seem to her to stretch out "uncontrollably" (p. 25; see also p. 187). She changes her response as Jim Burden had earlier in *My Ántonia*.

The white man's relationships with nature at this time are much more ambivalent than the aboriginal's had been with the prairie, the Big Woods, in his day. Lewis's own responses to the land outside Sauk Centre were both sensitive and vacillating. Like Willa Cather, he loved the land[7] and admired the peoples who settled it. He "drove into the countryside with his father to visit the farmhouses of the immigrant Germans and Scandinavians. . . . These people were part of his childhood and everything he wrote about them rang true."[8] And like her creator, Carol thinks that these "simple and hard-working" farmers are "bigger than we are" (p. 57). They have a "dignity and greatness" not to be found among the economically parasitic townsmen (p. 58). A Swedish housewife on a farm comes to the door "shining with welcome" (p. 56). There is "beauty in the children" and "homely ease" in the old men who "gossiped sometimes" while they "squatted on their heels on the sidewalk" (p. 63). Carol can admire the natural people, the workers, and even the formally uneducated social thinkers like the lovable Miles Bjorstam, and the farm girl and then housewife Bea. For brief moments Carol is able to lead the citizenry of the town to country joys. She inspires a skating party and a sliding party for once at least, but the people do not have the initiative to continue. Once, twenty people from Gopher Prairie ride in the moonlight on the lake on a bobsled (p. 205), but the pleasures of the outdoor world subside rapidly, and the proclivity to return to a dull domesticity always prevails. She enjoys a hunting trip with Will Kennicott which has some of the attractiveness of the hunting imagery and story of *The Green Hills of Africa*, but she almost ruins the tone with her delicate sensibility when she thinks that "she had no desire to slaughter birds" (p. 55).

Even pioneering on a farm is an ugly thing: during Carol's and Will's courtship he shows her, presumably as an attraction, "a photograph of a forest clearing: pathetic new furrows straggling among stumps, a clumsy log cabin chinked with mud and roofed with hay. In front of it a sagging woman with tight-drawn hair, and a baby bedraggled, smeary, glorious-eyed" (p. 18). The wilderness has been destroyed, and the farm has no cultivated neatness to replace the wild. It is a long way and time from the beauties of the primeval to the cultural sophistication Carol and Sinclair Lewis yearned for. Sometimes the earth and pioneer life upon it call for strength and courage in men. By the poor lamplight of a country home Kennicott, for example, cuts off the arm of a farmer who has been injured. Carol administers the ether. Not until later does Will tell her that the ether might have exploded and blown patient and attendants to bits. Lost in a snowstorm after the operation, he and Carol find a barn and spend the night with the stock rather than run the risk of getting lost in the storm between the barn and the house (pp. 190–194).

Carol was "lured" to Gopher Prairie by the "courageous venture" of a new home in an untamed world, but courage is not comfort and some of the new houses are "proud, unwise, . . . naked and ungraceful" (p. 187). One house has been painted "glossy white . . . and pink" and "every tree [around it] had been cut down" (p. 187). The transitions from wilderness to farm to town are accompanied by many degradations.

All this, then, in fiction was the history, the setting, the geography, the time and the place of Gopher Prairie as derived from the time and place of Sauk Centre and of all small towns in America and the world. Lewis's social and historical claim was egotistic, sweeping and all-inclusive. Gopher Prairie, he asserted in his initial proclamation, was America, all American small towns, and the climax of all civilizations. When Thomas Wolfe in the beginning of his first novel wrote that "each moment is the fruit of forty thousand years" and that "every moment is a window on all time," he was making a sweeping assertion about the state of man and his soul and imagination. Lewis's pronouncement was also partly that, but it was much more a cultural and social assessment of a kind of sensitive mind caught in what it regarded as an unattractive cultural environment.

The question about Gopher Prairie is what it is to Carol, to Lewis, and to the readers of the book. Provincial and social and critical answers have been abundant, but as MacLeish said, "A poem should not mean / But be" ("Ars Poetica"), and *Main Street* is not first a study but a work of art, a novel. MacLeish's statement in a sense is a denial of the possibility of fullness and accuracy in summary, interpretation, criticism. As history is a representation rather than the thing itself, criticism of *Main Street* is a condensed and incomplete representation of the town within its pages. Given the impossibility, then, what is Gopher Prairie?

The thing itself must be seen without Carol as point of view, and regardless of the relationship between Lewis and Mrs. Kennicott, the town itself must be seen as Lewis's, because he made it, and it is his. Some have even ventured to "prophesy that, a century from now, literate people will look to Sinclair Lewis to tell what this country was like in those four amazing decades from 1910 to 1950."[9] They assert what may be two impossibilities: that it is possible truly to know history over the barrier of time, and that the knowledge may come through fiction. Perhaps the most one may claim, on the other hand, is represented by William Styron's very controversial description of his book as a "meditation on history," that is, mere speculation about what history might have been.

History may be personal and unconscious, that is, written in fiction by an author who is unaware that he is for any purpose making an attempt to record time and place with accuracy for posterity. This sort of novelist may render a time and a place simply because he knew it and happens to tell what it was without any cultural or social axe to grind. Faulkner, for example, in his search for the spiritual and psychological truth of the mind of Darl Bundren might have placed that character in a world with much historical accuracy, but absolutely with no pretense of representing the social, economical, and historical implications of his way of life.

Main Street was a novel written with a painful pen. Women "in ten thousand Gopher Prairies" have "visions of a tragic futility" (p. 264). Towns are neither bucolic nor pastoral, but creations of a jaundiced malaise of the spirit. "Hundreds of thousands, particularly women and young men, . . . are not at all content" (pp. 264–265). They are victims of unimaginative standardization (Lewis's work here sounds like some of the scholarly descriptions of American culture a half-century later), "negation," "slavery," "dullness made God" (pp. 264–265). From the first, Carol and Lewis see "no dignity" in the town "nor any hope of greatness" (p. 26). This view constitutes an entire numbered section in a chapter in the middle of the book, and the only attributions of the view to the character rather than her creator are "asserted Carol" and "Carol insisted" (pp. 264–265). On the whole Lewis is more of an expository essayist in much of his fiction than an unobtrusive enactor who leaves the meanings of his creations to his readers' opinions. There is little of the ambivalence which makes the reader ask himself what the author did think. Sometimes Lewis steps altogether outside his character and away from her to interpret her surroundings in terms not at all her own: with some irony and perhaps some straightforwardness at the same time, Lewis compares the insignificant talk of a Gopher Prairie party to "cellar-plot and cabinet meetings and labor conferences in Persia and Prussia, Rome and Boston, and the orators who deemed themselves international leaders were but the raised voices of a billion Juanitas denouncing a million Carols, with a hundred thousand Vida Sherwins trying to shoo away the storm" (p. 91). Lewis is a satirist of small-town ways, but he is also intensely bored with the ways of men of high as well as low estate.

Without subtle satire or ridiculous and exaggerated humor, it may be impossible to write a good book about a stereotyped and shallow society. It is possible to write a good historical or social essay about a bad book, but it may be impossible to write good literary criticism of a bad and shallow book. Sometimes, however, it is a task one must attempt: one must know the good from the bad; weak fiction reveals true history; and one must account for the enormous popularity of shallow fiction which the world buys and reads late into the night. The reader may wish to see himself or to see others like himself without real self-recognition; or the half-educated one indulges in a feeling of superiority induced by reading about those no better than he. *Main Street* is a cultural and historical and even a literary phenomenon. It is a dull book about dull people. Would that it were not so.

Whether it is possible to create great art in fiction when the characters carry on their lives in social and cultural situations first as illustrations of the condition and only then as people is a question usually answered by the taste of the reader. It is difficult to conceive of *Main Street* with a title like *The Tragedy of Carol Kennicott* or of a critical article about the book as an artistic study of the psychology of the heart of a hero or a heroine. Sinclair Lewis did not write it that way, and his critics have not taken it that way. Granted for the moment that *Main Street* may be a superbly accurate fictionalized representation of a large part of American life over a substantially long period of time, it still may not be meritorious as art. The heroine is shallow; the other characters, except for a few undeveloped walk-on parts, are shallow and two-dimensional. Given such premises, can *Main Street* be a good book? It can be significant in history as a representation of a segment of American life, and it can be an important phenomenon in the study of American taste, what the people like to read. But it cannot be a great tragedy or a great novel, I believe, in any sense of the term. It follows, then, that there may be superb uses by scholars of *Main Street* for many purposes; it is a "document," [10] but there may not be profound or probing criticism of the subtle art of the novel.

Like all Gaul, the reactions of Sinclair Lewis to Gopher Prairie as an assembly of people is divided into three parts, or three emotional responses. He hated it, he liked it, and he was just not quite sure what he felt about it. The assumptions of modern criticism have been that certain characteristics of a novel and the responses to it prove greatness: much ambivalence in reactions to characters, widespread interest in the book, much and widely varying disagreement among leading critics about what it is and what it means, and sometimes widely divergent, even contradictory statements about the book itself by the author after he has written it. Sometimes it seems that no work is worthy of notice unless there are more interpretations of the book than there are arts and meanings in it. One hardly expects the diversity of response to *Main Street* to resemble that to *Moby-Dick* or to *Absalom, Absalom!*, but there is not a great deal of difference. Certainly the criticism of *Main Street* is more various than the book itself.

Lewis's own reactions, I believe, his prevailing attitudes, were marked by rejection and sometimes strong dislike. One of the most well-known criticisms of *Main Street* has called Lewis's hatred "cordial and malignant." [11] If as a native he had "the right," as he maintained in a speech at St. Cloud, "to criticize the things that I think are wrong in the small town,"[12] he sometimes attacked his home town in the mouth-twisted frenzy of those who espouse frantic causes, not in the tones of a gentle counselor. Given what Lewis was, his disposition, he would have been vehement in any time, but the particular phase of the town's history when he knew Sauk Centre or Gopher Prairie defined the nature of his animosities. His first wife, Grace Hegger, saw the problem as Lewis's hating his neighbors for claiming the virtues of the frontier and "the log-cabin tradition" while they enjoyed the ease of the age of automobiles.[13] Basically, this response is a hatred of hypocrisy. He wanted the small town to know and to be what it was and not to try to be what it was not.[14] If there was to be praise, it should come from without the town; self-praise is the boosterism of Babbitt,[15] or "smugness," a term which Lewis hurled at Sauk Centre time after time.[16]

The way the local citizenry spent their leisure time reflected their smug self-centeredness. A party given by young Mr. and Mrs. Lewis on Sunday morning offended delicate Puritan sensibilities.[17] The town's own imagination provided only dullness, typical local small-town parties or idle hanging about the drugstore in one classical American pursuit.[18] Lewis had a point of view with blinders. He "seemed never to have participated," Sherwood Anderson wrote in his *Memoirs*, "in the thrills and pleasures of the small town."[19] The citizenry gossiped themselves, but they could not tolerate criticism; they preferred "orderly, thought-stifling, conventional living."[20] The lack of depth enabled the Thanatopsis Club to cover "Scandinavian, Russian, and Polish literature, with remarks by Mrs. Leonard Warren on the sinful paganism of the Russian so-called Church" (p. 135). Physically, the streets of the town were "a black swamp from curb to curb" (p. 139). The architecture, which was as dull and false as the two-storied fronts on one-story buildings in the old West, made Carol in her usual foolish way think at least of rebuilding the town and at most of asking someone else to give it a start (pp. 135–137).

Carol Kennicott is an unusual perspective or point of view for an American author who writes autobiographical narrative about the country or the town of his origins. The tradition is that the author chooses a central character not unlike himself, especially in age and sex. Examples are numerous. Mark Twain was one of the best practitioners of the pattern in this phenomenon of literature in America. At least nine of Faulkner's novels (not counting the short stories) create the life of Yoknapatawpha County in a story that begins with the perspective of a boy growing up. Chick Mallison and Quentin Compson are most representative. Thomas Wolfe saw Altamont from the perspective of Eugene Gant and then Libya Hill from that of Monk Webber. The short stories of Sherwood Anderson and Ernest Hemingway tell of the movement from boyhood to maturity in Michigan and Ohio. Willa Cather's Ántonia moves from girlhood to a wise womanhood. Black authors such as Richard Wright and Ralph Ellison use narrators of the author's own sex and background. This kind of point of view provides a sensitive and usually a sympathetic outlook. A child awakening to life is not already bored with the routines of adults who may begin to ponder meaning without wonder, to puzzle over the repetitiousness of the same patterns day after day with little change. A child does not look at his home town with the sophisticated standards of a returned world wanderer. He may go away and come back as Mark Twain did in *Old Times on the Mississippi* or as Wolfe did in trying to come home again, but even then part of the old memories of beginning life return to the village with him.

Lewis's fictional study of a town breaks the pattern more completely perhaps than any other American book ever has. There are almost no children in Gopher Prairie. The characters are adults or babies, Carol's and Bea Bjornstam's. It is almost as if Lewis leaves a great generation gap in the town during the years of his own growing up. A few delinquents lurk around generally in undesirable hang-outs. Carol agonizes that "there was no youth in all the town . . . . they were born old, grim and spying and censorious" (p. 102). She might as well be speaking literally, because there is no teen-ager who is more than incidental in the book.

Lewis's onlooker is a woman, not a person of the author's own sex; she is not a native of the town but a stranger; nothing of the joys of childhood serves as a palliative in her acrimony; her attitude is overdelicately womanish, perhaps indicating something about the sensibilities of her creator; masculinity itself is thus one of the

causes of the boorishness of her environment. She might endure
the adventuresomeness of Ishmael, but Huck Finn or Ahab would
be simply boors. Much of the character of Sinclair Lewis may be
revealed by the choice of his heroine, but the effect on his fiction is
the point at hand. A delicate and foreign female sensibility almost
has to be an enemy to the ways of the town. Carol fancies herself in
all sorts of roles, but she is no Margaret Mead, no Lily Pons, no
Marilyn Monroe brought to perish in the boondocks.

So Sinclair Lewis hated Sauk Centre and Gopher Prairie, or said
he did. And he loved the towns, or said he did. On one occasion he
saw the progression of Sauk Centre's history as moving from
"tobacco-chewing to tea-drinking with gasping speed; we may as
quickly dash from boosting to a beautiful and languorous death."[21]
The dislike was not exclusively for Gopher Prairie, but an aspect of
the hatred of Sinclair Lewis, who on occasion was afflicted with a
general misanthropogeographical hatred. "In fact," he wrote in
Main Street, "the village longed for the elegance of city recreations
almost as much as the cities longed for city sports; and Gopher
Prairie took as much pride in neglecting coasting as St. Paul—or
New York—in going coasting" (pp. 82–83). All is malaise. In short,
you're damned if you're here and you're damned if you're there.
Ambivalence is to be expected in any expatriate, but not the wild
swinging contradictions of this man from the prairies. Further,
Lewis's statements of endearment seem usually for public benefits
and occasions, and most of them were made as he looked back over
long years during which time had ended the pain. In his later com-
pliments to the town, one modern citizen of Sauk Centre says, he
could afford to be genial because he had been a success. A decade
after Main Street Lewis stooped to write a sugary little piece for
the fiftieth issue of his high school annual, the O-Sa-Ge. Wherever
he went, he said, "New York, or Paris, or Berlin, or Stockholm,"
he carried fond memories of Sauk Centre, "its streets and its people and the familiar, friendly faces."[22] He described himself as a
critic, as censorious of the great cities and universities as he had
been of the small town. And criticism accompanies love. "I could
have been born and reared in no place in the world where I would
have had more friendliness." His memories of childhood differed

greatly from the stories of his isolation, withdrawal, and sufferings at the hands of maliciously teasing friends. He had not been active in the outdoors, but he remembered fun swimming and fishing in Sauk Lake, drifting on a raft, picnics, hunting, and all the joys of a Tom Sawyer boyhood. Indeed, he said even in 1924 that he had grown up in a place of great natural beauty. It is difficult to imagine how such wonders had permitted the eight-year absence from Sauk Centre which preceded his first trip home with his wife.[23]

It is the custom of vitriolic young authors to age and ripen and return to the old scene with sweet endearments in later years. The irreligious and sometimes spiteful Sinclair Lewis in 1942 was willing to make a speech to a seventy-fifth anniversary gathering of the Congregational Church. He even described himself as a Congregationalist! He admired it largely because of its "sanctity of scholarship where one had intellectual freedom,"[24] and it had also provided for its people education, music, love of the outdoors, paintings (though they were not good ones), "personal dignity," "marvelous friendship," and absorption of some of the German and Scandinavian cultures. His demand for the future of the church was "understanding between young and old." And his conclusion was even religious, at least in terminology: "Let's work together, live together, pray together for a better world." His talk was less than what he had always attacked as boosterism, but it was conventional, and it contained none of the elements that had made *Main Street* a hated and popular book. It was not Lewis as he really was, but Lewis as he was acting for the home occasion. By 1944 he said he saw Sauk Centre simply as "a pleasant village for people to live in," although he did not himself choose to make his residence there.[25] The changes of time and in Sinclair Lewis were almost too wondrous to believe.

The changes in the ways of life also create a difficulty in the interpretation of *Main Street* and make it impossible to assert a single even if complex view of Lewis or to define the relationship between Sauk Centre and Gopher Prairie or between Lewis and Carol. Her views may or may not be those of her author, and the relationship may vary from section to section. To Charles Breasted, Lewis asserted simply and with little amplification that "Carol is

'Red Lewis.' "[26] Lewis's wife Gracie and critics Grebstein, Dooley, and Schorer agree that "Sinclair Lewis did not intend deliberately to satirize her."[27] Although Heywood Broun sees Carol as "puerile," Lewis wrote that she was "sensitive and articulate," and Will and Carol were the "halves of his divided being."[28] She looks different to our age: Schorer remarks that Lewis "by no means thought of 'her superior culture' as 'chiefly bogus.' "[29] One critic apparently reads Carol not only as identification with Lewis but also as a developing character who ever moves toward more greatness of soul. She progresses from "rebellion, withdrawal . . . to reconciliation" and finally comes to love the town and to be "at home in Gopher Prairie in every sense of the word."[30] The tone of the article suggests triumph; it may in fact be defeat.

The novel itself provides no infallible statement or evidence that Carol is a heroine and a spokesman for her creator or that she is a fool and an intellectual blackguard. So instead of a mouthpiece, she is taken by many as Lewis's mouther of nonsense. Warren Beck ridicules her, especially in her "Winky Poo" dramatic appearance, but says that Lewis takes her seriously.[31] Her plans are "formless," because of her naiveté, and no character in the book represents the author's point of view.[32] Lewis is said even to sneer at her.[33] To another detractor she is a "featherbrained romantic."[34] Carol is an opportunity for many other critics to indulge in name-calling, enough to make her pitiable if not sympathetic. Thus some say that Lewis and Carol are not at all to be identified. Lewis satirized her[35] as "a null," "a blank at the center of the book."[36] Whether or not he changed his mind after he had considered all the reactions to his heroine and his book, he took elaborate pains to deny the identification of himself with his heroine. He said she was silly and had been at the time of her creation: "For example," Lewis explains his methods, "I deliberately had her decorate a room in bad taste. A couple of critics used that to show what a fool I was."[37] The climactic view of Lewis's attitude toward his heroine, perhaps, is the contention that he created her as the mouthpiece of his protest, later recognized that she was too conventional and naive to be associated with himself, and then turned on his own intended heroine.[38] Apparently an interpreter of *Main Street* can pay his money, but he had better not make his choice. The author (as well as his heroine) is "really not one person, but four or five people of various temperaments, all mixed together."[39]

If Lewis and Carol together and apart form a gallery of so many possible portraits, what can be said of what they see—the town itself? *Main Street* is "an affectionate story," according to its own author, who said he loved the town and the "dull people" who lived in it.[40] His friend William Rose Benét said he loved the "essential humanness of the people."[41] Again, "In the Midwest lies the hope of Carol—and of Lewis—for a richer and fuller life than has ever before existed."[42] It has been possible for one reader at least to wax poetic over the glories of Gopher Prairie and the small town as the gem of America if not the world. Lewis had dreamed that "small-town America was the place where democracy could thrive," and despite all the "distasteful culture" Lewis "instinctively wanted to believe in the goodness and healthiness of small-town life, and this instinct is manifest in *Main Street*." The novel has, indeed, a "feeling of wholesomeness."[43] The book is a paean of praise for what so many have regarded as cheap and shallow. More realistically, Sherwood Anderson felt that "Lewis never laughs at all," that he could not love life about him, and that he was "blind to the minor beauties our lives hold."[44] On the whole the criticism tends toward abuse of the town created in fiction, of all small towns, and of authors who condemn them in shallow books. If Lewis lacked, as Anthony Hilfer has said, "the subjective sensibility" to enable him to create the tensions of a character like Quentin Compson at the end of *Absalom, Absalom!*[45] he also lacked even the lyrical vacillation to express the ambivalence of Wolfe's Eugene Gant. He did not have the negative capability of the disciplined artist or the emotional response to pour words into uneven tomes of ranting and lyricism.

When a town passes away in time and the place changes, it is perhaps the primary truism of all that nothing can bring it back—neither history, fiction, pageants, nor festivals. The return of Sauk Centre or Gopher Prairie in *Main Street* is partial, as it has to be; but it seems finally less complete than the portraits of most well-known towns in literature. One perspective, written before the fiction, gives a different account of the town. Carol presumably settled with her new husband, Will, in Gopher Prairie in 1912, and there is at least one way of seeing what was going on in Sauk Centre at the time—the newspaper. These two versions—one of fiction, one of journalism—differ, of course, in form, but the content is dissimilar as well as the method.

So what does the newspaper say happened in Sauk Centre from January 1912 to the Fourth of July—about half a year? Except in violence and scandal politically ignored by local papers, the domestic life of the people might be about the same in the news and the novel. The activity—acceptable or not to Sinclair Lewis—is rather vigorous compared to the usual outsider's belief in a prevailing dullness. If the healthy and eligible citizens of Sauk Centre took part in what was available to them, they had social and professional lives as busy as their big-city counterparts.

The activities of the town were diverse. Elementary as it seems, they had a newspaper which reported local affairs extensively and, perhaps happily, left its readers mostly uninformed of wars and rumors of wars and the troubling affairs of the great world. Besides boiler plate and local news, it ran sentimental serial novels like those Thomas Wolfe read in the Asheville papers. In 1912 the Sauk Centre *Herald* published a novel with a title not altogether removed from daily reality, Randall Parrish's *Keith of the Border: A Tale of the Plains*. Also it carried the very impersonal personal notices from outlying communities which have always appeared in all local papers. At Easter there was even a colored front page for the issue. The barren culture of Gopher Prairie misrepresents in part the reality of this small town and the somewhat sophisticated culture of Sauk Centre. The folk music of the county, perhaps the most noteworthy entertainment, functioned as radio and television have for a later time, but in the Sauk Centre *Herald* there were announcements of numerous musical events worthy of the taste and accomplishment of the time and place: a church concert, a recital at the church organ, other musical events and recitations at churches, a children's musical program (perhaps no more stultifying culturally than the performances with kazoos of kindergarten orchestras in the big cities), musical entertainments at the

Methodist Church, the Kipp String Orchestra from Minneapolis with A. E. Kipp and three daughters (which spent three days in Sauk Centre), and a band concert. The twenty-three-piece Sauk Centre Band played classical selections as well as other kinds of music; it had a vocal soloist; and there was a high school male quartet and a Ladies Monday Musical Club. In April even the St. Paul Symphony Orchestra gave two separate performances (including Wagner) to two separate audiences.

In drama, there was a dramatic reading at the Methodist Church, a high school seniors' play, "Thompson and the 'Varsity' "; and a little theater group presented at the Grand Opera House the kind of drama which Lewis would have expected and the age would have enjoyed, *The Wolf*, "The Greatest Realistic Drama of This Century," the paper said. The quantity and variety of entertainments and parties in Sauk Centre can be demonstrated best by naming them. The Fire Department had a house-warming; a church had an open house. Others were a big bean bake; numerous card parties; afternoon sewings; a chafing dish party; a thimble bee; coffee and a supper at a store; regular meetings of a Commercial Club of forty members; the usual junior-senior banquet and the high school graduation. The Gradatim Club in the *Herald* is less ridiculous than the Thanatopsis in the novel. Instead of covering half the world in an afternoon, the members studied Japan for a year and lightened their labors with music, food for one hundred members at a meal, and "feminine sayings." One of the good members reported that "the feast of reason and flow of soul proceedings were exclusively feminine." Without Carol, the club built a rest room like that in *Main Street*. It was an entire building with chairs, places to eat lunch, a telephone, and reading materials. Nearly three thousand persons stopped by for some kind of rest during the second year it was open.

Other amusements seem less stilted, sometimes even less provincial; some seem worthy, but some show how Lewis did not need to change them much to make them ridiculous. On New Year's Night the "Sauk Centre Band gave one of their enjoyable dancing parties." There were pot dinners, social hops, dances in evening dress, reunions of Civil War soldiers and their wives. Intellectually and educationally, there were special courses in "agriculture, stock raising, dairying and kindred subjects, manual training and domestic science" and other farmers' short courses—the kind of thing Carol yearned for but could not establish. Joseph A. Caughren offered a $110 silver trophy for excellence in debating. Besides the State Industrial School for Girls, there was a business college and a parochial school as well as the high school, a twelve-thousand-dollar public library (remember the time and the size of the town) with ten thousand books. The president of the state university delivered a lecture in Sauk Centre. Farmers' clubs and meetings, several lodges, the organization of a Commercial Club, consultations of Associated Doctors at the Palmer House, and the order of Rebekahs kept the people busy.

The dismal and ugly little town which Carol saw when she came to Gopher Prairie was not to be seen in the Sauk Centre *Herald*. It proclaimed the glory, wealth, and beauty of the railroad, "the wonderful Park Region of Minnesota," ten-mile long Sauk Lake (there is "no finer Summer Resort on earth"), fifteen miles of sidewalk (Carol covered the paved walkways of Gopher Prairie in thirty-two minutes), at least twenty-six businesses and factories besides the stores, twenty-four-hour electric light service, sports (a ski tournament, basketball, fishing), and a school exhibit (which displayed the products of months of work of all the children). The celebration of the Fourth of July perhaps best symbolizes the vigorous activity of the little town. There were about thirty parades, games, contests, and concerts, dances which lasted from 9:00 in the morning until the last dance began at 9:30 in the evening. Of course, these were primitive events suitable for that time, not staged for later years. But, indeed, some modern festivities attempt to re-create them. At great modern celebrations and sports events the people watch and appreciate and exclaim and even cheer from the sidelines or on the living room sofa. In Gopher Prairie the people idled away their time and criticized the goings on of their neighbors; but in Sauk Centre, at least according to the newspaper account, the people themselves played, grunted and groaned in competition, and displayed their abilities and accomplishments. The comparison of hometown journalism and satirical fiction is unjust, but despite the accepted identification of Sauk Centre and Gopher Prairie, the novel creates a world vastly different from the life represented in the weekly paper.

Satire like that in *Main Street* can successfully ridicule examples of the foibles of the people of a town and place like Sauk Centre, but it cannot do so with the authenticity that has been ascribed to it by many critics. Lewis's method is too much like riding through a place on a train, looking out at only one side of the track, seeing only the face and the dress of people and the paint and structure of the houses. It is less than a "sociological caricature unmasking the small town."[46] It mirrors "banalities,"[47] true, but the mirror includes only a little of the landscape, and far in the background significant aspects of the life of the town appear in miniature rather than in fullness. Lewis Mumford was carried away with the historical accuracy of Lewis's account. The people were "of flesh and blood," truly "stodgy, self-satisfied" like their prototypes, representative of American life "all over the country," and so on.[48] But Lewis and Lewis Mumford created and criticized in half-truths, and their accounts ignore some of the actuality of life apparent in the walking flesh of the real prairie town and even in the reportage of the Sauk Centre *Herald*. Much of the inhumanity of Gopher Prairie derives from the eccentricities and fidgetings and boredom of its author. Culturally, agriculturally, socially, geographically, the potentialities for fullness of being were greater than those in Red Cloud, where Willa Cather saw people whole; and Sauk Centre provided a richness which its most famous son never saw.

My own experience in Sauk Centre was brief and late. I went to the town with a closed mind, expecting to react as Carol did, anticipating a haven of dullness. But In 1975 I could not imagine how Lewis's novel had been "true to actual conditions,"[49] "durable and to a large extent accurate,"[50] one of the best descriptions of "life in a small town" ever written (in the words of the secretary of the Swedish Academy).[51] I sat in the living room of a retired, unmarried teacher of history who vehemently denied that dullness in Sauk Centre is true to dullness in Gopher Prairie, and at the same moment a widow, a teacher of English, also a resident of the town, maintained that Lewis's novel is a fair and true representation of that way of life. The citizen, the reader, and the citizen-reader all arrive at their judgments. The reactions run in patterns, but few are exactly alike. What can the totality of judgments result in but chaoses of opinion and of criticism? Surely the reactions to *Main Street* may end somewhere besides the conclusion that attitude toward life and reactions to literature are so diverse that they are ultimately contradictory and meaningless. Perhaps one may conclude only that the good man and the great writer must see life and art in all their fullness. One must turn from horizon to horizon and observe all elevations in order to see men for what they are. To look at a town, a place, and a horizon at one time and to reach a judgment like that passed upon Gopher Prairie and Sauk Centre is to be harsh, incomplete, and untrue.

Sauk Centre was settled and built decades and even centuries after the towns and states to the east and the south. Red men or white, it had little past. The Indian had left no lasting structures or even trails, certainly nothing like the pueblo homes of the Southwest. The country around was farmland, and Anglo-Americans built a trade center to provide for and exploit the farmers who made the living for the area. Compared to Minnesota, Mississippi was almost an Old World culture. The local-color writers who discovered the quaint pockets of strange civilizations in remote places after the Civil War had for their materials wide divergences from person to person and local populations which seemed almost like fantasies to other American peoples. When the South already had national defeat as a tradition at once to honor and to overcome, Minnesotans were just beginning to dig their plows into virgin soil. In short, these people built their homes and immediately began to work toward the image of standardized America. Most of the racial differences in their land had already begun to melt into the common pot, and it was easy for one with the disposition of Sinclair Lewis to see little but dull uniformity, a town which had built itself into a new and universal pattern.

As towns go, Sauk Centre and Gopher Prairie are neither unique, exotic, nor quaint. There were no teepees, few cabins, no homes with elaborate Greek architecture. The town had natural beauties and some personality, but, as a younger child of the nation, it was more standard Anglo-American than communities with a single racial component, less varied in architecture than the plantations built with the labor of slaves, less differentiated than the various homes of the East, and less European than the southwestern cathedrals built on the bloody ruins of ancient Indian and Spanish civilizations. But Sauk Centre is a beautiful town in its limited way, as well as useful.

For what the vitriolic Lewis wished to write, Sauk Centre was a perfect subject matter. He yearned for the beauties and luxuries of pharaohs and kings, but he had to submit himself to a high school and the discipline of a stern and puritanical small-town physician father. Later he pursued a restless, wandering, and nervously dissipated life, but he had grown up reading a book as he mowed or was supposed to mow the lawn. The civilization of Sauk Centre and Gopher Prairie looks forward to what America as well as the small town became later in the century. Lewis was born to complain, and his people provided the opportunity. Even after half a century *Main Street* may help us see ourselves as we can be if all of us wish to be dull and alike. It is not a good novel; it is not a book wholly true of its own world or its country; it is a work to read and say, "God help us. May we never be like that." It is more message than fiction.

10

☙ TEN ☞

A Void New World

The American writer since 1850 has discovered a past and a culture which James Fenimore Cooper and his contemporaries did not believe existed. The eight novels studied here have portrayed cultures that are widely divergent from each other and from the standardized Anyplace of the twentieth century. In each instance the life of a people provided unique mores for a novel, even when the novelist was not altogether successful in capturing their spirit in the characters. Although nostalgia is seldom the dominant mood of the work, the ways of life of the people represented by these novels have vanished and are disappearing. Almost every place is becoming Anyplace. In varying degrees Americans and their likenesses in fiction will make themselves content with standardization or will revolt from it. Perhaps one who somewhat insensitively or unconsciously lives the life of the monotonous repetitions of Metropolis will adapt himself better than the novelist who must try to write about it, search out another culture, or become a student of history.

Two poems by American poets reveal in remarkably different ways the difference between the cultures we have given up and the worlds we are making, Robert Lowell's "The Mouth of the Hudson"[1] and Robert Frost's "Directive." The first is a horrifying description of a barren landscape near New York, a standardized city archetypically American. A lone man stands overlooking the mouth of one of the most polluted rivers in the world, but no trace remains of the fresh greenness of the New World (as it is described in *The Great Gatsby*) when Hudson discovered the river, and nothing in the poem mentions a vestige of the old Dutch settlers of New Amsterdam. The images of what had once been nature have been converted to those of foul pollution and destruction. The snow is "pepper and salt" with soot; the air is "chemical"; the sun, "sulphur-yellow"; "A Negro toasts / Wheat-seeds over . . . coke-fumes" (one of the foulest of fuels). The "unforgivable landscape" is littered with a cable drum and a punctured barrel. The movements of the "wild ice" are described in mechanical terms; twice the flow of the river is presented in an image of a mechanical ticking. The observer is alone and therefore altogether outside any community. Indeed, America cannot even be seen in the poem. It is not in this landscape, perhaps not anywhere anymore: "He cannot discover America by counting / the chains of condemned freight-trains / from thirty states." The factories stand in repetitious "ledges." Lowell has deliberately written a poem about the ugliest of land-scapes. "The Mouth of the Hudson" has no community, no human relationships; one observer can only stand "like a bird-watcher" in the hope of glimpsing something worth seeing. He sees a Negro, but the two share nothing. In short, none of the ingredients of fiction or beauty or any interrelationships are here. All is void.

Lowell describes the world we have made; Frost describes the places we have left behind. "Directive"[2] is set in a "country where two village cultures faded / Into each other. Both of them are lost." Both are lost in time, the past—the Indian village and the white settlement which succeeded it. Nature is here in excess, a second-growth nature now unpopulated: "Great monolithic knees the for-mer town / Long since gave up pretense of keeping covered." Most of man's marks are gone. A few remain: cellar holes, "pecker-fretted apple trees," "shattered dishes," "a broken drinking gob-let." Here too the materials of fiction have vanished. The poetry and songs of the past do not survive. The visitor to this extinct community is advised to "Make yourself up a cheering song of how / Someone's road home from work this once was." But he does not proceed to a fantasy of the lyrics "someone might have sung." Probably they too have been lost with the community.

Nature, community, family, the drama (or fiction) of interrela-tionships have been lost, then, in the world from which Americans have fled in vast movements of population. And large areas of the urban places to which the people have moved have been destroyed so that there would be places to run trains and automobiles, to dump garbage, to erect the enormous structures which house the offices, warehouses, and factories of the monsters needed to construct a mechanical world, and to build the tightly squeezed material structures to serve as bedrooms and kitchens for those who supervise and operate and build. The philosophy of the American home and the quantity of space around it—fields or lawn—has been completely abandoned; a flowerpot or at most a planter sometimes has to suffice. The change in the physical use of the natural world has affected the social use of the world man has about him. The stand-up cocktail party in one room or a few has replaced the Fourth of July celebration, the community Thanksgiving, or the family reunion. Some gatherings, such as those of large families before a funeral, have virtually disappeared.

Perhaps the novelist has retained better than most the image of a world where there is interchange between people and nature, people and people, and people and God. Many young Americans may know the mouth of the Hudson or something like it or even a park, but they do not know a community and cannot imagine the concept of a community. In short, the materials which have been used for fiction throughout all history can be known only vicariously to most readers of fiction and even to potential novelists. Perhaps this condition sounds like an expository statement of an abstract condition. Instead it is intensely personal and real and concrete. In 1973, for example, I asked each student in a composition class to write a short paper about a community where people were involved in the lives of one another. It was a cosmopolitan class with various origins: one of aristocratic European backgrounds, several from Florida, two from New York, one from the Midwest, several from Kentucky and Alabama and various other southern states, at least one from Atlanta. The assignment asked the impossible because not one of the fourteen students originated from anything that could be called a community. One did remember visiting her grandmother's rural Georgia home; another had spent a few weeks on some kind of welfare mission in Appalachia. But the others had nothing to write about. Not only were they without a community (sometimes even without anything that could be called an authentic home), but they were also without any concept of what a community might be for anyone else. They asked numerous questions about what the assignment meant, what they were supposed to do. They wrote character sketches of solitary individuals, portrayed elderly retired citizens on the streets of St. Petersburg, described an ocean shore, recounted the events of the way two boys played together for a day, and told about water sports. Not one student knew a community where people were involved in the lives of one another; not one knew at first hand anything a traditional novel could be written about. At the end of the term one student planned to visit places where he might see communities in the South. He wished to go to Oxford and to Asheville and to places where he might talk with people who did have communities. He would find that much of the idea of community is vanishing also in places where authors once lived. Julia Wolfe's Old Kentucky Home fronts on the parking lot of a skyscraper. He hoped to become a writer, and he wished to acquire a subject matter because he said he had not been born and raised with the materials of fiction.

The bare facts of this study have been that in eight novels the authors had available to them materials in which the human drama might work its way to interrelationships that resulted in humor, comedy, tragedy, and—to sum up—consequence. In the ways of human beings, some of these creators attained monumental art and some only wrote interesting books. It is the province of the critic to look back and see what the author did with the materials he had. In his own function it is never his prerogative to attempt to provide a way of life for an author, communal or religious or cultural or social. It is hardly the province of the critic to foresee the future of society or literature—as the social scientist or the psychiatrist may perhaps attempt to do—and to predict the state of the society and of the souls that will be. It is frustrating not to be able to step from the role of critic to the role of monarch and proclaim orders that worlds and communities may be created so that men may live in them happily and that writers may have happy people to write about or—even more important for literature—that they have happy and tragic people to write about.

All the critic can do is to study the fiction and the culture and to see what kind of fiction comes from what kind of culture. Thus the poor redneck Bundrens, as some would call them, lived a life that enabled Faulkner to make art of their lives; but the beautiful Scarlett O'Hara living her meaningless life in her unreal world, despite all her popularity, attains only a lowly state in art. Scarlett, as a sort of symbol of many Americans' notions of the high attainments of art, is a failure, though not a tragedy, with or without her husband, without any God, in her community or out of it, in her fiction or in the motion picture; hers is a world without the cultural complexities that seem necessary in all but the most introspective art.

Notes

Notes

CHAPTER ONE: THE MAKINGS OF AMERICAN FICTION

1. George K. Lewis, "Population Change in Northern New England," *Annals of the Association of American Geographers* 62 (June 1972): 307.

2. Robert Frost, "The Census-Taker" (*Complete Poems*, New York: Holt, Rinehart and Winston, 1961), pp. 216–217, however, is an early portrait of the world left by the multitudinous migration of Americans away from rural areas.

3. William Faulkner, "To the Editor of the Oxford *Eagle*" (March 13, 1947), in James B. Meriwether, *Essays, Speeches and Public Letters by William Faulkner* (New York, 1965), p. 202.

4. T. S. Eliot, *Notes towards the Definition of Culture* (New York, 1949), pp. 55, 125.

5. Wilbur Zelinsky, *The Cultural Geography of the United States* (Englewood Cliffs, N.J., 1973), pp. 125–126, 128.

6. Donald E. Stanford, "*Caroline Gordon: From* Penhally *to* A Narrow Heart," *Southern Review*, n.s. 7 (April 1971): xviii–xix.

7. C. G. Jung, "The Role of the Unconscious," in *Civilization in Transition*, vol. 10, *The Collected Works* (New York: Pantheon Books, 1964), 13, 49.

8. Lewis, pp. 326–327.

9. Graham Greene, *A Sort of Life* (New York, 1971), p. 205.

10. U.S. Bureau of the Census, *Historical Studies of the United States, Colonial Times to 1957* (Washington, D.C., 1960), p. 289.

11. Cleanth Brooks, "The Current State of American Literature," *Southern Review*, n.s. 9 (January 1973): 280.

12. The figures of the Bureau of Census here are not altogether consistent: "Prior to 1950 . . . a number of large and densely settled places were not included as urban because they were not incorporated." The Bureau in 1950 began classifying such areas as urban.

13. Jung, p. 254.

14. Brooks, p. 280.

15. Ibid., p. 275.

16. Zelinsky, p. 90.

17. Ibid., p. 86.

18. Ibid., p. 82.

CHAPTER TWO: *THE GRAPES OF WRATH*

1. Quoted in "Red Meat and Red Herrings," *Commonweal* 30 (October 13, 1939): 562.

2. H. A. Taine, *History of English Literature*, trans. H. Van Laun (New York, 1879), pp. 17–18.

3. Remarks by Hon. Lyle H. Boren, *Congressional Record*, Appendix 86, part 13 (1940), 140.

4. County Agent Houston B. Ward, quoted by Martin Staples Shockley, "The Reception of *The Grapes of Wrath* in Oklahoma," *American Literature* 15 (1944): 353.

5. Frank J. Taylor, "California's 'Grapes of Wrath,'" *Forum* 102 (November 1939): 232–238.

6. Carey McWilliams, "California Pastoral," *Antioch Review* 2 (Spring 1942): 104.

7. John Steinbeck, *The Grapes of Wrath* (New York: Viking Press, 1939), p. 3. All parenthetical references in the text are to this edition.

8. *The Grapes of Wrath*, p. 231; H. Kelly Crockett, "The Bible and *The Grapes of Wrath*," *College English* 24 (December 1962): 193.

9. Frederick F. Manfred, "Sinclair Lewis: A Portrait," *American Scholar* 23 (Spring 1954): 180.

10. Walter Fuller Taylor, "*The Grapes of Wrath* Reconsidered," *Mississippi Quarterly* 12 (Summer 1959): 139.

11. Robert Penn Warren, "The Blind Poet: Sidney Lanier," *American Review* 2 (November 1933): 37.

12. Quoted in "Red Meat and Red Herrings," p. 563.

CHAPTER THREE: *GONE WITH THE WIND*

1. Lion Feuchtwanger, *The House of Desdemona: Or the Laurels and Limitations of Historical Fiction*, trans. Harold A. Basilius (Detroit, 1963), p. 129.

2. Helen Cam, *Historical Novels*, no. 48, Historical Association (London, 1961), p. 18.

3. William Dean Howells, "The New Historical Romances," *North American Review* 171 (December 1900): 943.

4. William S. Howland, "Margaret Mitchell—Romantic Realist,"

Margaret Mitchell Memorial of the Atlanta Public Library (Atlanta, 1954), p. 5.

5. Robert Y. Drake, Jr., "Tara Twenty Years After," *Georgia Review* 12 (Summer 1958): 142.

6. Belle Rosenbaum, "Why Do They Read It?" *Scribner's Magazine* 102 (August 1937): 69.

7. Drake, p. 145.

8. See L. Hugh Moore, Jr., "Robert Penn Warren and History: 'The Big Myth We Live' " (Ph.D. dissertation, Emory University, 1964), pp. 13, 68.

9. W. J. Stuckey, *The Pulitzer Prize Novels: A Critical Backward Look* (Norman, Okla., 1966), p. 111.

10. Margaret Mitchell, *Gone with the Wind* (New York, 1936), p. 219. All parenthetical references in the text are to this edition.

11. Stuckey, p. 111.

12. Stephens Mitchell, "Margaret Mitchell and Her People in the Atlanta Area," *Atlanta Historical Bulletin* 9 (May 1950): 22.

13. Marian Elder Jones, "Me and My Book," *Georgia Review* 16 (Summer 1962): 184.

14. Finis Farr, *Margaret Mitchell of Atlanta: The Author of "Gone with the Wind"* (New York, 1965), p. 104.

15. Andrew Nelson Lytle, "The Image as Guide to Meaning in the Historical Novel," *Sewanee Review* 61 (1953): 410–411.

16. See burning cotton or consult with J. W. McCarty, of the Georgia Institute of Technology and consultant with the Georgia Department of Agriculture.

17. Alan Conway, *The Reconstruction of Georgia* (Minneapolis, 1966), p. 44.

18. Sheldon Van Auken, "The Southern Historical Novel in the Early Twentieth Century," *Journal of Southern History* 14 (May 1948): 185.

19. Richard Chase, *The American Novel and Its Tradition* (London, 1957), p. 20.

20. Thomas Wolfe, *Look Homeward, Angel* (New York, 1929), p. 273.

CHAPTER FOUR:
THE CONFESSIONS OF NAT TURNER

1. Interview with William Styron, June 18, 1974. Hereafter cited in text as "interview."

2. William Styron, *The Confessions of Nat Turner* (New York, 1967). All parenthetical references in the text are to this edition.

3. Henry Irving Tragle, *The Southampton Slave Revolt of 1831: A Compilation of Source Material* (Amherst, Mass., 1971), p. 6.

4. Martin Boyd Coyner, Jr., "John Hartwell Cocke of Bremo: Agriculture and Slavery in the Ante-Bellum South" (Ph.D. dissertation, University of Virginia, 1961), p. 397.

5. John W. Blassingame, *The Slave Community: Plantation Life in the Antebellum South* (New York, 1972), pp. 95–96.

6. Coyner, p. 89.

7. Blassingame, p. 153.

8. Quoted by Alan Holder, "Styron's Slave: *The Confessions of Nat Turner*," *South Atlantic Quarterly* 68 (Spring 1969): 169.

9. Frances Anne Kemble, *Journal of a Residence on a Georgian Plantation in 1838–1839*, ed. by John A. Scott (New York, 1970), p. 305.

10. Coyner, p. 16.

11. Ibid., p. 305.

12. Ibid., p. 394–396.

13. Quoted by Holder, p. 167.

CHAPTER FIVE: *MY ÁNTONIA*

1. Robert Louis Stevenson, *From Scotland to Silverado*, ed. by James D. Hart (Cambridge, Mass., 1966), pp. 124, 125, 123.

2. Willa Cather, *My Ántonia* (Boston, 1926), p. ix. All parenthetical references in the text are to this edition.

3. Stevenson, p. 123.

4. Ellen Churchill Semple, *Influences of Geographic Environment on the Basis of Ratzel's System of Anthropo-Geography* (New York, 1911), p. 619.

5. Interview, Professor Bernice Slote, 1974.

6. David Stouck, "*O Pioneers!*: Willa Cather and the Epic Imagination," *Prairie Schooner* 46 (Spring 1972): 27.

7. Walter Havighurst, ed., "Prairie Life in *My Ántonia*," *My Ántonia* (Boston, 1946), p. vi.

8. Martha Ferguson McKeown, *Them Was the Days* (Lincoln, Neb., 1961), p. 99.

9. Ellsworth Huntington, *The Character of Races as Influenced by*

Physical Environment, Natural Selection and Historical Development
(New York, 1924), p. 29.

10. Semple, p. 477.

11. Ibid., p. 19.

12. Ibid., p. 20.

13. Roderick Peattie, *Geography in Human Destiny* (New York, 1940),
pp. 201, 218, 213, 216–217.

14. Ibid., p. 38.

15. Don D. Walker, "The Western Humanism of Willa Cather,"
Western American Literature 1 (Spring 1966): 75.

16. Many interpreters of Willa Cather's fiction have written about the
prairie world of *My Ántonia*, and several, especially Bernice Slote and
Mildred Bennett, have commented on her attitudes toward the land and
Nebraska. I am indebted to several scholars, but my indebtednesses are
general and seldom call for particular footnotes.

17. Willa Cather, *Early Stories of Willa Cather*, ed. by Mildred Bennett (New York, 1957), pp. 10–11.

18. Bernice Slote, "Writer in Nebraska," *The Kingdom of Art: Willa
Cather's First Principles and Critical Statements 1893–1896* (Lincoln,
Neb., 1966), p. 107. Anthony Channell Hilfer, *The Revolt from the Vil-
lage 1915–1930* (Chapel Hill, N.C., 1969), p. 87.

19. Willa Cather, "On the Divide," *Willa Cather's Collected Short
Fiction*, ed. by Mildred R. Bennett (Lincoln, Neb., 1970), pp. 493–496.

20. Bennett, "Introduction," *Collected Short Fiction*, p. xviii.

21. James Woodress, *Willa Cather: Her Life and Art* (New York,
1970), pp. 77–79.

22. Willa Cather, "Eric Hermannson's Soul," *Collected Short Fiction*,
pp. 363–364, 368–369.

23. Willa Cather, "El Dorado: A Kansas Recessional," *Collected Short
Fiction*, p. 293.

24. Lincoln *Courier*, June 22, 1901.

25. "Willa Cather Talks of Work: *Special Correspondence of the
Philadelphia Record*," in Slote, *The Kingdom of Art*, pp. 448, 449.

26. Willa Cather, *O Pioneers!* (Boston, 1941), pp. 15, 48, 187, et
passim.

27. Ibid., p. 65.

28. Webster County *Argus*, September 29, 1921.

29. Ibid.

30. Hastings *Daily Tribune*, August 27, 1927.

NOTES

31. *Argus*, September 29, 1921.

32. Willa Cather, "Nebraska: The End of the First Cycle," *Nation* 117 (September 5, 1923), 236–238.

33. Ibid., p. 238.

34. Omaha *Daily Bee*, October 29, 1929.

35. Willa Cather was not buried in Virginia, Nebraska, or the Southwest. When she died, her friend Edith Lewis informed the Cather family that she had left instructions that she was to be buried in a mountainous area of New Hampshire. Rumors are that the family never saw the request by Willa Cather in writing and that they doubted Miss Lewis's statement. Miss Lewis did not like to travel, and the family believed also that she had prevented Willa Cather from returning to Nebraska on trips in the later years.

36. *O Pioneers!*, p. 19.

37. *Commercial Advertiser*, November 16, 1921.

38. Semple, p. 48.

39. John Randall III, *The Landscape and the Looking Glass: Willa Cather's Search for Value* (Boston, 1960), p. 105.

40. Superior *Express*, [no month, no day] 1921.

41. Lincoln *Star*, November 16, 1921.

42. Mildred R. Bennett, *The World of Willa Cather* (Lincoln, Neb., 1961), p. 201.

43. Webster County *News*, April 19, 1912.

44. Quoted by Ethel M. Hockett, "The Vision of a Successful Fiction Writer," Lincoln *Daily Star*, October 24, 1915, in *The Kingdom of Art*, p. 452.

45. *Commercial Advertiser*, November 16, 1921.

46. Webster County *Argus*, September 29, 1921.

47. Mildred R. Bennett, "Catherton," *Prairie Schooner* 23 (1949): 281.

48. F. H., "Willa Cather Talks of Work," in *The Kingdom of Art*, p. 448.

49. Rose Rosicky, *A History of Czechs (Bohemians) in Nebraska* (Omaha: Czech Historical Society of Nebraska, 1929), p. 207.

50. Terence Martin, "The Drama of Memory in *My Ántonia*," *PMLA* 84 (March, 1969): 306.

51. Cather, "Nebraska."

52. Blanche H. Gelfant, "The Forgotten Reaping-Hook: Sex in *My Ántonia*," *American Literature* 43 (March 1971): 63.

53. Bennett, *World of Willa Cather*, p. 29.

54. See Richard Giannone, *Music in Willa Cather's Fiction* (Lincoln, Neb., 1968), p. 114.

55. Cather, "Nebraska," p. 237.

56. Mariel Gere to Mildred R. Bennett, February 6, 1956.

CHAPTER SIX: *DEATH COMES FOR THE ARCHBISHOP*

1. Willa Cather, *Death Comes for the Archbishop* (New York, 1957). All parenthetical references in the text are to this edition.

2. James Woodress, *Willa Cather: Her Life and Art* (New York, 1970), pp. 225, 219.

3. Willa Cather, "A Letter from Willa Cather," *Commonweal* 7 (November 23, 1927): 714.

4. Mildred R. Bennett, *The World of Willa Cather* (Lincoln, Neb., 1961), p. 222.

5. Woodress, pp. 217–220; Edith Lewis, *Willa Cather Living* (New York, 1953), pp. 96ff.

6. Edward A. Bloom and Lillian D. Bloom, *Willa Cather's Gift of Sympathy* (Carbondale, Ill., 1962), p. 212.

7. Cather, "A Letter," p. 32.

8. Hippolyte Delehaye, *The Legends of the Saints: An Introduction to Hagiography*, trans. V. M. Crawford, introduction by Richard J. Schoeck, 1907 (Notre Dame, 1961), p. 10.

9. See H. Newstead, "Legends, Medieval," *New Catholic Encyclopedia* (New York, 1967), 8: 610.

10. *The Golden Legend of Jacobus De Voragine*, translated and adapted from the Latin by Granger Ryan and Helmut Ripperger (London, 1941), p. x.

11. Clara Reeves, *The Progress of Romance through Times, Countries, and Manners*, quoted in Robert Scholes and Robert Kellogg, *The Nature of Narrative* (New York, 1966), p. 6.

12. Northrop Frye, *The Anatomy of Criticism* (Princeton, 1957), p. 33.

13. Fred S. Perrine, "Military Escorts on the Santa Fé Trail," *New Mexico Historical Review* 2 (April 1927): 179, n. 7; John D. Lee, "Diary of the Mormon Battalion Mission," ed. by Juanita Brooks, *New Mexico Historical Review* 42 (October 1967): 282.

NOTES

14. Cather, "A Letter," p. 173.

15. Pueblo: Colorado, 1908. This source and many other sources for the novel were first discovered by the Blooms.

16. Jean Baptiste Salpointe, *Soldiers of the Cross: Notes on the Ecclesiastical History of New Mexico, Arizona and Colorado* (Albuquerque, 1967; originally published 1898), p. 275.

17. Howlett, p. 29.

18. Willa Cather knew of two white mules like Contento and Angelica, but Mexicans owned them, not the priests (letter to Carrie Miner, April 29, 1945; Howlett, pp. 216–217).

19. Earl R. Forrest, *Missions and Pueblos of the Old Southwest* (Cleveland, 1929), p. 167.

20. Ralph Emerson Twitchell, *The Leading Facts of New Mexican History* (Albuquerque, 1963; facsimile of 1911 and 1912), 2:339.

21. See also ibid., pp. 331–332.

22. Forrest, p. 92; Oliver La Farge (with the assistance of Arthur N. Morgan), *Santa Fé: The Autobiography of a Southwestern Town* (Norman, Okla., 1959), p. 44.

23. Ralph Emerson Twitchell, *The History of the Military Occupation of the Territory of New Mexico from 1846 to 1851 by the Government of the United States* (Chicago: Rio Grande Press; originally published 1909), pp. 287–301.

24. M. Morgan Estergreen, *Kit Carson: A Portrait in Courage* (Norman, Okla., 1962), p. 124.

25. Twitchell, *Military Occupation*, pp. 124ff.

26. Salpointe, p. 163.

27. Forrest, p. 206.

28. Elizabeth Shepley Sergeant, *Willa Cather: A Memoir* (Philadelphia, 1953), p. 235.

29. Howlett, pp. 174–175.

30. Cleve Hallenbeck and Juanita H. Williams, *Legends of the Spanish Southwest* (Glendale, Calif., 1938), pp. 289–293; Twitchell, *Leading Facts*, 2:153; Josiah Gregg, *Commerce of the Prairies; or, The Journal of a Santa Fé Trader*, in Reuben Gold Thwaites, ed., *Early Western Travels, 1748–1846* (Cleveland, 1905), 20: 38ff.; *Death Comes for the Archbishop*, pp. 46ff.

31. Probably Willa Cather found the stories in Francis Palou, *Life of Ven. Padre Junípero Serra*, trans. J. Adam (San Francisco, 1884), pp. 12–13, 21–22; they are also recounted by Maynard J. Geiger, *The Life and Times of Fray Junípero* (Washington, D.C., 1959), 1: 84, 85, 154.

32. Sister Lucy Schneider, "Cather's 'Land-Philosophy' in *Death Comes for the Archbishop*," *Renascence* 22 (Winter 1970): 81.

33. On Mexican art see Richard Giannone, *Music in Willa Cather's Fiction* (Lincoln, Neb., 1968), p. 199.

34. John Ruskin, *The Stones of Venice*, in *The Works of John Ruskin*, 10 vols. (London, 1904), 2: 181.

35. Charles Fletcher Lummis, *A New Mexico David and Other Stories and Sketches of the Southwest* (Freeport, N. Y., 1969), p. 197.

36. Twitchell, *Military Occupation*, pp. 287–301.

37. Lewis, p. 142.

38. See Bloom and Bloom, p. 231.

39. Maynard Fox, "Proponents of Order: Tom Outland and Bishop Latour," *Western American Literature* 4 (Summer 1969): 111–112. Schneider, pp. 81–82.

40. Lummis, *A New Mexico David*, p. 52.

41. Alfred Vincent Kidder, "Pecos, New Mexico: Archaeological Notes," *Papers of the Robert S. Peabody Foundation for Archaeology* 5 (1958): 227.

42. Kidder, p. 228; Lummis, *Mesa, Cañon and Pueblo* (New York, 1925), p. 148.

43. Lummis, *Mesa*, p. 148.

44. Forrest, p. 103.

45. Kidder, pp. 232, 234, 235.

46. Twitchell, *Leading Facts*, 2: 303.

47. Ibid., p. 434.

48. Lawrence C. Kelly, *Navajo Roundup: Selected Correspondence of Kit Carson's Expedition Against the Navajo, 1863–1865* (Boulder, Colo., 1970), p. 165.

49. Lt. James H. Simpson, *Navajo Expedition*, ed. by Frank McNitt (Norman, Okla., 1964), p. 197.

50. Bloom and Bloom, p. 216.

51. Frank McNitt, *Navajo Wars: Military Campaigns, Slave Raids and Reprisals* (Albuquerque, 1972), p. 265.

52. *New Mexico: A Guide to the Colorful State*, American Guide Series, new edition by Joseph Miller (New York, 1962; originally published 1940), p. 341.

53. Hubert Howe Bancroft, *History of Arizona and New Mexico, 1530–1888* (New Mexico Foreword by Clinton P. Anderson; Arizona Foreword by Barry Goldwater [Albuquerque, 1962; facsimile of the 1889 edition]), p. 182, n. 10.

54. Henry Nash Smith, *Virgin Land: The American West as Symbol and Myth* (Cambridge, 1950), p. 85.

CHAPTER SEVEN: *HOUSE MADE OF DAWN*

1. N. Scott Momaday, *House Made of Dawn* (New York, 1968), p. 5. All parenthetical references in the text are to this edition.

2. N. Scott Momaday, "The Morality of Indian Hating, *Ramparts* 3 (Summer 1964): 40.

3. Elsie Clews Parsons, *Pueblo Indian Religion* (Chicago, 1939), 2: 940.

4. Edward P. Dozier, "Spanish-Catholic Influence on Rio Grande Pueblo Religion," *American Anthropologist* 60 (1958): 447.

5. Ibid., p. 446.

6. Elsie Clews Parsons, *The Pueblo of Jemez* (New Haven, 1925), p. 68.

7. Edgar L. Hewett, *Ancient Life in the American Southwest* (Indianapolis, 1930), p. 128.

8. Alfred Vincent Kidder, *Pecos, New Mexico: Archaeological Notes*, Papers of the Robert S. Peabody Foundation for Archaeology (Andover, Mass., 1958), 5: 227.

9. Charles F. Lummis, *Some Strange Corners of Our Country* (New York, 1892, p. 67.

10. Ibid., p. 68.

11. Albuquerque *Journal*, December 7, 1958, p. 4.

12. Ibid., December 9, 1958, p. 10.

13. Ibid., February 21, 1959, p. 11.

14. Parsons, *Religion*, 1: 44, 215, 524; *Jemez*, p. 29.

15. Parsons, *Jemez*, p. 139.

16. Parsons, *Religion*, 2: 820–821.

17. Harvey Fergusson, *Rio Grande* (New York, 1967), p. 35.

18. Parsons, *Jemez*, p. 118.

19. Ibid., p. 90.

20. Momaday, "The Morality of Indian Hating," p. 40.

21. Parsons, *Jemez*, p. 76.

22. Interview with Paul Toya, Jemez Pueblo, June 1971.

23. Parsons, *Religion*. 1: 425.

24. Ibid., 2: 795.

25. "The Morality of Indian Hating," p. 40.

26. Esther Schiff Goldfrank, *The Social and Ceremonial Organization of Cochiti, Memoirs of the American Anthropological Association*, No. 33 (1927), pp. 84–85.

27. Ibid., p. 88.

28. Parsons, *Jemez*, 62.

29. Albert B. Reagan, "The Jemez Indians," *El Palacio Santa Fe, New Mexico* (April 1917): 4: 47.

30. Interview at Jemez Pueblo, June 1971.

31. Parsons, *Jemez*, p. 62.

32. Interview with N. Scott Momaday, Santa Fe, N.M., June 1971.

33. Kidder, p. 296.

34. T. M. Pearce, assisted by Ina Sizer Cassidy and Helen S. Pearce, *New Mexico Place Names: A Geographical Dictionary* (Albuquerque, 1965), p. 150.

35. Leslie A. White, *The Pueblo of Santa Ana, New Mexico*, Memoir Series of the American Anthropological Association, No. 60, Vol. 44, *American Anthropologist*, new ser. (October–December 1942): 256–257.

36. Ibid., p. 264; *House Made of Dawn*, pp. 38–39.

37. White, p. 265.

38. Ibid., p. 258.

39. Parsons, *Jemez*, p. 136.

40. The Atlanta *Journal*, August 25, 1971.

41. Weston La Barre, *The Peyote Cult*, enlarged ed. (New York, 1972), p. 50, n. 108.

42. *House Made of Dawn*, p. 131. A very similar version of this Kiowa tale was told me by Ella Poolaw, Anadarko, Okla., July 1971.

43. Mildred P. Mayhall, *The Kiowas* (Norman, Okla., 1962), p. 265.

44. J. S. Slotkin, *The Peyote Religion* (Glencoe, Ill., 1956), p. 23.

45. T. D. Allen, *Navahos Have Five Fingers* (Norman, Okla., 1963), p. 168. Interview with Helen Daw, Wide Ruins, Ariz., July 1971.

46. Washington Matthews, *Navaho Legends*, Memoirs of the American Folk-Lore Society, Vol. 5 (1897), p. 275.

47. Interview with Helen Daw.

48. Matthews, *Navaho Legends*, pp. 104–105.

49. Memoirs of the American Museum of Natural History 6 (1902).

50. J. W. Powell, "Introduction," *Fifth Annual Report of the Bureau of Ethnology* (Washington, D.C.: Government Printing Office, 1887), p. xlvi.

51. Matthews, *Night Chant*, p. 271.

52. Matthews, *Navaho Legends*, p. 25.
53. Matthews, *Night Chant*, p. 271.
54. Matthews, *Navaho Legends*, p. 24.
55. Matthews, *Night Chant*, pp. 142–143.
56. Matthews, *Navaho Legends*, p. 275.
57. In the free translation, Matthews renders this "In Tsegíhi (oh you who dwell!)."

CHAPTER EIGHT: *AS I LAY DYING*

1. Even uneducated southerners, whites and blacks, often used classical names.
2. Cassius Q. Benbow in *The Unvanquished* is called Cash. See Frances Willard Pate, "Names of Characters in Faulkner's Mississippi" (Ph.D. dissertation, Emory University, 1969), pp. 80–81. William Faulkner, *Faulkner in the University*, ed. by Frederick L. Gwynn and Joseph L. Blotner (Charlottesville, Va., 1959), p. 115.
3. William Faulkner, *As I Lay Dying* (New York, 1967), p. 7. All parenthetical references in the text are to this edition.
4. One that I have heard of used his coffin as a storage place for apples.
5. William Faulkner, *The Hamlet* (New York, 1940), p. 226.
6. Cleanth Brooks, *William Faulkner: The Yoknapatawpha Country* (New Haven, 1963), pp. 143–144.
7. In many communities the story was of a man so lazy that the people decided to bury him before he died. Someone on the way to the cemetery, sorry for the man, offered him some corn. Sitting up in the wagon, he asked, "Is it shelled?" When they told him no, he said, "Well, just take me on."

CHAPTER NINE: *MAIN STREET*

1. Mark Schorer, "Afterword," Sinclair Lewis, *Main Street* (New York, 1961), p. 434.
2. Ivy Louise Hildebrand, "Sauk Centre: A Study of the Growth of a Frontier Town" (M.A. thesis, St. Cloud State College, 1960), p. 16, n. 54.
3. Sinclair Lewis, *Main Street* (New York, 1920), p. 151. All parenthetical references in the text are to this edition.
4. Walter Lippman, *Men of Destiny* (New York, 1927), p. 84.

5. Mark Schorer, "Main Street," *American Heritage* 12 (October 1961): 76.

6. Lewis, "Minnesota: The Norse State," *Nation* 116 (May 30, 1923): 624.

7. Grace Hegger Lewis, *With Love from Gracie: Sinclair Lewis, 1912–1925* (New York, 1955), p. 96.

8. Grace Lewis, p. 92.

9. Harry E. Maule and Melville H. Cane, "Introduction," *A Sinclair Lewis Reader: The Man from Main Street: Selected Essays and Other Writings* (New York, 1953), p. xiv.

10. Donald Schier, "Main Street," *Carleton Miscellany* 4 (Fall 1963): 101.

11. T. K. Whipple, *Spokesmen* (New York, 1928), p. 219.

12. Sauk Centre *Herald*, July 20, 1922.

13. Grace Lewis, p. 97.

14. *Herald*, July 20, 1922.

15. Ibid.

16. Lewis Gannett, "Sinclair Lewis: 'Main Street,'" *Saturday Review of Literature* 32 (August 6, 1949): 31.

17. Grace Hegger Lewis, "When Lewis Walked Down Main Street," *New York Times Magazine*, July 3, 1960, p. 28.

18. Grace Lewis, *With Love*, p. 95.

19. John T. Flanagan, "A Long Way to Gopher Prairie: Sinclair Lewis's Apprenticeship," *Southwest Review* 32 (Autumn 1947): 404.

20. Grace Lewis, "When Lewis Walked," p. 29.

21. Lewis, "Minnesota: The Norse State," p. 626.

22. Lewis, *A Sinclair Lewis Reader*, p. 272.

23. Grace Lewis, *With Love*, p. 88.

24. *Herald*, May 21, 1942.

25. Ibid., January 18, 1951.

26. Mark Schorer, *Sinclair Lewis: An American Life* (New York, 1961), p. 286n.

27. T. J. Matheson, "Lewis's Assessment of Carol Kennicott," *Sinclair Lewis Newsletter* 5 (1973–1974): 12.

28. Schorer, "Main Street," p. 31.

29. Schorer, "Introduction," *Sinclair Lewis: A Collection of Critical Essays* (Englewood Cliffs, 1962), p. 3.

30. Stephen S. Conroy, "Sinclair Lewis's Sociological Imagination," *American Literature* 42 (November 1970): 350, 351.

31. Warren Beck, "How Good Is Sinclair Lewis?" *English Journal* 37 (January 1948): 4.

32. Daniel R. Brown, "Lewis's Satire—A Negative Emphasis," *Renascence* 18 (Winter 1966): 65.

33. Lucy Lockwood Hazard, *The Frontier in American Literature* (New York, 1927), p. 281.

34. Glen A. Love, "New Pioneering on the Prairies: Nature, Progress, and the Individual in the Novels of Sinclair Lewis," *American Quarterly* 25 (December 1973): 565.

35. Matheson, p. 12.

36. Schier, p. 98.

37. Allen Austin, "An Interview with Sinclair Lewis," *University of Kansas City Review* 24 (Spring 1958): 204.

38. Joseph Wood Krutch, "Sinclair Lewis," *Nation* 172 (February 24, 1951): 179.

39. W. E. Woodward, "The World and Sauk Center [*sic*]—I," *New Yorker* 9 (January 27, 1934): 24.

40. Gannett, p. 31.

41. William Rose Benét, "The Earlier Lewis," *Saturday Review of Literature* 10 (January 20, 1934): 422.

42. D. J. Dooley, *The Art of Sinclair Lewis* (Lincoln, Neb., 1967), p. 70.

43. George H. Douglas, "*Main Street* after Fifty Years," *Prairie Schooner* 44 (Winter 1970–1971): 340–342.

44. Sherwood Anderson, "Four American Impressions," *New Republic* 32 (October 11, 1922): 172.

45. Anthony Channell Hilfer, *The Revolt from the Village 1915–1930* (Chapel Hill, 1969), p. 158.

46. Ibid., p. 160.

47. Flanagan, p. 403.

48. Lewis Mumford, "The America of Sinclair Lewis," *Current History* 33 (January 1931): 530.

49. Fred Lewis Pattee, *The New American Literature 1890–1930* (New York, 1930), p. 342.

50. John T. Flanagan, "The Minnesota Backgrounds of Sinclair Lewis' Fiction," *Minnesota History* 37 (March 1960): 1.

51. Erik Axel Karlfeldt, "Sinclair Lewis and the Nobel Prize," *Saturday Review of Literature* 7 (January 10, 1931): 524.

CHAPTER TEN: A VOID NEW WORLD

1. Robert Lowell, "The Mouth of the Hudson," *For the Union Dead* (New York, 1965), p. 10.

2. Robert Frost, "Directive," *Complete Poems of Robert Frost* (New York, 1968), pp. 520–521.

Index

Index

INDEX

INDEX

Sallisaw, Oklahoma, 20

Salpointe, Jean Baptiste, 112

San Ysidro, New Mexico, 158

Sandia Pueblo, New Mexico, 139

Sandoval County, New Mexico, 157

Santiago, 150–152

Santa Ana Pueblo, New Mexico, 150–151

Santa Fe National Forest, 157

Santa Fé, New Mexico, 106–107, 111, 112, 118, 119–120

Sauk Centre, Minnesota, 193–213

Sawish, 62, 69

Scalawags, 44

Schorer, Mark, 206

Scott, Sir Walter, 43

Secretariat, 186

Semple, Ellen Churchill, 77

Sentimental novels, 208

Sentimentalism, 87, 106

Sermons, 28

Serra, Father Junipero, 112

Sex, *The Grapes of Wrath*, 25

Sexuality, *Gone with the Wind*, 44–46

Seytokwa Pueblo, 158

Shakespeare, William, 8, 76

Shegog, Reverend, 28, 160, 180

Sherwood, Carrie, 84

Shiprock, Arizona and New Mexico, 127–128

Slavery, 34, 39–40, 51–70 passim; burial customs, 59–60; in *Death Comes for the Archbishop*, 129; moral and psychological aspects, 58; parallels to, 55–57; personality types, 60; private life, *The Confessions of Nat Turner*, 68–70; selling slaves, 63–64; sex, *The Confessions of Nat Turner*, 68–70

Small towns, 10–12, 97–100, 198–200, 202–205, 212–213

Snake, Pecos, 138–139

Snopeses, 100, 182

Social novel, 20

Social theme, *The Grapes of Wrath*, 26, 29

Sound and the Fury, The, 28, 180

Sources, fiction, 93, 106, 119, 121–123

South, the, 98–99, 212

Southampton Slave Revolt of 1831, The, 54

Southampton, Virginia, 52

Southern writers, 79

Southwest, 5; in *Death Comes for the Archbishop*, 106–130 passim

Spanish, 105, 133; explorers, 135; Fathers, 111–119 passim; friars, 113

"Spotted Horses," 10, 12

Squaw dances, 164

Standardization, 4–5, 14

Steinbeck, John, 4, 8, 19–29, 53

Stevenson, Robert Louis, 73–74, 75

Styron, William, 33–34, 51–70, 199

Suicide, *As I Lay Dying*, 178–179

Sun Also Rises, The, 14

Sun Dance, 162

Supernatural, the, 109–114 passim, 133–171 passim

Sutpen, Thomas, 13

Tai-me, 160

Taine, Hippolyte, 20

Taos, New Mexico, 105, 111, 116

Taos Pueblo, 123

Tarahumares Indians, 144

Tate, Allen, 60, 79

Taylor, Walter Fuller, 27

Teah-whau, 141

Thoreau, Henry David, 79

Timrod, Henry, 34, 43

To Kill a Mockingbird, 43

Town, The, 12

Town vs. country, 176–177

Towns. *See* Small towns

Toya, Juan, 144

Toya, Rafael, 140

INDEX